# Purposeful Speaking

# Purposeful Speaking

## ARTHUR KOCH

*Milwaukee Area Technical College*

Boston ■ New York ■ San Francisco
Mexico City ■ Montreal ■ Toronto ■ London ■ Madrid ■ Munich ■ Paris
Hong Kong ■ Singapore ■ Tokyo ■ Cape Town ■ Sydney

**Editor-in-Chief, Communications:** Karon Bowers
**Development Editor:** Hilary Jackson
**Assistant Editor:** Jenny Lupica
**Marketing Manager:** Suzan Czajkowski
**Production Supervisor:** Liz Napolitano
**Editorial Production Service:** Progressive Publishing Alternatives
**Composition Buyer:** Linda Cox
**Manufacturing Buyer:** Joanne Sweeney
**Electronic Composition:** Progressive Publishing Alternatives
**Interior Design:** Progressive Publishing Alternatives
**Photo Researcher:** Laurie Frankenthaler
**Cover Designer:** Joel Gendron

For related titles and support materials, visit our online catalog at
www.ablongman.com.

Between the time website information is gathered and then published, it is not
unusual for some sites to have closed. Also, the transcription of URLs can result in
typographical errors. The publisher would appreciate notification where these errors
occur so that they may be corrected in subsequent editions.

**Library of Congress Cataloging-in-Publication Data**
Koch, Arthur
  Purposeful Speaking/Arthur Koch.
  Includes index.
  ISBN 0-205-53231-4
  1. Public Speaking. I. Title.

PN 4129.15.K62 2008
808.51—dc22

                                        2006047979

Printed in the United States of America
11   12   V092   16   15   14

# Brief Contents

# Contents

# 2
# *Audience Analysis*   26

# 3
# *Determine Your Purpose and Subject*   42

# 4
# *The Introduction and Conclusion* 56

# 5
# *Gathering Supporting Material* 72

# 6
## *Supporting Your Ideas*   86

# 7
## *Preparing the Content of Your Speech*   104

# 8
# *Delivering Your Speech*     122

# 9
## *Informing* 148

# 10
## *Persuasion* 168

# 11

## *Group Communication* 192

# Preface

Numerous rewards await the person who can communicate successfully through speech. Improved self-concept, increased confidence, greater employability, and the ability to get along better with others are just a few of these benefits.

*Purposeful Speaking* is designed to help speakers develop the skills they need to prepare and deliver effective speeches. It is geared toward the student who wants practical advice and hands-on experience in speaking. This new, full-color version of *Speaking with a Purpose* continues to offer the concise, practical, step-by-step approach to the speechmaking process that has made *Speaking with a Purpose* successful through seven editions, while being enhanced by a colorful, updated design and expanded pedagogy.

*Purposeful Speaking* is based primarily on a traditional public-speaking approach combined with up-to-date communication theory. It is intentionally brief in order to give the reader more time to prepare, practice, and present speeches. After more than thirty years of teaching speech to graduate and undergraduate students and business and professional people, I am convinced that the best way to learn the skills of speaking effectively is by successfully delivering speeches. The step-by-step approach of the book allows students to concentrate on the speechmaking process.

*Purposeful Speaking* is written in a reader-friendly style. Most reviewers who critiqued the book labeled the readability, writing style, level, and pace of the book as "excellent." One said that every student in the class "reacted favorably to Koch's approach, tone, and handling of the subject matter." Another commented, "I have looked at, read, and considered at least a hundred speech texts and always come back to *[Purposeful Speaking.]* Mr. Koch is commended for his work—there is no other text quite like this one. I believe *[Purposeful Speaking]* is the best short book available on the subject."

Retaining the hallmark brevity and practical approach of *Speaking with a Purpose*, *Purposeful Speaking* offers an attractive new design, colorful photographs and illustrations, and a complete package of pedagogical aids. Each chapter now features chapter outlines, boldfaced key terms, a marginal glossary, a "Checklist for Success," and a bulleted chapter summary to help students review and retain important chapter concepts. New exercises at the end of chapters provide thought-provoking questions and activities to encourage students to apply basic principles. Recognizing the pervasive influence of technology in our world today, and the importance of using the Internet to research speech topics, new "Working with the Web" boxes have been developed in each chapter. These boxes provide current online web sites and other electronic resources to guide students' efforts in finding, using, and evaluating material for their speeches.

Other useful pedagogical aids new to the book include "Checklist for Success" a box containing practical tips and guidelines, and a new "Personal Inventory" in Chapter 3 to give students a starting point to brainstorm for speech topics. New Appendices after the informative and persuasive speaking chapters offer a range of sample speech topics to facilitate these brainstorming efforts. The sample speeches, evaluation forms, audience analysis guides, and speech assignments available in past editions of *Speaking with a Purpose* combine with these new features to offer a complete pedagogical package that guides the reader in reviewing and applying important concepts.

The arrangement of *Purposeful Speaking* is logical. Chapter 1 discusses the importance of speech, guidelines to successful speechmaking, listening, note taking, projecting confidence, the speech-communication process, and ethics in communication. Chapters 2 through 8 follow a seven-step approach on how to prepare and deliver a successful speech, highlighting the importance of combining personal knowledge and experience with modern technology. Chapter 9 covers speaking to inform and Chapter 10 presents an in-depth study of persuasion and persuasive speaking.

A feature of Chapter 11, the group communication chapter, is the inclusion of case problems as topics for discussion. These human relations problems, which involve situations that group members are likely to encounter in everyday life, have proven effective in stimulating group participation.

---

## ✔ *Checklist* FOR SUCCESS

**PERSONAL INVENTORY**

Taking inventory of subjects that you know something about or that are of particular interest to you is a useful way of brainstorming about potential speech topics.

For each category in this personal inventory, write down as many ideas as you can. When the list is complete, look over each idea to determine which one would be a good topic for a speech.

| Music: Groups and Songs | Sports: Issues and People |
| --- | --- |
| Technology: Issues and Innovations | Global Issues |
| Family and Friends | National Issues |
| People: Celebrities | Local Issues |
| Mass Media | Campus Issues |
| Crafts/Hobbies | Vacation Spots |
| Public Policy: Issues and Questions | Religious Issues |

Adapted from Seiler/Beall: *Communication: Making Connections*, 6/e, Allyn & Bacon, 2005.

## SUPPLEMENTARY MATERIALS

Adopters of the text have access to an *Instructor's Manual/Test Bank* to assist with preparation for the classroom. In addition, a computerized version of the *Test Bank* and a PowerPoint presentation package for the book are available for adopters to download from our Instructor's Resource Center at *www.ablongman.com/irc*. Finally, for technology resources to accompany the text, MySpeechKit *(www. myspeechkit.com)* is available as a package option with new copies of the book (access code required). MySpeechKit offers book-specific learning objectives, chapter summaries, flashcards, and practice tests, as well as video clips and activities to aid student learning and comprehension. Also included in MySpeechKit are Research Navigator and live weblinks, both of which provide assistance with and access to powerful and reliable research material. For more details and ordering information, please contact your Allyn & Bacon publisher's representative, located at *www.ablongman.com/ replocator.*

## ACKNOWLEDGMENTS

I want to thank Brent W. Bean, Brigham Young University, Idaho; Barbara Hebel, Riverland Community College; Raymond Ide, Lancester Bible College; Kay Rutherford, Seattle Central Community College; Michael Severson, Sacramento City College and Will Tomory, Southwestern Michigan College, for their valuable suggestions in reviewing this book. I am also indebted to Marion Tyndale Carter, Crafton Hills College, California, for her section on controlling nervousness in Chapter 1, and to my ex-wife, Marion and sons, Carl, Kai, and Christian, for their contributions to the book. I also want to thank the following people who prepared the book's supplements: *Instructor's Manual/Test Bank* and MySpeechKit: J.P. Williams, Defiance College; and PowerPoint presentation package: Daniel Paulnock, Saint Paul College. Finally, I am indebted to Karon Bowers, Editor-in-Chief, Jenny Lupica, Assistant Editor, who has provided valuable in-house oversight of the project, Hilary Jackson, whose editing knowledge and insight has sharpened the book in many ways, and to the many other people at Allyn & Bacon who have made this new version of the text possible.

# *Purposeful Speaking*

CHAPTER

1

*Speech*

COMMUNICATION

SPEECH COMMUNICATION involves the ability to understand and be understood. One of life's most important functions is the ability to communicate effectively with others. Becoming a better speaker involves learning to get your ideas across to others in an easy-to-understand, interesting way. *Purposeful Speaking* is designed to assist you in learning to prepare, organize, and deliver purposeful audience-centered speeches. Good speakers are not born with the ability to speak effectively; they develop the ability to speak well as the result of commitment and hard work. The key to success in speaking is practice. The more speeches that you prepare and present successfully, the more proficient, relaxed, and confident you will become.

# THE COMMUNICATIVE ACT

**Speech communication process:** The act or process of sending and receiving a message, involving five elements: a speaker, a message, a channel (through which the message is sent), an audience, and a response.

Five elements are involved in the **speech communication process**: a speaker, a message, a channel (through which the message is sent), an audience, and a response (Figure 1.1). Each time a speaker communicates a message to others, these elements are present. In speaking situations, these elements interact with each other. A simple speech situation can be summarized as follows:

1. A speaker wants to communicate an idea.
2. The speaker encodes the idea in a message.
3. The message is sent through a channel to an audience.
4. The audience receives and decodes the message.
5. The audience responds to the message.

As you can see, the communication process is complex. To understand it better, it might be helpful to consider each of the five elements in the process separately.

## SPEAKER

In the previous model, the process of communication begins with a speaker who wants to communicate an idea or some ideas. The image that the audience has of the speaker affects the message. Those in the audience who perceive a speaker as being a person of competence, integrity, and goodwill are most likely to believe what the speaker says.

## MESSAGE

The second element in the communication process is the message. To ensure that the listener attends to the message and understands it, the speaker must encode it in a language that is both interesting and clear. Emphasis, variety, and descriptive language help make material interesting. Words that are specific and familiar help make a message clear.

## CHANNEL

The channel is the means through which a message is transmitted. In the speaking situation, the channel can involve all the senses through which each member of the audience receives the information. Messages can be transmitted through hearing, seeing, smelling, tasting, and touching channels. A speaker can choose words that appeal to the audience's five senses, include sensory aids in the message, or add nonverbals to the message to make it more meaningful.

## AUDIENCE

Without an audience, communication does not take place. A person stranded on an island can put a note in a bottle or stand on the shore screaming for help. However,

**SPEAKER**
Speaker wants to communicate idea.

**MESSAGE**
Speaker encodes idea into message.

**CHANNEL**
Message is sent through channel to audience.

**AUDIENCE**
Audience receives and decodes message.

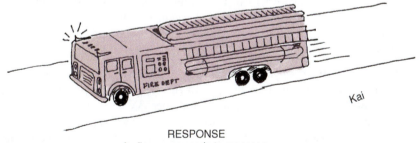

**RESPONSE**
Audience responds to message.

**FIGURE 1.1 ▪ How Communication Works**

In a communication event, the elements of communication flow from one to another and become part of a process. Examining the steps involved in a communicative act will help you better understand this process. This model demonstrates how the communication process works.

unless someone reads the note or hears the screams, nothing will have been accomplished. This emphasizes the fact that all communication by a speaker must be audience centered. Unless a message is encoded with a specific audience in mind, it is liable to fail.

## RESPONSE

In the final analysis, the success or failure of a communication is determined by audience response. The title of this book, *Purposeful Speaking*, underlines the fact that in order to be successful when communicating, the speaker's purpose—to inform, to entertain, or to persuade—must be achieved. Therefore, the success or failure of a communication is measured by whether those in the audience are informed, entertained, or persuaded.

## COMMUNICATION BREAKDOWNS

**Communication breakdown:**
A failure in the communication process traced to one of the five elements in the process.

A **communication breakdown** occurs because of a failure in the communication process. If you invite a friend to your house for a Friday night dinner and he or she comes Thursday night, the message you gave him or her was either inaccurate or misunderstood. If you fail to hear your instructor announce that the next class meeting has been called off, because you were daydreaming, you might be the only class member present on that day. Communication breakdowns occur at some point during the speech situation. Perhaps the speaker has failed to analyze the audience correctly. Maybe the message has been encoded in technical terms that the audience cannot understand. Or it might be that the microphone the speaker is using significantly distorts the message. Any of these factors could result in a breakdown of communication.

Communication breakdowns can usually be traced to one of the five elements in the communication process: speaker, message, channel, audience, or response. Consider the following situations and determine where the breakdowns in communication occurred:

1. Some of the members of your audience fail to understand parts of your speech on computer database technology because of the terminology you use. (Remember, you are most likely to talk to a general audience. What is clear to those who are computer literate might seem like gibberish to those who are not.)
2. What you are wearing draws attention to itself, interfering with your message. (The clothes you wear should not distract or detract from what you are saying. Dressing too flamboyantly or too casually can conflict with what you are saying.)
3. The overhead projector you brought to show your charts malfunctions. (A good rule of thumb when planning to use visual aids in a speech is "be prepared to do without them if need be." An audience will admire the speaker who is able to do this.)

4. The room you are speaking in is large, so it is difficult for those in the back to hear you. (If you haven't checked this out beforehand, you can only ask those in the back to move forward or increase your volume.)
5. Some type of external noise interferes with your audience's ability to hear you. (Remain silent until the noise stops. Unless your audience can hear you, communication is not taking place.)

## LISTENING

To get those in your audience to listen to what you are saying, you have to first get their attention and then give them a reason for continuing to listen. Unless there is a barrier that prevents them from listening, your audience will pay attention to something they find interesting or useful to them. Suggestions for developing an attention-getting introduction can be found in Chapter 7. Make note that two functions of the introduction are to capture the attention of the audience and to give each of them a reason for listening. If you maintain eye contact with your audience, you will be able to determine by their facial expressions, eye contact, posture, and gesture how many of them are actively listening.

Listening is an active process involving both concentrating on and thinking about the speaker's ideas.

Listening is an active process involving both concentration and thinking. Sometimes there is a barrier that interferes with the listener's concentration. Following are eight barriers to concentration in listening.

## BARRIERS TO LISTENING

**EXTERNAL NOISE.**    External noise includes noises both inside and outside the listening area. Talking, footsteps, whispering, coughing, and street noise are some of the things that make it difficult to pay attention to a speaker. As a listener, you can avoid such distractions by arriving early enough at a speech or lecture to get a seat where you can see and hear easily. As a speaker, you can aid your audience by remaining silent until an emergency vehicle passes by or a bell stops ringing.

**INTERNAL NOISE.**    Sometimes inner distractions caused by personal problems or concern about others can be so intense that it is extremely difficult to listen carefully. This internal "noise" can often be more distracting than a baby crying. When you are concerned about an upcoming test, a broken relationship, or a similar concern, you must redouble your efforts to concentrate.

**BIAS TOWARD SPEAKER.**    If a speaker's voice or appearance or mannerisms annoy you, listening carefully will become difficult. An instructor whose voice is raspy, who paces the floor, or who prefaces everything with *you know* can make a semester seem like an eternity. Work to overcome this listening barrier by concentrating on the content of the speech rather than the delivery.

**EMOTIONAL REACTION.**    Sometimes a word or phrase can cause a negative response that can interfere with a listener's ability to concentrate. Loaded words like *honky* or *greaser* or the use of profanity can trigger emotional responses that interfere with a person's ability to listen effectively. Try to screen out emotional reactions by resolving to hear everything a speaker has to say before making a judgment.

**DAYDREAMING.**    Who hasn't at one time or another drifted off into a pleasant daydream rather than pay attention? The tendency to daydream is influenced by two factors. First, a listener is able to think at a much faster rate than a speaker can speak. Consequently, while the speaker is talking at about 130 words per minute, the listener has plenty of thinking time left over. Second, attention is intermittent. That is, it stops and starts again at intervals. Daydreaming can be a serious barrier to listening. Learning to listen actively can help you avoid the tendency to daydream.

**FAKING ATTENTION.**    Faking attention is a technique that is usually learned in the first or second grade. There students learn to sit at their desks while leaning forward with hands propped under their chins and an interested expression on their faces. Regardless of whether we learned it in school, we have all at one time or another been guilty of faking attention. The problem with faking attention is that it can be a difficult habit to break.

**FATIGUE.**    Listening is an active process that requires the energy of the listener. If you are tired from too much studying or partying the night before, you will find it difficult to concentrate on what the speaker is saying. If you know that you will be attending an important speech or lecture, make sure that you are well rested.

**IMPROPER NOTE TAKING.**    Taking notes ineffectively is worse than not taking notes at all. Students who attempt to write down too much of what a speaker is saying often wind up missing the point the speaker is trying to make. The way to avoid this problem is to develop note-taking skills.

## WAYS TO IMPROVE LISTENING

**PREPARE TO LISTEN.**    The first thing to do before attending a speech or lecture is to prepare yourself to listen. This means knowing something about the subject beforehand so that you can listen actively rather than passively. The first step in preparing to listen is to determine the subject from the title of the speech or lecture. Next you must think about what you already know about the subject. Chances are that you know something. If your knowledge is limited, you can go to the library or read your textbook to obtain information that will help you better understand what the speaker has to say. Preparing to listen is the first step to improving your listening skills. It is unlikely that you could listen with any degree of understanding to a subject you know "nothing" about.

**AVOID DISTRACTIONS.**    As indicated previously, distractions can interfere with concentration and make it difficult to listen. To limit external distractions, arrive early enough to get a centrally located seat close to the speaker. If that is impossible, avoid sitting near windows or an entrance or exit.

Internal distractions are harder to screen out. The fact that you are aware that you are being bothered by them should alert you to redouble your efforts to concentrate.

**IDENTIFY THE CENTRAL IDEA.**    If the speech you are listening to has been well prepared, the central idea should be stated in the introduction. You might have already gotten a clue as to the central idea from the title. However, whether the speaker states the idea as a complete sentence or it is implicit in the message, as the listener you must be aware of what it is because the central idea is the main point of the speech.

**IDENTIFY THE MAIN POINTS.**    Most effective speeches involve a central idea supported by a number of main points. The listener's job is to sort out these main points from the supporting materials. This takes thinking and concentration. When identifying main points, listen for signals: "Some of the reasons that . . ." or "In addition. . . ." Phrases like these tip you off to the fact that important ideas are forthcoming.

**THINK ALONG WITH THE SPEAKER.**    To listen actively you must think along with the speaker. As you are listening, try to reconstruct the organizational pattern of the speech. Determine whether the speaker is supporting each new idea with a variety of supporting materials. Relate what the speaker is saying to your own knowledge and interests. Responding to the speech in this way will not only improve your active listening but will provide insights that will aid you in developing your own speeches.

**TAKE EFFECTIVE NOTES.**   Learning to take effective notes is an excellent way to improve your listening skills. Note taking promotes active listening and concentration. Rather than just listening passively to a speaker, the note taker must listen with the mind in order to identify the speaker's important ideas. It takes clear thinking and concentration to sort out main ideas from supporting details.

## NOTE-TAKING TIPS

**WRITE DOWN ONLY IMPORTANT IDEAS.**   A good speech is planned around a central idea and several main points. The central idea is usually stated in the introduction of the speech. Sometimes a speaker will also list in the introduction the main points to be covered. Listen for signals that indicate that main ideas are forthcoming. Words like *specifically*, *further*, and *first* indicate that a speaker is moving from one point to another.

Taking good notes is an excellent way to improve your listening skills. You need to actively engage in what the speaker is saying in order to identify the main points of the speech. This will enhance your overall understanding.

**WRITE LEGIBLY.**    Sometimes note takers write so hurriedly that when they finish, they can't read their own notes. If your notes are illegible, you are probably writing down too much.

**KEEP UP.**    If you find that you are falling behind in your note taking, skip a few lines and begin again. Later, when you expand your notes, you can fill in the missing information.

**USE YOUR OWN WORDS.**    One of the best ways to show that you understand something is to be able to explain it in your own words. When you translate the ideas of another into your own vocabulary, they will be easier to understand and remember.

**BE BRIEF.**    A common mistake among inexperienced note takers is the tendency to write down too much. Don't try to write down everything the speaker says. A set of notes should be a summary of a speaker's main ideas.

**DON'T ERASE.**    Rather than waste time erasing, draw a line through the mistake and continue. Remember, the notes you are taking are for your own use. If you want your notes to be neat, you can rewrite or type them later.

**DON'T WORRY ABOUT SPELLING.**    If you're not sure about how a word is spelled, write it phonetically. You can check the spelling later when you expand your notes.

**DATE YOUR NOTES.**    Whether you are taking notes on a lecture or a public speech, you should get into the habit of dating them. This will enable you to pinpoint a missed lecture or the specific date of a speech.

**EXPAND YOUR NOTES.**    If the notes you are taking are for the purpose of helping you remember information or to aid you in studying for an exam, it is wise to expand them as soon after a lecture as possible.

## GETTING STARTED

If you are like most students, the thought of taking a speech course far from excites you. Perhaps you have some anxiety about standing up in front of a group of class-mates to deliver a speech. You might be unclear as to how to develop a clear and inter-esting message. Possibly you are afraid you might forget what you planned to say in your speech, say the wrong thing, or say it ineffectively and be embarrassed.

A key feature of this text is that it is "brief and concise." *Purposeful Speaking* is intentionally brief to allow you plenty of opportunity to learn by doing. It is designed to give you the information necessary to begin delivering speeches as soon as possible. The step-by-step approach allows you to concentrate on the speechmaking process.

In today's society, the person who can't communicate effectively is operating at a distinct disadvantage. People who are successful at the corporate level are invariably required to speak both within and outside the organization. Business and industrial employees are often required to take courses at the company's expense in order to improve their speech skills. Make no mistake, the ability to communicate effectively can often mean the difference between success and failure in the workplace.

People tend to equate the ability to speak well with the ability to think well. To a great extent, this is due to the fact that effective speakers are able to get their ideas across to others in an easy-to-understand, interesting way. Remember, every time you speak you are communicating something about who you are to others. If you want others to see you as an effective communicator, two broad guidelines can help ensure success: (1) Say something worthwhile, and (2) say it in a confident, natural way.

## SAY SOMETHING WORTHWHILE

**Content:** What is said in a speech, including the subject, main idea, supporting materials, organization, and the way the speech is worded.

When you prepare a speech, you are concerned with two things: what you want to say and how you want to say it. What you say is called the **content** of your speech, which includes your subject, main idea and supporting material, organization, and the way you word your speech. Whenever you can, you should choose a worthwhile subject from your own area of interest so that you are familiar with what you are talking about and have some concern for your subject. Next, you must develop the subject with your audience in mind. An audience will pay attention to something that is either useful or interesting to them. If you can show your audience that your subject is useful to them, this will give them a reason to pay attention. Point out how your speech will be useful to your listeners in the introduction. If your subject is interesting to them, you can get their attention in the introduction and hold it throughout the speech.

If, however, your subject does not seem useful to your audience, is not interesting in itself, yet you still want to choose it because you believe it is worthwhile, in order to hold their attention you must make it interesting to them. Suggestions for getting and holding the attention of your audience are found in Chapter 2. Keep in mind that the less interesting or useful a subject is, the more difficult it will be to hold the audience's attention. For example, unless you were in a class of art students, an informative speech on Salvador Dali's contribution to modern art would take a lot more imagination and effort to make it interesting to a typical audience than a speech on the Beatle's influence on rock and roll.

Similarly, your listeners would be more likely to see the usefulness of a speech on the effects of alcohol on the mind and body than on one demonstrating how to make an arrow. Almost everyone takes a drink now and then or knows someone who does, perhaps taking more than he or she should. Knowing the positives and negatives of drinking alcohol would most likely seem useful to many. In contrast, knowing how to make an arrow would probably only seem useful to a bow hunter or avid archer.

This does not mean, however, that a speech demonstrating how to make an arrow could not be made interesting to a general audience. A number of years ago, one of my students, a Native American from a Wisconsin Chippewa tribe, delivered a speech on how to make an arrow. He brought in a modern apparatus for aligning the feathers and the arrowhead on the arrow shaft so that the arrow would be in perfect balance. He showed us a variety of modern arrows and bows. Then he showed us a number of bows and arrows that had been made by the members of his or other Ojibwa tribes over one hundred and fifty years earlier. The arrowheads were flint and the feathers had come from eagles or hawks. When he put the primitive arrows on the apparatus they were way out of balance. The bows were obviously nowhere near as powerful as the ones made today. He explained that Indians wore moccasins and learned to walk without making a sound so that they could get close enough to hit whatever they were stalking with their primitive weapons. The speech was interesting and informative. It cleared up some misconceptions the class had from watching cowboy and Indian movies and gave the class a greater appreciation of the contributions and resourcefulness of Native Americans.

## SAY IT IN A CONFIDENT WAY

The way you say something is called **delivery**. Delivery includes such things as eye contact, facial expression, body movement, personal appearance, and voice. Effective delivery should seem confident and natural. Besides an increase in volume for a larger audience, there are a number of differences between platform speaking and ordinary conversation. First, platform speaking is intentional. As the title of this text emphasizes, a speech is delivered with a clear purpose in mind. Second, a speech is more carefully prepared than everyday conversation. A subject is chosen and developed with a specific audience in mind, and words are chosen more carefully. If you want to deliver an effective speech, you must be clear about what you want to say and whom you are trying to reach. Remember, in most cases, the only interaction with your audience that you have in a speech situation is their nonverbal response.

**Delivery:** The way the speech is communicated, including through eye contact, facial expression, body movement, personal appearance, and voice.

Your delivery will seem more confident and natural if you use a conversational style. A conversational style makes frequent use of the personal pronoun, which gives it an air of familiarity, as if the speaker were talking to close friends. Use your own vocabulary but eliminate words that might be considered overly casual or inappropriate. If you try to use words with which you are unfamiliar, your style will seem stilted and unnatural. You should, however, choose your words carefully. Keep in mind that speech is more formal than ordinary conversation, and your language should be a bit more formal, too.

The advantage of using your own vocabulary when delivering a speech is that you will feel more natural and comfortable. Talking about something you believe is important and about which you are sincere will help you exude confidence.

At this point, you might be asking yourself, "How can I exude confidence, when the thought of giving a speech gives my stomach butterflies?"

# PROJECTING CONFIDENCE

Keep in mind that if you choose a topic from your own area of interest that you believe is worthwhile, prepare your speech carefully with a clear purpose and your audience in mind, and adequately practice your delivery beforehand, you will project confidence when delivering your speech. You might feel anxious (or nervous) before and during the speech, but unless you tell your audience that you are nervous, most likely they won't know.

For years I taught a course for business and professional people at a local university. The course was designed to improve speaking ability, particularly in the area of delivery. Most of the students who took that course were successful executive types with high-level jobs who were highly motivated to improve their ability to communicate effectively. The course met for three hours once a week, and each time every person in the class delivered a speech that was videotaped during the first half of the class and shown and discussed during the second half. The students soon discovered that although some felt nervous while delivering their speeches, this nervousness was not discernible on the videotape playback. If someone said, "Boy, was I nervous," the response would invariably be, "You didn't look nervous. What did you do to show that you were nervous?" Once it became clear that their nervousness was not apparent to their classmates, the butterflies disappeared.

Another benefit of the course was that delivering a speech at every meeting gave each student important experience in speaking in front of a group. Because everyone was in the same boat, the group was highly supportive. The more speeches those students gave, the better they got. There is nothing like success to boost your confidence.

On the positive side, being a bit nervous before giving a speech is an indication that you are "keyed up," a desirable reaction. Have you ever watched a performer pace back and forth before going on stage or an athlete bending, stretching, or just moving around before competing? They are keyed up, and they are letting off a bit of the nervous energy or excitement that is building up for that moment on stage, on the field, in the ring, or wherever they are going to perform. This energy works to their advantage, and it can work to yours, too, when you let it help you deliver an enthusiastic speech.

## ENERGIZE YOURSELF

**Isometric exercise:**
A procedure during which you contract a muscle for about 8 to 10 seconds, against resistance, in order to release nervous energy.

When you will be giving a speech in class, you won't be able to pace the floor, jump up and down, or do knee bends, but you can exercise isometrically, which should help you release some of your nervous energy. An **isometric exercise** is a procedure by which you contract a muscle for about eight to ten seconds against some immovable resistance, for example, a chair, table, or floor. Here are some isometric exercises you can try:

1. While sitting on a chair with your feet flat on the floor, grasp each side of the chair and attempt to lift yourself.
2. Sit on a chair with your feet flat on the floor. Put your hands on top of your knees while drawing in your abdominal muscles. Attempt to lift your heels off the floor.
3. While sitting on a chair, place the palms of your hands on the sides of the chair and press inward as hard as you can with spread fingers.

Material on pages 14–20 is taken with permission from Marian Tyndale Carter, *Content and Delivery*, 2nd ed. (Beaumont, CA: Maple Leaf, 1995).

A few minutes before it is your turn to speak, breathe in slowly and deeply through your nose until your lungs are full. Hold the breath for a count of four or five and slowly breathe out with jaw and lips relaxed, as if you are yawning. Repeat three or four times. Then, when it is your turn to speak, stand up and walk briskly and confidently up to the podium to deliver your speech.

## THE TRUTH ABOUT NERVOUSNESS

Nervousness is learned behavior. Several years ago in a psychology class called "Self-Confidence," a young mother brought her four-year-old son to the final exam class because of a mix-up with a sitter. The final exam was a short talk about some of the ideas learned in the class and how they had made life better. There were eighteen students in the class and as we listened to the talks we heard people sharing many wonderful changes that they had created in their own feelings, in their relationships, and in their school and career successes. The group was supportive and warmly applauded each speaker. When the last student finished, the little boy slipped off his chair and went to the front of the group. He said, "I want to talk." He then talked for one or two minutes about his dog, how they played, and how happy his dog made him feel. The applause was loud, and there were quite a few of us with suspiciously bright eyes. When he went back to his mother, we all heard him say, "That was fun. I liked it." I have never forgotten this precious child who had never learned to be afraid of standing in front of an audience. I was so impressed that, first, he perceived the caring and connection that was experienced as these students shared of themselves and were acknowledged lovingly by their classmates. He knew this was a good thing, and he wanted to experience it. Second, even this young child perceived accurately that the speakers were telling about things in their own lives and sharing their emotional feelings, so he just unself-consciously shared something important from his life and the emotions he felt of happiness. Right on target! I have often pondered the possible results if we could but teach public speaking to young children before they learn to be so afraid.

Public speaking is probably the course feared by more students than any other. The reasons for this fear are numerous and not all negative. However, in my experience, many students have horror sto-

**Overconcern:** The anxiety about what others will think of us.

ries to tell about being laughed at or humiliated in elementary school. This particular fear usually yields quite easily to the confidence-building sequence of easy speaking activities in the early part of the semester. The positive feedback from classmates and from your own videotaped performances is very powerful and when supplemented with positive self-talk is very effective in replacing those fears from childhood. A more appropriate or rational nervousness is created because you care about what the audience thinks about you. This is especially true when you stand before a group of your peers. This concern for the opinion of your fellow human is appropriate if not carried too far. Appropriate caring causes you to do all you can to do your best. It gives you the extra rush of energy that you need to be really alive in front of an audience. Albert Ellis said in his book *A New Guide to Rational Living* that 98 percent of our anxiety is **overconcern** about what others will think of us. Overconcern is then the problem.

Overconcern is usually stimulated and reinforced by negative self-talk such as, "I'm so nervous!" "I can't do this!" "I know I'll forget everything!" or that old classic self-fulfilling prophecy, "When I get in front of an audience my mind goes blank!" Say any of these affirmations enough and they tend to become the truth. Your strongest "word of honor" seems to be that spoken of yourself to yourself!

One really fascinating view of nervousness is that on a physiological level the physical signs of nervousness parallel the physical signs of excitement. That is to say that two people may experience the same symptoms and one may name it *nervousness* and the other may name it *excitement*. I urge every student to rename their nervous feelings sincerely as *excitement* and see how that changes their perception of their feelings.

For several semesters, I had students rank themselves as speakers and the audience rank the speaker in terms of how nervous they were. I used a scale of zero to twenty. It was quite consistent that the speaker perceived himself to be twice as nervous as the audience would perceive him to be. That is, if a speaker said he was an eighteen on the nervousness scale, the audience on the average would perceive him to be close to nine on that same scale. It is reassuring to realize that as a speaker a person only appears half as nervous to the audience as he thinks he appears.

## HOW TO DEVELOP SELF-CONFIDENCE

As the oft-quoted saying "Nothing succeeds like success" implies, the experience of doing well in the speech activities in class will go a long way toward helping you develop greater self-confidence. To this end, always talk about something you really know, prepare, and practice a lot. Be sincere and talk about things that really matter to you. Never ever try to "con" an audience into believing that you know something you do not. You cannot fool an audience. They can almost always tell exactly how much you do or do not know, how much time you have spent preparing, and above all how much time you spent rehearsing. Being well prepared and well rehearsed create almost certain success. This is what builds confidence.

Physically there are several important things you can do to build self-confidence. First, be sure that you do not form the habit of holding your breath or breathing shallowly. Many people, without even realizing it, breathe less deeply or even hold their breath when they experience stress. This can really backfire, because it can diminish the flow of oxygen to the brain, which may trigger a fear response that is mistaken for nervousness, not a physical reaction to lack of oxygen. Posture is also important in developing self-confidence. If you stand with your weight evenly balanced on both feet, spine erect, head up, and arms loose at your side, your body will experience balance and comfort.

Psychologically there are several important steps you can take to develop greater self-confidence. You can practice positive self-talk, repeatedly saying to yourself with as much conviction as you can create, "I can do this," "I can take it one step at a time," "I can become an excellent speaker," "This class is getting easier every week," and "I really want to learn to be a powerful speaker!" A second physiological exercise is to banish all talk of fear and nervousness. Substitute other less loaded words when you talk of your concerns. From now on, instead of "I'm really nervous," say "I'm really excited." If you are compelled to acknowledge your previous levels of nervousness, always say "In the past I have had some problems with nervousness, but it is getting better all of the time." Such relanguaging or renaming something is a powerful way to gain control over your psychological reactions. Constantly using "I am very excited" and eliminating the fear and nervousness talk is a powerful technique for changing your whole response pattern to the public-speaking situation. For this to be effective in lessening nervousness, you do not have to believe strongly in your positive self-talk, but you *do* have to eliminate negative self-talk, or the positive and negative statements will cancel each other, leaving you to experience little growth in this area.

Another powerful psychological idea is to change your focus from concern for yourself to concern for the audience. All too often a speaker is so focused on the impression he is making that he forgets to be really focused on how well the audience is hearing, seeing, understanding, and so forth. When your attention is turned back on yourself, your mind will be filled with questions like "Do I look scared?" "Do I sound stupid?" "What if I forget?" "Can they see my knees shaking?" and on and on. The speaker who can forget himself and really be concerned if the audience is understanding the important ideas he is sharing will experience a genuine shift to a nurturing connection with the audience. This is the feeling that causes many a speaker to get "hooked" on public speaking. It is a powerful feeling when you realize that you can share an idea that could change someone's life. This can only happen if you talk about things that are so interesting and important to you that you truly want every person in the audience to understand. This means preparing well and working on that shift of focus. I have seen speakers experience this shift of focus and when they had that experience, it eliminated most of their excessive nervousness.

## STRETCH YOUR COMFORT ZONE

Your **comfort zone** is defined by your self-concept, your family culture, your community and national culture, and so on. As long as you are not violating any of the "rules" of these belief systems, you are in your comfort zone. Some of these rules are appropriate, but many are just habits handed down that end up creating a big rut that controls the direction of our life more than most of us realize. A more general approach to building confidence is to look constantly for opportunities to stretch your comfort zone in every area of life. If you are more comfortable waiting for someone else to speak first, push yourself to speak first as often as possible. Be on the lookout for little ways you can stretch that comfort zone. Push yourself in class. Ask more questions in a store. Ask for information. Try dressing differently. Seek leadership roles. Volunteer some time at the library literacy program. Go to a town council meeting and ask a question. Take voice lessons. Take flying lessons. Go horseback riding. Drive somewhere you have never been. Challenge yourself to be aware and to act by choice, not by habit. Try out for a role in a community theater play.

**Comfort zone:** Your self-concept and the belief systems and rules established by past experiences and personal knowledge.

## VISUAL IMAGERY IS A POWERFUL TOOL

**Visual imagery:** A technique for behavior change; when used to mentally rehearse a speech, helps develop confidence in public speaking.

The next delivery topic is a **visual imagery** technique specifically for developing confidence in public speaking. Mental rehearsal is another name for visual imagery. This technique is a fascinating tool for changing behavior, and the same procedure presented on the next few pages can be adapted to create behavior change in any area of life. You could even use it to practice remembering more and scoring better on the quizzes and to stop procrastinating and do that paperwork and other preparation early. Be creative and see how many areas you can find to try the three-step method of visual imagery you are now going to learn.

## VISUAL IMAGERY FOR CONFIDENCE IN PUBLIC SPEAKING

Visual imagery for behavior change is a powerful technique that gained broad exposure during the Olympic Games in Los Angeles. In TV interviews, sports coaches of a wide variety of different events explained how this technique, used as a *regular* part of daily practice, had helped athletes improve their performances. From divers to gymnasts, visual imagery was found to be a valuable tool.

The subconscious mind does not seem to differentiate between actual physical rehearsal and mental rehearsal (visual imagery) when the mental rehearsal is done with the same concentration and vivid feelings associated with the actual physical rehearsal. The benefits from mental rehearsal done well are many. The rehearsal is completely under the control of the person doing the imagery; therefore, each rehearsal can be a positive, strengthening experience. The time involved is much less than actual practice requires, so more practice can be done. The troublesome spots in an activity can be practiced over and over easily. The subconscious mind can build a store house of "success" feelings about an activity. These feelings then encourage continued successful performance just as actual successful rehearsal would.

The visual imagery pattern I recommend for speech students desiring to experience more confidence and greater speaking skill in front of an audience is a simple three-step pattern. It is suggested that you practice using this pattern (or your own personal version of it) at least three times a day. Each session should be brief (two to five minutes) but as intensely vivid and "real" as you can create it. Do this brief visual imagery three or more times a day for two to three weeks or longer and you will find a tremendous development of skill and confidence as the result. Each session should take only two to five minutes. Visual imagery can be done in any place where you can be uninterrupted for a few minutes. The best schedule is morning, midday, and evening. Detailed instructions for using the visual imagery pattern follow.

For a more in-depth discussion of visual imagery, you will enjoy reading the books *Psycho-Cybernetics* by Maxwell Maltz, *Visualization* by Adelaide Bry, *The Mind's Eye* by Arnold Lazarus, *Creative Visualization* by Shakti Gawain, and *Visualization for Change* by Patrick Fanning. There are also subliminal tapes available that seem to help some people develop greater confidence in public speaking.

## Working WITH THE WEB

The Internet can be a useful tool in all phases of developing a speech. Throughout this edition of *Purposeful Speaking*, Internet addresses are provided that may be helpful to you as you develop your speech. You may want to begin with:

www.abacon.com/pubspeak/

Developed and maintained by the publisher of this book, this is an excellent, comprehensive site that provides insight into all facets of speech development and public speaking. In addition, as you read through this chapter, you may want to check out these two sites, which offer a wealth of information on public speaking anxiety:

www.speakeeezi.com/page4.htm
www.speech-anxiety.healthyplace2.com

## A SCRIPT FOR USING VISUAL IMAGERY TO DEVELOP CONFIDENCE IN SPEAKING

### STEP ONE: SYSTEMATIC RELAXATION

Pay particular attention to shoulders, face, and stomach muscles. The purpose of step one is to focus attention away from your outer environment onto your physical body, and then to relax your body sufficiently to avoid its becoming a distraction later in the process when you focus your attention within yourself. Sit in a centered posture—do not recline. Start with your toes and systematically relax every part of your body up to the top of your head. Tensing and relaxing is good if at first your shoulders or other large muscle groups are very tense.

### STEP TWO: FAVORITE PEACEFUL PLACE

Picture a vivid sensory-rich scene in nature. You should use this same scene over and over or at least until you change projects. I usually use the beach. Focus on all the sensory details possible—sky, water, waves, sunlight, sun's warmth, sounds of birds and water, feel of sand underfoot, and so on. See yourself walking along the beach experiencing the colors, sights, sounds, touches, and freedom of the beach as vividly as you can.

### STEP THREE: REHEARSING YOUR DESIRED BEHAVIOR

Picture yourself doing the behavior you desire to do just as perfectly as you hope to learn to do it—speaking with confidence and skill. The sequence I recommend is to see yourself sitting at your desk, aware that you are the next speaker. When it is your

Practicing your speech will increase your confidence, minimize mistakes, and help you work through any nervousness you feel about speaking in public.

turn you rise confidently and walk to the podium. You look confidently at individuals in the audience, then begin with a ringing powerful opening statement. See yourself standing and speaking with real authority and clarity. You do not have to "hear" any actual words. Feel the energy and enthusiasm in your delivery. See people in the audience nodding their heads in agreement with your ideas. Feel your strong desire to communicate the interest and the importance of the information you are sharing. See yourself finishing with a strong dynamic ending statement. Hear the loud spontaneous applause as your audience acknowledges your excellent speech. Notice how you really enjoy the feeling of having done a good job. Feel this enjoyment. This is an important ingredient in the visualization—your enjoyment of your success. See yourself now returning to your seat with the same sincere and confident attitude. See yourself sitting with a big smile on your face—pleased with yourself. Enjoy and strengthen this feeling for a few moments before you open your eyes and are finished with the session.

## ETHICS IN COMMUNICATION

**Ethics:** The moral standards and values that influence our decisions and behaviors.

**Ethics** in communication requires honesty. It requires a communicator to give only truthful and accurate information to an audience. This is an important responsibility and one not to be taken lightly.

Unfortunately, there are those in our society who believe in getting by any way they can. Too many political candidates offer us whatever it takes to ensure their election. We get daily accounts of those in government and business who have violated our trust in order to further their own causes. Too many advertisers justify their sales pitches with the slogan *caveat emptor* (let the buyer beware).

We are constantly bombarded with TV and radio commercials that promise us instant satisfaction if only we buy the advertised product. "Brush with our brand of toothpaste" or "buy our hair spray and shampoo"—these hucksters tell us—and we will be successful, approved of, popular, or whatever we desire. Too often, even though we realize that what we are receiving is often fabrication and misrepresentation, we just shake our heads and do nothing but regret that we can't trust many of the advertisers, politicians, elected officials, and others who have a direct influence on our lives. That is unfortunate because as receivers we have the right to demand that those who communicate to us provide us with honest and accurate information.

Most of the ethical decisions that we make in our lives are based on our moral standards and values. Our decisions to respect the rights of others, to treat others with dignity, and to be true to our word are all ethical choices we make based on the value system to which we ascribe.

As a speaker, you have an ethical responsibility to your listeners to give them the same kind of honest and accurate information you would want them to give you. Document the statistics you use in your speech. Avoid using vague phrases such as "recent studies indicate" or "the latest surveys show." Instead, indicate exactly when and by whom the statistics you are stating were compiled. This will increase your credibility in the minds of your listeners. Chances are that some in your audience have been misled in the past by statistics. Pointing out exactly where your statistics came from and who compiled them will make the statistics you are using both reputable and unbiased and will set your audience's minds at ease.

When you back up your statements with the testimony of others, make sure you choose experts your audience will consider well qualified and objective. If the experts are unknown to your audience, give information about them that will establish their qualifications and objectivity.

Be especially careful when citing information you have obtained from the Internet. It is a good idea to save the material you are citing so that you can compare it to other sources you are using. When evaluating information you find on the Internet, make sure the material is current and objective. The better the reputation of the author or the reliability of the sponsoring organization, the more likely it will be that the information is accurate.

Always make sure that your purpose is absolutely clear to the audience. For example, if your purpose is to persuade your audience to vote against establishing the death penalty in their state, let them know early on that that is what you are asking them to do. In the interest of fairness, it is also wise to present some of the arguments from the other side. This will demonstrate to your audience that you are interested in their reaching a well-informed decision. Furthermore, it will enable you to point out some of the weaknesses in the opposing viewpoint as well.

Whenever you use the ideas of others, you must give them credit. Even if you put their opinions or assertions in your own words by paraphrasing them rather than quoting them verbatim, you have a responsibility to acknowledge the source of information that is not your own. Presenting their words or ideas without giving them

**Plagiarism:** Presenting someone's words or ideas as your own, without giving proper or adequate credit.

credit is **plagiarism**. Plagiarism can involve either presenting the ideas of others word for word as they were written or spoken or paraphrasing the ideas in your own words. It makes no difference. Whenever you use the ideas of others without giving them credit, you are stealing from them. It doesn't matter whether you do this intentionally or through carelessness; it is stealing nonetheless.

Sometimes you may engage in plagiarism without intending to or even being aware of it. Suppose, for example, that you are a member of a group opposed to the manufacturing and sale of land mines in the United States. Because you have attended many meetings and are preoccupied with the issue, you have accumulated a substantial amount of material on this topic. Certainly some of the information from fliers and other handouts could have been taken from unidentified sources. Some of the ideas that you now embrace as your own could have come from others. Presenting them without giving credit to these sources would make you guilty of plagiarism. You can protect yourself by indicating to your audience that some of your ideas have come from the anti-land-mine organization of which you are a member. An added benefit will be that indicating your membership in the organization will also increase your credibility.

Make no mistake, plagiarism is the presenting of someone's words and ideas as if they were your own regardless of whether intentional, and the penalties for plagiarism at many schools are often severe, ranging from a failing grade on the assignment to failing the course or even being expelled from school. Some of the synonyms for plagiarism listed in *Roget's Thesaurus* are counterfeit, filch, lift, pinch, pirate, sneak, steal, and swipe.

Those who are caught plagiarizing outside the school often suffer significant penalties as well. Careers have been ruined, promotions denied, elections lost, and reputations irreparably damaged all because someone used the words or ideas of others in spoken or written communication without giving the originator of those words or ideas credit.

Obviously then, you must be careful to take comprehensive notes that include the name of the author, the title, the call number of the book or periodical, the publisher, and the place and date of publication when gathering information for your speech. If you are quoting the material exactly, use quotation marks and make sure of the word order and punctuation. If you are paraphrasing, make sure you capture the author's meaning. When you record information, use a speech notebook, note cards, or computer file.

An ethical speaker avoids exaggeration and distortion. While we expect our friends to increase the size of the deer they shot or the length of the fish they caught when telling us about it, overstating the facts in a speech is unacceptable. Your audience deserves honest and accurate information. Equally unacceptable is distortion or misrepresentation of the facts. Unfortunately, one of my former students learned this the hard way. In delivering a speech on the evil of drinking and driving, she told the audience in graphic detail how her brother, his wife, and two little children had been killed by a drunken driver in an auto accident a few months earlier. The speech was very moving, and many in the audience had tears in their eyes. As the class was leaving, someone asked her how the rest of the family was holding up under the strain and she said she had made the story up to make the speech more effective. As a result of this misrepresentation, her reputation in the class was damaged and she suffered a loss of credibility for the rest of the semester. What it all boils down to is this: An ethical speaker has a responsibility to present accurate and honest information that is free from exaggeration, distortion, or bias.

An ethical speaker must be tolerant of others. The strength of the United States lies in its diversity. We are a melting pot of people from all over the world who came to these shores to live in freedom, equality, and harmony. These people brought with them their own values, mores, and customs. Some of them will no doubt be different from ours, but an ethical speaker has a responsibility to respect the different viewpoints, beliefs, and values of others. The use of biased language or unkind references to others because of their race, ethnic background, religion, sexual orientation, or viewpoints is unacceptable. As an ethical speaker, you must be willing to listen to views that are different from your own. That does not mean that you have to agree with an opposing view, but learning about others will help you understand them better and help you when you are preparing your speech.

Finally, what an audience thinks of you has a definite effect on their reaction to what you are saying to them. If they see you as being ethical, friendly, and competent, they will respond to you in a receptive and friendly manner. What is even more important is that you see yourself as being ethical, friendly, and competent. The more accurate a picture you have of yourself and your self-worth, the more likely it will be that you will communicate ethically, accurately, and successfully. The following poem aptly points out how important it is to understand and be honest with yourself. Keep it in mind as you plan and prepare the speeches you will deliver to your audience.

*When you get what you want in your struggle for self,*
*And the world makes you king for a day;*
*Then go to your mirror and look at yourself;*
*And see what that guy has to say.*
*For it isn't your father or husband or wife,*
*Whose judgment upon you must pass;*
*The fellow whose verdict counts most in your life,*
*Is the guy staring back from the glass.*
*He's the man you must please, never mind all the rest,*
*For he's with you right up to the end;*
*And you've passed your most difficult dangerous test,*
*When the man in the glass is your friend.*
*You may be like little Jack Horner and "chisel" a plum,*
*And think you're a wonderful guy;*
*But the man in the glass thinks you're only a bum,*
*If you can't look him straight in the eye.*
*You can fool the whole world down the pathway of years,*
*And can get pats on the back as you pass;*
*But your final reward will be heartache and tears;*
*If you've cheated the man in the glass.*

AUTHOR UNKNOWN

# Chapter Review

After reading this chapter, you should be able to

- Describe each of the five elements of the speech communication process and how they interact with each other.
- Describe some typical barriers to listening and how each one interferes with the listener's ability to concentrate on the speaker's message.
- Identify ways to improve your own listening and avoid common communication breakdowns.
- Understand the factors that contribute to nervousness in a public speaking situation and how to develop more self-confidence.
- Explain each of the steps in the visual imagery technique.
- Define plagiarism.
- Name at least three qualities of an ethical speaker.

# Key Terms

Speech communication process (p. 4)    Overconcern (p. 15)
Communication breakdown (p. 6)    Comfort zone (p. 17)
Content (p. 12)    Visual imagery (p. 18)
Delivery (p. 13)    Ethics (p. 20)
Isometric exercise (p. 14)    Plagiarism (p. 22)

# Exercises

1. Describe at least two instances of communication breakdowns in your own experience and identify the cause of those breakdowns. What could have been done to improve the communication? How would other people, such as friends, family, a teacher, a coach, or your parents, rate you as a listener? Make an assessment and then compare with their actual ratings.
2. Think of two or three situations, beyond public speaking, where you could try the visual imagery method. Describe each one, explaining what you would do in each step of the visual imagery technique.
3. On one side of a piece of paper, develop a list of experiences when you weren't nervous sharing something personal. On the other side, explain what made the difference between confidence and nervousness.
4. With a classmate or friend, share a list of five things you can do to stretch your comfort zone.
5. Do you have a "peaceful place"? Describe it.
6. Tell of an instance when plagiarism got someone you knew or read about in trouble. Was the plagiarism intentional or unintentional? How do you know?

# Speech Assignments

1. *Introduce a Classmate*

   In your interview with her, question her about her hobbies, goals, attitudes, accomplishments, or anything you believe will be of interest to the class. Take careful notes. Then have your classmate interview you. Develop your material in an interesting way and put it in an order that will be easy for you and your audience to remember. Deliver the speech as your instructor directs.

   ### Suggestions

   1. Pronounce the classmate's name clearly and distinctly.
   2. Be as enthusiastic and friendly as you can.
   3. Be accurate. Check the facts before you deliver the speech.
   4. Be familiar with your material. If you need notes, use only one note card.

2. *Introduce Yourself*

   This speech should be delivered extemporaneously (preferably without notes). Develop your presentation in an interesting way that will be easy for you and your classmates to understand and remember. Deliver the speech as your instructor directs.

   ### Suggestions

   1. Give your name and hometown. Pronounce them distinctly.
   2. Be as friendly and enthusiastic as you can.
   3. Indicate your major or what major you are considering.
   4. Describe a special interest or talent.
   5. Tell why you are taking this course and how it will benefit you.
   6. Tell about the things you believe are important.

# CHAPTER 2

# *Audience* ANALYSIS

AFTER YOU have selected a subject and determined your purpose, you are ready to think of the speech in terms of your audience. An audience is an indispensable part of communication. If your audience fails to understand or pay attention to your message, communication does not take place. Therefore, when you develop your speech, do so with your audience in mind.

A speech that is prepared with a specific audience in mind is one that is audience centered. To aid in preparing an **audience-centered speech**, ask yourself the questions discussed in this chapter.

**Audience-centered speech:**
A speech that is prepared with a specific audience, a specific collection of individuals, in mind.

# WHO EXACTLY IS MY AUDIENCE?

As you prepare the content of your speech, consider who is in your audience. Your boss or teacher? Your coworkers or classmates? Even if there is only one male or one female in an otherwise all-female or all-male audience, you must consider this person when preparing your speech. A surprising number of communications fail because the sender has been unclear as to the composition of his or her audience.

Take the case of George Scott, assistant cashier of a small midwestern bank. George came home in a state of dejection one night after having been passed over for promotion for the third time. He called his sister-in-law Phyllis, a close friend of the bank president's wife, and asked her to try to find out why. She learned the following: George considered himself a great storyteller and was particularly fond of ethnic jokes. He often told these jokes, both at the office and at holiday and other office get-togethers. What George failed to realize was that a number of people, including the bank president, found this sort of humor at the expense of others patently offensive. Whenever an opportunity for advancement occurred, George was rejected as being too insensitive. He paid a high price for not knowing his audience.

**Audience analysis:** The collection and consideration of information about the characteristics, values, and attitudes of your listeners.

**Audience analysis** involves the collection and analysis of information about your listeners. As you listen to your classmates' speeches and talk to them, consider your audience carefully, make note of their interests, consider their backgrounds, knowledge, and attitudes toward your subject, and then develop your speech accordingly.

# WHAT RESPONSE CAN I REASONABLY EXPECT FROM MY AUDIENCE?

No matter how good a speech looks on paper or how well it is delivered, its success or failure must always be measured in terms of audience response. A salesperson who doesn't sell the product will soon be out of a job, the comedienne who doesn't evoke laughter will fall flat on her face, and the politician who doesn't get votes will not get elected. Therefore, when developing your speech, you must always consider whether the response you are seeking is realistic.

Some responses might be unattainable. Your audience might not have the background or experience necessary for you to be able to teach them how to repair a computer or sew a dress. A lack of time or resources might prevent you from showing your audience how to give a permanent or tile a floor. Your audience's attitude might be so opposed to your subject that they reject it at the outset. An example of the last would be trying to promote the legalization of marijuana in the United States. Although some in your audience would be for it, others would be impossible to approach. In such cases you would be better off choosing another, more realistic purpose that could achieve a reasonable response.

## WILL MY AUDIENCE FIND THIS SUBJECT USEFUL?

People willingly pay attention if they will gain something from doing so. You pay attention to the directions for filling out your income tax forms because you have something to gain if you do—and something to lose if you don't. You listen to a dull story told by your boss or prospective in-law and laugh because it is in your best interest to do so.

If for some reason members of your audience need to know the information you will be giving them in your speech, tell them they do. If they will prevent possible costly repair to their cars by engaging in a do-it-yourself lubricating program, if they have a responsibility to act against the growing problem of child abuse, or if they might possibly save a life by taking a Red Cross CPR course, let them know at the beginning of the speech. To show an audience how to react to an accident at home and then explain to them only at the conclusion of your speech that the majority of accidents occur at home would be to leave a number of those in your audience thinking, "I guess I should have listened."

Whenever possible, give your listener a reason for listening, and do it during the introduction to your speech.

The success or failure of a speech will be measured in terms of the audience response to it.

## WILL MY AUDIENCE FIND THIS SUBJECT INTERESTING?

The second reason that people pay attention is to satisfy an interest. Less effort is required to pay attention to what is interesting than to what is useful. Consider your own experience. Have you ever watched an unimaginative educational film because you knew there would be an exam about it? Have you listened to an uninteresting lecture because you knew it would have an effect on your grade? How much did you learn in that course? How much do you remember? In both cases, you had, in effect, something to gain by paying attention. Did it pay off? Now compare the uninteresting educational film or the lecture to the educational TV program *Sesame Street*. It is estimated that *Sesame Street* has a viewing audience of ten million. The people who write and produce the program handle their material in such an interesting way that paying attention (and thus learning) is no longer a chore—it is fun. Your job as a speaker is to develop your material interestingly. Although you can do this with someone you know quite well, how can you do it with strangers?

If you are familiar with the subject you have chosen, you should be able to make an educated guess. Suppose you choose to speak about one of your two hobbies, raising tropical fish or restoring antique cars. The majority of your friends have shown more interest in your antique cars than in your fish. Some might have even changed the subject when you asked if they wanted to see your baby swordtails. Probably, a general audience would have greater initial interest in antique cars. This, however, does not mean you could not choose to speak about raising tropical fish. You can do it effectively if you build your audience's interest to gain and maintain their attention. You might begin by introducing your listeners to the piranha, one of the most interesting fish you own. A description of this voracious, sometimes man-eating creature as even more dangerous than the great white shark is a surefire attention-getter.

## WHAT IS MY AUDIENCE'S KNOWLEDGE OF MY SUBJECT?

Considering what your listeners already know about your subject is an important part of audience analysis. A too technical approach could leave them thoroughly confused; repeating what they already know is sure to bore them.

If your audience has little or no knowledge of your subject, you must explain unfamiliar terminology and concepts to them. Keep in mind that this lack of knowledge will have an effect on their ability to respond. You could not expect those in your audience who have little idea of what is under the hood of a car to learn how to adjust a set of points or time a car after your speech to demonstrate. Nor could a nonsewer be expected to know how to install a zipper or cuff a pair of pants after a speech to demonstrate. Your educated guess as to the audience's knowledge of your subject should be an important consideration in terms of your choice of subject and purpose for each speech you make.

# WHAT DEMOGRAPHIC CHARACTERISTICS SHOULD I CONSIDER ABOUT MY AUDIENCE?

The word *demography* is derived from the Greek word *demos*, meaning "people." **Demographic audience analysis** has to do with their vital statistics: age, education, beliefs, special interests, and so on. These characteristics can often help you in determining how to handle your subject. For example, as a rule, young people tend to be more physically active than older people, more inclined to engage in sports rather than watch them. Consequently, when talking about a particular sport, you might treat it as a participation sport for a younger audience and as a spectator sport for an older group.

> **Demographic audience analysis:** The collection and consideration of the audience's vital statistics, including age, gender, educational level, and ethnic, cultural, or racial background.

The educational level of your audience could be important to you for a number of reasons. One of these has to do with the relationship between education and vocabulary. You must speak to an audience in familiar words that they can understand instantly. For example, you wouldn't explain the process of osmosis to your eleven-year-old sister in the same way you'd explain it to your college speech class. Another consideration is that a well-educated audience will be more aware of vital issues and current events than will a less educated one.

How many members of your audience come from different cultures? Never before in our history has the ethnic, cultural, and racial population in our country been so diverse. Each of us belongs to a variety of groups that have a distinct effect on the way we communicate. As indicated in Chapter 1, communication breakdowns occur even when communicating with those who are members of the groups to which we belong. Even more common are communication breakdowns between people from different cultures and subcultures. In analyzing your audience, try to consider any cultural characteristic, attitude, or sentiment that might bear on your speech topic.

Do those in your audience have similar attitudes and beliefs? Do they have special interests in common? Are they rich or poor, Democrat or Republican, conservative or liberal? Any of these demographic characteristics might be important to you as you prepare your speech. Remember, the success of your speech is always determined in terms of audience response. Did your audience get the information you wanted them to have? Were they entertained? Did you get them to take the action you wanted? The more you know about your audience, the more likely it will be that you will achieve your purpose.

# IS MY AUDIENCE'S ATTITUDE FAVORABLE, INDIFFERENT, OR OPPOSED?

## A FAVORABLE AUDIENCE

Perhaps the greatest advantage to dealing with a favorable audience is that they are usually both supportive and attentive. Your goal when communicating to them is to reinforce their positive attitudes. If they enjoy humor, the more effectively you entertain

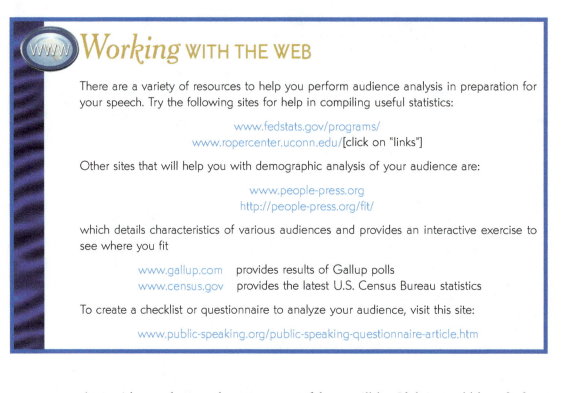

**www** *Working* WITH THE WEB

There are a variety of resources to help you perform audience analysis in preparation for your speech. Try the following sites for help in compiling useful statistics:

www.fedstats.gov/programs/
www.ropercenter.uconn.edu/[click on "links"]

Other sites that will help you with demographic analysis of your audience are:

www.people-press.org
http://people-press.org/fit/

which details characteristics of various audiences and provides an interactive exercise to see where you fit

www.gallup.com    provides results of Gallup polls
www.census.gov    provides the latest U.S. Census Bureau statistics

To create a checklist or questionnaire to analyze your audience, visit this site:

www.public-speaking.org/public-speaking-questionnaire-article.htm

them with your humor, the more successful you will be. If they would benefit from some tips on simple car maintenance, their satisfaction will be measured by how clearly you can explain your directions. The more effectively you can reinforce their positive attitudes, the more likely you will be to move them to action.

## AN INDIFFERENT AUDIENCE

When you feel that many in your audience will be indifferent to your subject, your job is to stimulate their interest. Make it clear to the audience why they should listen to your speech. You might point out why the subject is useful to them and how they will gain something from listening, you might give them information that will trigger their curiosity or interest, or you might point out how the problem affects them and why they need to listen to your plan for solving the problem. In each case, the action must be taken early in your introduction in order to gain the attention of your audience and hold it.

E. Fuller Torrey, psychiatrist, author, expert on mental illness, and president of the Treatment Advocacy Center, an Arlington, Virginia-based nonprofit group working to strengthen mental illness treatment laws, tells us how the case of the seriously mentally ill in twentieth-century United States affects us all.

When states began closing psychiatric hospitals three decades ago, nobody anticipated that our nation's cities would bear the brunt of a failed social policy known as deinstitutionalization which dumped hundreds of thousands of mentally ill individuals into communities without ensuring that they would get the medication that they needed to remain well. The National Advisory Mental Health Council has estimated that forty percent of the 3.5 million individuals with schizophrenia and manic depressive illness—or 1.4 million people—are not being treated. People with untreated mental illness are walking time bombs in the community. Repeated studies have shown it is not a question of whether violence will occur, it is a question of when. Random acts of violence committed by individuals whose mental illness is not being treated terrorize the residents of our cities.

Although Americans with untreated mental illness represent only 1% of the population in this country, they commit more than 1,000 homicides each year. At least a third of the estimated 600,000 homeless individuals have untreated schizophrenia or manic-depressive illness. At least 10 percent of the prisoners in our jails and prisons suffer from these illnesses, costing U.S. taxpayers $8.5 billion a year. A study released in 1999 by the MacArthur Foundation revealed that those who received proper treatment for their mental illness were no more violence prone than the rest of the population. Unfortunately, however, inadequate treatment laws in this country result in a person with untreated mental illness more often facing a policeman rather than a psychiatrist.

Because of the lack of community supports, deinstitutionalization not only has contributed to the nation's rate of violence, but also has affected our quality of life. We see it especially clearly in our big cities—the deterioration of public transportation facilities, loss of use of public parks, and disruption of public libraries are a few examples. The presence of even nonviolent mentally ill homeless in the streets and parks creates an inescapable sense of squalor and degradation. These people often end up victimized, in jail for misdemeanors, or prematurely dead from accidents, suicide, or untreated illnesses.

What can we do to ensure adequate treatment for these patients? First, change the standard. The legal standard for assisted treatment should be inability to help oneself, not, as it is now "danger to self or others." Society has an obligation to save people from degradation, not just death. This does not mean that we will have to reopen all the psychiatric hospitals that have closed as a result of deinstitutionalization.

Second, require compliance. Most individuals with severe mental illnesses can live in the community. But that must be conditioned on continued medication compliance. Outpatient commitments, conservatorships, and conditional hospital releases should be used widely to ensure that discharged patients comply with the requirement that they take their medication.

Third, build support in the community. For assisted treatment to work, states must build a network of outreach services in their communities to ensure compliance and to provide the supports needed for daily living and to prevent relapse. It means building the services that were promised to replace the closed state psychiatric hospitals.

Finally, demand accountability. States have had the responsibility of caring for individuals with mental illness for 150 years, but most have no internal monitoring system to assess those services. As a condition for receiving federal mental health block grants, states should be required to institute such programs. The data could then be sent to the Institute of Medicine under the National Academy of Sciences, which would submit an annual report to Congress.

The case of the seriously mentally ill in 20th-century America has been a public disgrace. More than 150 years of warehousing patients in inhumane state hospitals has been followed by almost 40 years of dumping them into bleak boarding homes or onto the streets. As we enter the next millennium, it is time to help individuals with severe mental illness become life's victors and not remain its victims.*

A successful speech to an indifferent audience was given by Erik Jackson, a second-year photography student. From conversations he had with them, Erik was aware that many of his classmates did not share his interest in photography and did not own expensive cameras or equipment. So, rather than delivering a complicated speech involving f-stops or light meters, Erik decided to give his speech class information about photography that would be useful to them regardless of what kind of equipment they had.

Erik began his speech by showing those in his audience several pages of pictures from a photo album. He had enlarged each of the pictures so that they could easily be seen, even by those in the back of the room. He called his classmates' attention to the fact that other than there being different people in each, the photos were very much alike. In each snapshot, people stood rigidly together in a line with smiles on their faces.

Next Erik showed the class a few variations of the first pictures he had shown. Although the people in them were the same, these snapshots were much more interesting than the first set. In some the arrangement of people was much more imaginative. In others the background made the group stand out much more vividly. By explaining about camera angle, posing, and picture balance, Erik demonstrated to his audience that with a little imagination they could take pictures that were more interesting.

## AN OPPOSED AUDIENCE

Perhaps the hardest audience to deal with is one that is opposed to your point of view or dislikes your subject. Who hasn't spent hours arguing about religion or politics only to wind up even more convinced than ever that he was right and the other fellow wrong. It is difficult to convince a person to change a point of view or opinion that may have taken her years to form. By the time a person reaches adulthood, many of his attitudes are pretty well fixed. Studies indicate that there is little change in viewpoint among those who listen to or read things with which they strongly disagree.

Fortunately, occasions are rare when a speaker or writer must address an audience opposed to her subject or viewpoint. It is difficult, for example, to imagine a pro-choice article in the *Catholic Herald Citizen* or to picture Elton John delivering a speech on same-sex marriages at a Promise Keepers convention.

Perhaps the best example of changing the viewpoint of a hostile audience is found in *Julius Caesar* by William Shakespeare. Mark Antony faces an audience that has been convinced by Brutus that Caesar was an ambitious tyrant who was justifiably killed for the good of Rome. He takes on the seemingly impossible job of persuading the Roman citizens that Brutus, whom they hold in high regard, is actually a despicable assassin.

---

*Remarks by E. Fuller Torrey, president. Treatment Advocacy Center, Arlington, VA. Used with permission.

The most difficult audience to address is most likely one with a viewpoint opposed to your own or with strong opinions about a controversial subject.

Antony begins by establishing a common ground with his audience. They are his "friends," his "fellow Romans," his "countrymen." He has not come to praise Caesar, whom the crowd hates, but to bury him as any friend would do. (His audience can understand this kind of friendship.) He shows respect for the audience's friendship toward Brutus by speaking of the "noble" Brutus. At this point, Antony raises the first question he wishes his audience to consider. "Brutus hath told you that Caesar was ambitious. If it were so, it was a grievous fault. And grievously hath Caesar answered it." This issue is, *was* Caesar ambitious? At this point, the crowd is convinced he was.

Antony acknowledges that Brutus permitted him to speak. He calls Brutus an "honorable" man. All those who were

ANTONY: Friends, Romans, Countrymen, lend me your ears; I come to bury Caesar, not to praise him. The evil that men do lives after them; The good is oft interred with their bones. So let it be with Caesar. The noble Brutus hath told you Caesar was ambitious. If it were so, it was a grievous fault, And grievously hath Caesar answered it. Here under leave of Brutus and the rest (for Brutus is an honorable man; So are they all, all honorable men), Come I to speak in Caesar's funeral.

involved in the assassination were "honorable" men. Antony's tone of voice when he says "honorable" should suggest that he might mean just the opposite. Have you ever said one thing and meant another? Have you ever asked someone for a favor and received the response, "I don't mind," when you could tell by the tone of voice that the person really did mind? The *way* you say something can communicate a great deal to others.

Antony begins questioning whether Caesar actually was ambitious. Brutus said he was, but what are the facts? If Caesar filled the treasury with money, where is the personal gain? If Caesar refused a kingly crown, where is the ambition? Note the reference to the personal experience of the listeners in the words, "You all did see . . ." "*Brutus* tells you that Caesar was ambitious," says Antony, "but you all have seen that he wasn't."

Notice that Antony is still careful not to say anything against Brutus. Even though the audience can see the weakness in Brutus's argument, Antony still avoids attacking him. After all, Brutus was held in high regard by the crowd for his patriotism and self-sacrifice, and there still may be respect in the minds of some.

The response of the audience onstage should indicate that Antony has changed their point of view. Although Brutus convinced them that Caesar was murdered to protect them from his ambition to become a dictator and make them his slaves, the fact that Caesar never profited from his position and three times refused the crown proves that he wasn't ambitious. Antony clearly established his image as a faithful friend by what he says and by what he does. He even weeps for Caesar. The crowd responds, "There's not a nobler man in Rome than Antony." From this point on, Mark Antony is speaking to friendly citizens who have been won over to his point of view.

ANTONY: He was my friend, faithful and just to me; but Brutus says he was ambitious, and Brutus is an honorable man. He hath brought many captives home to Rome, whose ransoms did the general coffers fill. Did this in Caesar seem ambitious? When that the poor have cried, Caesar hath wept; Ambition should be made of sterner stuff. Yet Brutus says he was ambitious; and Brutus is an honorable man. You all did see that on Lupercal I thrice presented him a kingly crown, which he did thrice refuse. Was this ambition? Yet Brutus says he was ambitious and sure he is an honorable man. I speak not to disprove what Brutus spoke, but here I am to speak what I know. You all did love him once, not without cause. What cause withholds you then to mourn for him? Oh, judgment, thou are fled to brutish beasts, and men have lost their reason! Bear with me. My heart is in the coffin there with Caesar, and I must pause till it come back to me.

This speech exemplifies two useful suggestions for dealing with an audience opposed to your subject or viewpoint: (1) establish a common ground with the audience, and (2) clear up any lack of understanding or misinformation your audience may have about your point of view or subject.

Mary Smith, a junior college freshman, used a **common-ground approach** in preparing a speech to inform on one of her favorite subjects, opera. She had found that most of her classmates were apathetic or even hostile to her subject. One fellow named Ron intended to cut class on the day of her speech because opera, especially Wagnerian opera, Mary's favorite, really "turned him off."

> **Common-ground approach:** A way of dealing with an audience opposed to your speech topic or viewpoint by finding a means of identifying with audience members.

On the day she delivered her speech, Mary identified with many in her audience by beginning:

> You know, like many of you I was really turned off by opera until two years ago, when I realized that I didn't like opera because I didn't know anything about it. Well, ever since then the more I got to know about it, the more I got to like it. I'm sure when you get to know enough about it, you'll like it, too.

Mary realized that she needed a fresh, imaginative approach to hold the attention of her audience. She prepared carefully and thoughtfully, and delivered to the class a humorous plot summary of Wagner's opera *Tannhauser*, which ended to even Ron's delight with the heroine getting stabbed right between the two big trees.

Mary took what many in her audience believed was a dull, boring topic and made it exciting and interesting. She used humor, novelty, conflict, and suspense to hold their attention, and the result was a successful speech.*

## Chapter Review

After reading this chapter, you should be able to

- Define audience analysis and the steps involved in preparing an audience-centered speech.
- Assess how useful your speech topic will be to your potential audience, and determine if members of your audience *need* the information you will be sharing with them.
- Determine the demographic characteristics of an intended audience, such as your classmates or another group to which you might give a speech.
- Assess your audience's attitude toward your intended speech topic.
- Determine how to overcome potential indifference or hostility/opposition to your point of view and develop a common-ground approach to your speech.
- Develop the appropriate strategy for your next classroom speech based on an analysis of your audience.

---

*Materials on pages 33–35 used with permission from Arthur Koch and Stanley B. Felber, *What Did You Say?*, 3rd ed. (Upper Saddle River, NJ: Prentice-Hall, 1985).

## Key Terms

Audience-centered speech (p. 27)          Demographic audience analysis (p. 31)
Audience analysis (p. 28)                Common-ground approach (p. 37)

## Exercises

1. Analyze five different magazines to determine the audience to which each appeals. What specific features did you notice?
2. Analyze your class as an audience. In what ways are your classmates similar? In what ways do they differ?
3. Keeping your analysis in mind, prepare a list of topics that would be *useful* to your audience.
4. Again, with your analysis in mind, prepare a list of topics that would be *interesting* to your audience.
5. Pick a highly controversial issue such as embryonic stem cell research. Write a statement that favors or opposes it. Estimate how many in your class would agree with your statement, be indifferent to it, or oppose it. Survey the class to check your estimates.
6. Analyze a popular TV show. To what age group is it directed? How do you know? Describe the characteristics of a "typical" viewer for this show.
7. Fill out a copy of the audience analysis form (Figure 2.1) during the planning of your speech. Many of the answers you put down on the form will be educated guesses about your audience. After your speech, have your classmates fill out the audience analysis evaluation form (Figure 2.2) to give you feedback on how successful you were at analyzing and adapting to your audience.

## Speech Assignments

1. *The Humorous Story*
Everybody loves a funny story, but not everyone can tell one well. If you have a favorite story or anecdote that you believe is genuinely funny, try your hand at using it for this assignment.

*Delivery.* This speech must be delivered extemporaneously. Your audience will expect you to have total eye contact when telling a story. The more spontaneous and relaxed you are, the more your audience will enjoy your presentation.

### Suggestions

1. Use vivid colorful language to stimulate the senses of your audience.
2. Organize your story in a clear chronological order.
3. Keep your story short enough to hold the interest of your classmates.

### Horseback Riding

A school principal calls a local minister to ask if he could fill in for a speaker who couldn't make it to deliver a speech on sex education that night at the local high school. "Glad to help," says the minister and goes home to shower and change

AUDIENCE ANALYSIS FORM

Name _____ Date _____

Title of Speech _____

(Answer each question completely.)

THE COMMUNICATOR

1. Why have I chosen this subject?

2. What qualifies me to deal with this subject?

THE MESSAGE

3. What is my specific purpose?

4. What response can I reasonably expect?

THE AUDIENCE

5. Will my audience find this subject interesting?

6. Will my audience find this subject useful?

7. What is the audience's probable knowledge of my subject?

8. What characteristics of my audience should I consider in preparing my subject?

**FIGURE 2.1** ■ **Audience Analysis Form**
This form is designed to help you understand your audience better. Fill out a copy of the form during the planning of your speech.

clothes. As he walks in the door, he yells to his wife that he'll be late for dinner because he has to give a lecture at the high school. "I'm in the living room dear," she replies. When he walks into the living room he is surprised to see a room full of churchwomen. "What's the lecture on dear?" she asks. "Ah, uh, horseback riding," he says. "Do a good job dear," she replies and he leaves.

The next day, the wife takes their little boy to the barbershop for a haircut. "I heard your husband's lecture at the high school last night and he did a good job," the barber told her. "That's strange," the wife says. "He's only tried it twice. The first time his new hat blew off and the second time he fell off and broke his leg."

AUDIENCE ANALYSIS EVALUATION FORM

Name _____

1. What was the communicator's subject?


2. How interesting was this subject to you?

   low        high

3. How useful was this subject to you?

   low        high

4. How effectively did the communicator get attention during introduction?

   low        high

5. How much preparation was put into this communication?

   low        high

6. What was the communicator's specific purpose? (one simple,
   declarative sentence)

   low        high

7. How effective was the conclusion to the communication?

   low        high

8. How well did the communicator accomplish his purpose?

   low        high

COMMENTS:

**FIGURE 2.2 ■ Audience Analysis Evaluation Form**
Have your classmates fill out this form to give you feedback on how well
you analyzed and adapted to your audience in planning and giving your speech.

**2.** *Reading Poetry*

Select poetry that falls within a one-to-two-minute time limit. Pick something you think your listeners will like and that you can handle intelligently. Study it carefully in regard to mood and purpose. Practice it so that you can read it effectively.

*Delivery.* Speak clearly and distinctly using variations in pitch, volume, rate, and inflection to make your reading interesting. Know your selection well enough so that you can maintain adequate eye contact.

**National Brotherhood Week**

*Oh, the white folks hate the black folks*
*And the black folks hate the white folks—*
*To hate all but the right folks*
*Is an old established rule.*

*But during National Brotherhood Week,*
*National Brotherhood Week,*
*Lena Horne and Sheriff Clark are dancing cheek to cheek.*
*It's fun to eulogize the people you despise.*
*As long as you don't let them in your school.*

*Oh, the poor folks hate the rich folks*
*And the rich folks hate the poor folks—*
*All of my folks hate all of your folks,*
*It's American as apple pie.*

*But during National Brotherhood Week,*
*National Brotherhood Week,*
*New Yorkers love the Puerto Ricans cause it's very chic.*

*Step up and take the hand of someone you can't stand;*
*You can tolerate him if you try.*

*Oh, the Protestants hate the Catholics*
*And the Catholics hate the Protestants*
*And the Hindus hate the Muslims*
*And everybody hates the Jews.*

*But during National Brotherhood Week*
*National Brotherhood Week,*
*It's National Smile at Oneanotherhood Week.*
*Be nice to people who are inferior to you;*
*It's only for a week, so have no fear—*
*Be grateful that it doesn't last all year!**

---

*Copyright 1965 by Tom Lehrer. Used by permission.

# 3

# *Determine Your*
## PURPOSE AND SUBJECT

TO DEVELOP an effective speech, you must have a clear purpose in mind. The title of this book, *Purposeful Speaking*, emphasizes the importance of *purpose* in oral communication. Your aim as a speaker should be to fulfill a **general purpose** by achieving a desired response. Your success in informing, entertaining, or persuading must always be measured in terms of the response your receiver gives to your message. Beginning speakers often fail because they pay too little attention to purpose and audience response when planning their speeches. Following are the major purposes in speaking:

> **General purpose:** A clear goal established for your speech, with a desired response from the audience: informing, persuading, or entertaining.

1. *To entertain*—to elicit a pleasurable response, to provoke curiosity, to provide suspense, or to amuse. Treating a serious subject lightly

or a light subject seriously and describing an unusual or exciting experience are examples of communication to entertain.

2. *To inform*—to add to the knowledge or understanding of the listener. Demonstrating how to do something, explaining a process, reporting on a meeting, and describing an event are examples of communication to inform.

3. *To persuade*—to convince, to reinforce, or to actuate. Because persuasion is more complex than entertainment or information, the three types of persuasion will be treated separately.

   a. *To convince*—to change your listener's opinions or to commit them to a point of view about which they are undecided. Persuasion to convince occurs frequently in debate and in problem-solving discussion. In both, information is given to listeners in an attempt to get them to change their minds or to form an opinion on something about which they are undecided. Persuasion to convince relies heavily on a logical approach using reasoning, statistics, testimony, comparison, and factual examples.

   b. *To reinforce*—to arouse and invigorate an audience already in agreement with the speaker's point of view. A speech at a pep rally in the school auditorium before a football or basketball game is a good example of persuasion to reinforce. The students do not have to be convinced about the importance of their team's winning. The idea is to strengthen their attitude about winning, to build a fire under them so that they are prepared emotionally and enthusiastically for the game. Persuasion to reinforce largely employs a psychological approach—appealing to the attitudes, beliefs, sentiments, and motives of the audience.

**c.** *To **actuate**—*to put into action. In the previous example, the speaker's job is to stimulate the members of the student audience to become even more excited than they already are about the upcoming game. However, they are not given specific instructions as to what to do in terms of that excitement. In persuasion to actuate, the audience should be told exactly what action you want to be accomplished. A speech by the coach to the team in the locker room before the game is a good example of persuasion to actuate. The team is told specifically to go out and "win one for the alma mater." The speech to actuate asks the audience to buy, to sell, to join, to march, or the like. Although it can employ persuasion to convince or to reinforce or both, it is by far more successful when directed to an audience who has already agreed. Obviously, if you want to get your audience to do something, you are bound to be more successful if it is already predisposed to act that way.

> **Actuate:** To put into action; in the case of a persuasive speech, gives audience instruction as to what action you want them to take: to buy, to sell, to join, to protest, and so on.

## SELECTING A SUBJECT

Once you clearly understand the general purpose of your speech, you are ready to choose a subject. There will undoubtedly be times when you will be asked to deliver a speech on a topic that has already been determined. For example, you are asked to give a report on a convention you attended as a delegate. Or as a member of a symposium you are assigned to speak on one aspect of a subject. In a different situation the occasion might determine what your subject will be. However, more often than not, you will need to select your own subject. It may be that when you find you must deliver a speech, you immediately think of a subject you have interest in and that you believe will be interesting to your audience. If this happens, you can immediately begin developing your speech. However, if you can't think of an appropriate subject, take out a sheet of paper and write down as many things as you can that you are interested in or have experience with. There is no better place to look for a subject than in your own background. Did you grow up on a farm? Did you come from a different part of the country? Where have you traveled? Do you have special skills in athletics, music, graphic arts, theater, or fashion design? What hobbies do you have? What are your political views? What issues turn you on? What do you talk about with close friends? With some imagination and hard work, you can make these subjects interesting to your audience.

# *Checklist* FOR SUCCESS

## PERSONAL INVENTORY

Taking inventory of subjects that you know something about or that are of particular interest to you is a useful way of brainstorming about potential speech topics.

For each category in this personal inventory, write down as many ideas as you can. When the list is complete, look over each idea to determine which one would be a good topic for a speech.

Music:  Groups and Songs

_____

_____

_____

Sports:  Issues and People

_____

_____

_____

Technology:  Issues and Innovations

_____

_____

_____

Global Issues

_____

_____

_____

Family and Friends

_____

_____

_____

National Issues

_____

_____

_____

People:  Celebrities

_____

_____

_____

Local Issues

_____

_____

_____

Mass Media

_____

_____

_____

Campus Issues

_____

_____

_____

Crafts/Hobbies

_____

_____

_____

Vacation Spots

_____

_____

_____

Public Policy: Issues and Questions

_____

_____

_____

Religious Issues

_____

_____

_____

Adapted from Seiler/Beall: *Communication: Making Connections*, 6/e, Allyn & Bacon, 2005.

## ✔ *Checklist* FOR SUCCESS

When determining which subject to choose, ask yourself the following questions:

1. Is the subject suited to my purpose?
2. Is the subject interesting to me?
3. Am I qualified to speak on this subject?
4. Will my audience find this subject interesting?
5. Will my audience find this subject useful?
6. Is my subject sufficiently narrowed?

## IS THE SUBJECT SUITED TO MY PURPOSE?

Suppose you are asked to deliver a speech whose general purpose is to inform. Because you have recently begun studying the U.S. Army School of the Americas in your Latin America history class, you decide to deliver an informative speech about this school, which was established in 1946 at Fort Benning, Georgia. As you begin developing the speech and find out more about the school, however, you learn that during the last fifty years, the School of the Americas has trained more than 87,000 Latin American and Caribbean soldiers, many of whom have committed some of the worst human rights violations in our hemisphere, and that officers who studied at the school are responsible for the torture, killing, and maiming of hundreds of thousands of innocent people in Latin America and that many graduates have destabilized democratic institutions or overthrown their governments. This would most likely give your listeners a highly negative view of this school which one Central American newspaper dubbed "School of the Assassins." This subject would be better suited as a speech with the general purpose to persuade and the specific purpose to actuate your audience to write their representative in Congress to support the Kennedy Bill, HR 2652, which will cut off funding for the School for the Americas, effectively closing it down.

## IS THE SUBJECT INTERESTING TO ME?

Whenever possible, choose a subject you find interesting. Enthusiasm is a key factor to successful speaking. If you talk enthusiastically about something, this enthusiasm is bound to rub off on your audience. Are you excited about a particular kind of music or art form? Are you into alternative rock or zydeco? Do you jog or lift weights? Collect coins? With a little imagination and some effort, you can make what interests you interesting for your audience.

When you have difficulty finding a subject that interests you, try a technique called **brainstorming**. Take out a blank sheet of paper and jot down as many potential speech topics as you can. Don't worry about the quality of these topics; aim for quantity. After you have listed

**Brainstorming:** A technique used to generate ideas for speech topics by spontaneously coming up with as many ideas as possible, without pausing to evaluate them.

In selecting a speech topic, consider your own qualifications to speak about a specific subject. Drawing on your own experiences, interests, and hobbies may help you develop a more interesting and useful presentation.

as many as you can, put the sheet away for at least eight hours. When you return to it, you may find that you have listed a number of topics of interest to you that you hadn't thought about.

## AM I QUALIFIED TO SPEAK ON THIS SUBJECT?

What are your qualifications for dealing with a particular subject? The fact that you are interested in a subject does not necessarily mean that you are qualified to speak on it. If your interest is recent, you might lack sufficient knowledge or experience to prepare the subject effectively. In some cases, it might be better to select a subject with which you are more familiar. Are you qualified because of background or skill? Do you speak from personal experience? What are your credentials? Do you have special skills in real estate, music, computers, or sewing? Sometimes the perfect speech topic is so close that the speaker doesn't see it. A speech by a student in the dental technology program on caring for teeth will undoubtedly be well received by classmates. If you have expertise or special knowledge or experience about your speech topic, indicate this to your audience in your introduction. If you have access to special information through a friend or relative who is an expert, indicate this as well. Even if your knowledge about the topic comes only through research, you want to let your audience know that what you are telling them is accurate and carefully prepared.

## (WWW) *Working* WITH THE WEB

The Internet Public Library is an excellent place to go for ideas on a subject for your next speech. You can visit this site at

www.ipl.org

Another excellent site for subject ideas is the Librarian's Index to the Internet, where you can find different categories of subjects already indexed for you, such as business, sports, health, science, or news and media. Go to

www.lii.org/search

An interesting source of speech topics is the Invisible Web, which indexes archives, databases, and search engines, and includes a "Hot List" of categories of current interest. Visit this site at

http://invisibleweb.com

## WILL MY AUDIENCE FIND THIS SUBJECT INTERESTING?

It takes little effort to pay attention to a subject that is interesting. Therefore, you will hold the attention of your audience if your subject is interesting to them. If you are not sure it will be, you must work to make it so. An effective way to do this is to use **attention factors**—humor, novelty, suspense, and the like. You will find a discussion of attention factors on pages 58–63.

**Attention factors:**
Techniques, such as humor, suspense, and novelty, used to get and hold the attention of your audience.

## WILL MY AUDIENCE FIND THIS SUBJECT USEFUL?

People will willingly pay attention to a communication if they expect to gain something useful from doing so. Consider your own experience. Have you ever followed a set of instructions on how to operate a computer, bake a cake, or ferment your own wine? Have you ever attended a lecture on what to expect on the final exam? Have you ever bought a do-it-yourself book and tried to follow the *simplified instructions*? Did you pay attention? Of course you did. If the subject you choose will benefit your audience in some way, it will quite likely hold their attention. If you believe that the usefulness of your subject will not be readily apparent to your audience, tell them in your introduction how they will benefit from listening to your speech.

## IS MY SUBJECT SUFFICIENTLY NARROWED?

In most cases, you will be given a definite time limit when you are asked to give a speech. If you exceed this time limit appreciably, you are bound to annoy your audience. Many beginning speakers try to cover too much in the time available to them. It is far better to deal with a restricted subject in detail than to cover too many points.

Remember, if you cover too much material without supporting it adequately, your audience is unlikely to remember it regardless of the length of your speech.

## SPECIFIC PURPOSE

**Specific purpose:** A more detailed statement of what you want to accomplish with your speech.

After you have chosen your subject in accordance with the considerations above, you are ready to formulate a **specific purpose**. Earlier I classified the general purposes for speaking: to entertain, to inform, and to persuade. Specific purposes illustrate your intent more precisely. They indicate in more detail exactly what you hope to accomplish. Note the following examples:

1. *General purpose*: to entertain
   *Specific purposes*:
   a. to amuse my audience by explaining how to wash a bull elephant
   b. to hold my audience in suspense while telling about the time I was robbed
   c. to amaze my audience with a demonstration of magic
   d. to fascinate my audience with a story about my first parachute jump
2. *General purpose*: to inform
   *Specific purposes*:
   a. to explain the art of tree dwarfing
   b. to demonstrate how to make an omelet
   c. to show how to take an effective snapshot
   d. to report the results of a recent experiment
3. *General purpose*: to persuade
   *Specific purposes*:
   a. to motivate my audience to contribute to CARE
   b. to prove to my audience that my new plan for ending the arms race will work
   c. to increase my audience's reverence for our flag
   d. to modify my audience's attitude about socialized medicine

Note that the specific purposes are phrases that begin with the infinitive form of a verb, which clearly relates to one of the three general purposes of speech. Thus, speeches to entertain, amuse, fascinate, amaze, delight; speeches to inform, explain, make clear, demonstrate, report; and speeches to persuade, motivate, prove, increase, modify.

## THE CENTRAL IDEA

**Central idea:** A clear, one-sentence statement or thesis around which the entire speech is developed.

Once you have phrased your specific purpose statement, it is time to develop your **central idea**. The central idea may be thought of as the thesis, the key statement, or the controlling idea of the speech. Although it is related to the speech purpose, it is worded differently. A specific purpose statement is worded as an infinitive phrase. A central idea is worded as a complete sentence. The specific purpose statement always includes the infinitive form of the verb that clarifies what your purpose is, that is to persuade, to inform, or to entertain. The central idea statement is a digested version of what you will be talking about in your speech. It is a one-sentence statement around which the entire speech is developed. The following guidelines will help you in developing your central idea statement.

The central idea statement is the key statement around which the entire speech is based. It is usually developed as you research and gain more information about your topic.

## THE CENTRAL IDEA SHOULD BE A COMPLETE SENTENCE

In most cases, a central idea should be stated as a simple complete sentence. Phrases, questions, or compound and complex sentences are usually not appropriate for central ideas.

| | |
|---|---|
| *Good*: | Being a single parent is tough. |
| | (Simple, declarative sentence) |
| *Bad*: | Are single parents getting a bad rap? |
| | (Question) |
| *Bad*: | Single parent problems |
| | (Phrase) |
| *Bad*: | After I raised Alex, I discovered being a single parent is tough. |
| | (Complex sentence) |

## THE CENTRAL IDEA SHOULD BE A STATEMENT YOU MUST EXPLAIN OR DEFEND

Your central idea should be a statement that requires clarification or reinforcement. Once you have developed your central idea, your next step will be to choose main points to support it. Following that you will choose supporting points to support the main points, and so on. Therefore, you must develop your central idea with thoughtfulness and care so that the supports that you use will seem clear and logical to your audience.

In some cases, your central idea will break up quite naturally into three or four main points or logical divisions. For example, consider a speech with the central idea "Walking is the ideal exercise." You might support it with these three main points: (1) it can be done by almost anyone at any age, (2) it conditions the mind and body, and (3) it removes unwanted fat. In other cases, the main points supporting your central idea might be a series of steps like the four steps involved in making lasagna, the three steps in refinishing furniture, and so on. Perhaps the main points supporting your central idea will be the reasons you give to convince your audience that your central idea is true.

## THE CENTRAL IDEA SHOULD BE SPECIFIC

State the central idea in specific rather than general terms. When you give your audience terms that are instantly understandable to them at the outset of your speech, they will be able to follow you more easily, and you won't have to waste their time defining terms for them as you unfold your ideas.

*Vague*:     The U.S. Social Security System is in crisis.
*Specific*:   The five-step Ball Plan can save Social Security.

## THE CENTRAL IDEA SHOULD COVER A SINGLE TOPIC

Combining more than one topic in a speech will create frustration and confusion for both the speaker and the audience.

*Bad*:      Unless we stop the influx of drugs into this country and stiffen the penalties for using and dealing, drug use by our youth will double in the next five years.
*Good*:     There are three steps that must be taken to stop the influx of drugs into this country.

## THE CENTRAL IDEA SHOULD BE AUDIENCE CENTERED

Because you developed your subject and purpose with your audience in mind, you must show them that you considered them carefully when phrasing your central idea statement.

*Good*:     Walking is the ideal exercise.
            (Includes practically everyone)
*Bad*:      Walking is a good way to shed those extra pounds.
            (Not everyone is overweight and someone who is might resent the comment.)

## THE CENTRAL IDEA SHOULD RELATE TO PURPOSE

Stating the central idea as a complete sentence will help you plan your communication more effectively. Following are three central idea statements related to three of the specific purpose statements:

1. *Specific purpose*—to amuse my audience by telling them how to wash a bull elephant.
   *Central idea*—Washing a bull elephant isn't all that easy.
2. *Specific purpose*—to explain the art of tree dwarfing.
   *Central idea*—The secret of tree dwarfing is twofold: cutting the root and branch system properly and maintaining the tree correctly.
3. *Specific purpose*—to motivate my audience to contribute to CARE.
   *Central idea*—CARE is the most efficient and effective charity in the world.

As you can see, the central idea statement is a clear statement of the way in which you plan to develop your speech. For example, the first purpose above is to entertain, specifically to amuse the audience by telling them how to wash a bull elephant. The central idea—Washing a bull elephant isn't all that easy—implies that the speech will involve some of the humorous problems that could arise when trying to wash the elephant. The second purpose—to explain the art of tree dwarfing—is to inform. Its central idea indicates that the speech will deal with the two most important principles in tree dwarfing: cutting the roots and branches properly and maintaining the tree correctly. The third specific purpose—to motivate my audience to contribute to CARE—is to actuate. The central idea clearly indicates that you will develop the speech by talking about the efficiency and effectiveness of CARE.

## Chapter Review

After reading this chapter, you should be able to

- Determine a general and a specific purpose for your speech.
- Distinguish among the general purposes in giving a speech: to entertain, to inform, and to persuade.
- Define and give examples of the three types of persuasion: to convince, to reinforce, and to actuate.
- Brainstorm a list of subjects, and select a topic for your next classroom speech that will be suited to your purpose and interesting and useful to your audience.
- Understand how to formulate a specific purpose statement that conveys precisely the intent of your speech.
- Describe the difference between the specific purpose and the central idea.
- Construct a clear central idea statement that relates to the specific purpose statement of your speech.

## Key Terms

| | |
|---|---|
| General purpose (p. 43) | Attention factors (p. 48) |
| Actuate (p. 45) | Specific purpose (p. 49) |
| Brainstorming (p. 47) | Central idea (p. 50) |

## Exercises

1. State whether the general purpose in each of the following situations is to inform, to entertain, to convince, to reinforce, or to actuate. Be prepared to explain and defend your answers.
   a. The reading of a will
   b. A TV soda commercial
   c. A newscast
   d. A debate

    **e.** A eulogy at a funeral

    **f.** A campaign speech

    **g.** A TV soap opera

    **h.** A TV talk show

    **i.** An ornithology lecture

2. Write a general purpose statement, a specific purpose statement, and a central idea statement for any of the following subjects, as your instructor directs:

    **a.** Global warming

    **b.** Alcoholism

    **c.** Hobbies

    **d.** Parking on campus

    **e.** Internet security

    **f.** Identity theft

    **g.** Education

    **h.** Immigration

    **i.** Terrorism

    **j.** Steroid use in Major League baseball

3. Prepare to listen to a class lecture by recalling what you already know about the subject. Go to the library or log on to the Internet and obtain information that will help you better understand what the speaker will say.

4. During the next classroom speech that you attend, translate the speaker's main ideas and supporting details into your own words and write a full sentence outline of the speech. How easy was it to determine the general purpose, specific purpose, and central idea of the speech?

5. Tune in to C-SPAN, where members of Congress might be speaking, or to a national news show with guests speaking on different sides of an issue. Do you have an opinion about the topic? Does that bias affect your ability to listen to the speaker's words? Explain.

## Speech Assignments

1. *A Speech of Criticism*

    Deliver a two-to-three-minute speech criticizing a person, policy, or organization. Express your views in a direct, to-the-point manner, emphasizing your annoyance with the language you choose.

    *Delivery*. This is an expression of viewpoint. You are not attempting to persuade someone to agree with you. Communicate your annoyance with appropriate gestures, facial expression, and tone of voice.

    ### Sample Topics

    1. Harry Potter is all hype.
    2. Embryonic stem cell research is murder.
    3. My cousin is an idiot.
    4. Fad diets don't work.
    5. Welfare is another word for stealing.
    6. Let's get the bigots out of our judicial system.
    7. Pluto should be a planet.

### *Where Does This Hero Rest?*

MR. CONYERS: Mr. Speaker, not too long ago a young black American named William Terry volunteered to serve in the U.S. Army. Proudly he assumed the uniform of his country, and willingly took his training and was sent to Vietnam.

Private First Class Terry wore his uniform proudly, even though it may have been woven by a company which would not have hired or promoted him. And he fought for his country, even though he and 24 million of his countrymen were denied the rights due to them as full-fledged American citizens. And, not long afterwards, Private First Class Terry, only 20 years old, gave his life to his country—killed in action in defense of a government that renounced the same freedoms he was told he was fighting for.

Bill Terry did not think of the slave ships, the auction blocks, Jim Crow, or Judge Lynch. He did not allow himself to be swayed by those who would destroy the dreams of himself and his fellows, by those who would segregate his schools, isolate his jobs, hurl threats or even bombs at his doorways. Instead, he thought only of what he conceived to be his duty to his country. He fought for what he thought right and he died for it.

And then, in a Government-issue coffin, he came home to his family—in Birmingham, Ala.

His family asked that he be buried in Birmingham, in a place called the Elmwood Cemetery. But the Elmwood Cemetery said no, only white people could be buried there. So, because he was black, Bill Terry was buried in another cemetery outside of Birmingham, where only blacks were interred. And he was buried in an unmarked grave.

Just as it is a source of pride to relatives of others who lie with him that he is there, so it is a source of shame to our country that he was forced to lie there. What was he to America, even in death? What was his family to America? And now, what is America to them?

In recent days we have heard much of patriotism and our country. Many speeches have been delivered. With all those flags flapping in the breeze, I wonder whether all those speakers included Bill Terry in their thoughts. Did they count him in? Did they care?

Maybe Bill Terry even heard them, there in that place where he rests.

2. *Pet Peeve Speech*

Deliver a one-to-two-minute speech about a situation, policy, person, or organization that really annoys you. Emphasize your irritation in your tone and the language you use.

*Model.* One thing that really ticks me off is being assigned a book for class and then hardly ever using it. Last semester, I had to buy two books for a class that cost over thirty dollars apiece. Most of the chapters we read were from one of the books, but only two were from the other. When I sold that book back to the bookstore it was in practically new condition, but I only got half my money back. That stinks!

---

*Congressional Record.* Speech given by Hon. John Conyers, Jr., of Michigan in the House of Representatives, November 25, 1969.

# The Introduction
## AND CONCLUSION

# OBJECTIVES OF INTRODUCTIONS

Now that you have determined your purpose and subject, you are ready to begin developing your **introduction**. In most cases, an introduction to a speech has five objectives: (1) it should capture the audience's attention, (2) it should present the central idea of the speech, (3) it should indicate your qualifications, (4) it should give the audience a reason for listening, and (5) it should preview the ideas to be covered in the speech. Keep in mind that although an introduction will often include all five of these elements, at times one or more of them may be omitted.

**Introduction:** An opening that gets the audience interested in listening to the speech, presents the central idea, and previews the main points.

1.  *Capture attention*—The first goal of the speaker is to get the attention of the audience. You cannot communicate to an audience that is not paying attention to you. Ten suggestions for getting the attention of your audience are given in the next section. They are designed to put your audience in a good frame of mind and to prepare them to listen to you.
2.  *Present central idea*—You should present the central idea of your speech early in your introduction. It should be a declarative statement about your subject that you must explain or defend rather than a fact that no one can deny. The central

idea may be thought of as the key statement or thesis of your speech. It should be worded as a simple sentence. Phrases, questions, or compound and complex sentences are not appropriate for central idea statements.

3. *Indicate your qualifications*—If you can show your audience that you have appreciable knowledge about your subject, it will motivate them to listen to you. If you've always had an interest in the subject and researched it carefully, reveal this to your audience. If you have had personal experience with a topic, tell them about it. If you are an expert on a subject, don't be modest about it, let them know.

4. *Give reason for listening*—The next step is to make it clear to the audience why they should listen to your speech. You might show how a problem affects them or others they are concerned about and why they need to listen to your plan for solving the problem; you might explain why the subject is useful to them and how they will gain something by listening; or you might give them some background information that will trigger their curiosity or interest.

5. *Preview main points*—The **preview statement** gives your audience a clear explanation of the main ideas to be covered in your speech. It is important because it prepares your audience to listen for and retain key information. The preview statement is the last thing you say in the introduction and should provide a transition into the body of the speech. If you've prepared your speech carefully with your audience in mind, your preview statement will hold the attention of your audience and give them something to look forward to.

> **Preview statement:** A clear explanation of the main ideas to be covered in the speech.

## ATTENTION STEP IN INTRODUCTIONS

Besides fulfilling some or all of these objectives, an effective introduction should smoothly lead into the body of the speech. The first objective of the introduction is to get the attention of the audience. Following are ten methods for accomplishing this. Each is followed by a model.

### Start Off with Humor

When I was preparing this speech, I was reminded of the story of the woman who called up the fire department and screamed, "Come quick! My house is on fire." When the fireman on the other end of the line responded, "OK lady, but how do we get there?" she replied, "Don't you have that big red truck anymore?" Now that story is kind of silly, but there's also a certain amount of truth to it. It won't be long before fire departments will no longer have red trucks.

Now that science has found that pastel colors are considerably more visible than red, more and more fire departments are changing to yellow or lime-green vehicles. However, this is only one of many changes fire departments have made over the last ten years. Today I'm going to tell you about some of the most interesting of these changes. Some of them you won't believe.

## Begin with a Brief Story

Julia is a forty-two-year-old single mother with a high school diploma. She works at a fast-food restaurant in Evansville, Indiana, for $7 an hour with no benefits. She ended a twenty-year marriage with the father of her three children when he became abusive after losing his job. The court ordered him to pay alimony and maintenance for his children, but he has left the state and cannot be located. To stretch her paycheck and feed her family, Julia restricts her heat and electricity usage and her phone calls and she shops only for necessities. She also visits the food pantry at a church nearby her home. According to a study by the U.S. Center on Budget and Policy Priorities, the poverty rate among working families has increased by nearly 50 percent, and 70 percent of poor families with children in the United States include a person who works. Today I'm going to tell you how the 1996 welfare law has failed.

## Ask a Rhetorical Question

Did you know that sports utility vehicles, minivans, and light trucks spew out three to five times as much air pollution as automobiles? Did you know that because they guzzle almost twice as much gas as automobiles they emit twice as much carbon dioxide into the air we breathe? Because these vehicles make up nearly 50 percent of new cars sold today, they are significantly damaging our environment and have become a large and growing contributor to global warming. Today I'm going to tell you what you can do to help clean up this significant source of environmental damage to the United States.

> **Rhetorical question:** A question used to gain listeners' attention, where the audience is not expected to give an answer out loud.

## Begin with a Statistic

More than 1.3 billion people live in abject poverty in this world. They live in garbage dumps, dried-up river beds, and land without resources. The United Nations estimates that another 100 million people will be added to the poverty list by the beginning of the twenty-first century. The World Bank estimates that number to be 200 million. One and one-half billion people have little or no medical care or clean drinking water. Every year one-half a million women die from pregnancy problems because they lack medical aid. Yet, 358 billionaires (with a collective wealth of $760 billion) have as much wealth as more than 40 percent of humanity. Twenty percent of the world's population owns 83 percent of the world's wealth. This same 20 percent, of which the United States is a major member, consume 80 percent of the world's resources. There is something that each of us can do to help, and today I'm going to tell you what that is.

## Refer to a Previous Speaker

I really enjoyed Marion's speech on how to save by buying generic. I had no idea how many products were sold under the generic label. Some of the prices

Beginning your speech with a startling statistic, such as stating the number of people living in abject poverty in the world, makes a strong introduction and is a good way to capture your audience's attention right away.

she quoted were incredibly low. What an easy way to save money! Today I'm going to tell you how the money you save by buying generic could help build a world in which no family will go hungry. Did you know that we produce enough food in the world to feed every man, woman, and child? Still, 841 million people in this world go hungry every day? Since 1945, when CARE began supplying food in CARE packages to desperately needy people in war-torn Europe and Asia, CARE has remained dedicated to alleviating hunger. I've been giving to CARE since I was a senior in high school. I figure I'm much better off than the people CARE is helping, so I give what I can. If you haven't given to CARE before and would be interested, I've put a stack of envelopes and forms on the back table. Pick one up, put a five or ten dollar check or money order in it, put a stamp on it, and mail it; it will make you feel good. I guarantee it.

## Refer to Familiar Terms

What images come to mind when you hear the words redmen, chiefs, or warriors? For many people, these words are synonymous with sports. Maybe some of you went to a school whose sports team had an Indian name. Perhaps some of you have a favorite professional team that has an Indian name like the Washington Redskins or the Atlanta Braves. Over the last few years, I've talked to many people who do not understand why American Indians object to "Indian" team names, mascots, and logos being used in school athletic programs and professional sports. "How can you complain? We're proud of our teams!" they say. "We love our Seminoles, our Chiefs, our Warriors. You should feel honored that we respect Native Americans enough to name our teams after them and display their logos on our posters and t-shirts."

Well, we don't feel honored. As an American Indian and member of the Potawatomi Nation, I'm here to tell you why using "Indian" names and images for sports teams, logos, and mascots is highly insulting to American Indians.

## Begin with a Definition

A hate crime is a crime committed against a class of people because of their race, religion, sexual orientation, or ethnic group. Common victims of hate crimes are blacks, Jews, homosexuals, Asians, American Indians, and Hispanics. Hate crimes are usually not directed at a specific individual. Those who commit hate crimes will choose anyone from the group that they hate. For example, a homophobic will commit a hate crime against a person because he or she is gay. It doesn't matter who the gay person is. The fact that the person is gay is all that counts. Although a horrendous number of hate crimes are committed against people of different races or religions, in 2002, the biggest reason for hate crimes was sexual orientation. Homosexuals are far more likely to be victims of violence than any other group. A recent study by the Southern Poverty Law Center in Montgomery, Alabama, found that 45 percent of lesbians and 29 percent of gay men have suffered physical attacks because of their sexual orientation and that they are six times more likely to be victims of hate crimes than Jews, Indians, Asians, or Hispanics and twice as likely as blacks. Hate crimes are on the rise in our country, and they threaten our security. Not surprisingly, hate crimes are caused by prejudice and fear. This afternoon I'm going to tell you about hate crimes and the people who commit them. Then I'm going to tell you what you can do to stop hate crimes in your community.

## Begin with a Startling Statement

More than one-half a million women are raped each year in the United States. Many more suffer intimidation, sexual abuse, physical abuse, and even death at the hands of men. Sexual abuse is even worse for women who are incarcerated. According to Amnesty International, "Sexual abuse is virtually a fact of life for incarcerated women in the United States. They are frequently the targets of sexual abuse by correctional officers, from groping to rape to coerced sex in exchange for work assignments, sanitary products, or shampoo. And they face retaliation if they dare to report threats and ill treatment by male guards." Today I'm going to talk about this problem, legislation that would mete out tough sentences to those responsible for sexual misconduct against women, and the steps that would protect victims from retaliation.

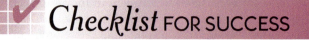

## Checklist FOR SUCCESS

Tips for Attention-getting Introductions:

- Start off with humor—engages the audience immediately and sets a positive tone
- Start off with a brief story—makes the material interesting
- Ask a rhetorical question—gets the audience thinking
- Begin with a statistic or several startling statistics—engages the audience
- Refer to a previous speaker—makes a connection
- Refer to familiar terms—lets the audience know your speech will be accessible
- Begin with a definition—again, makes the material accessible
- Begin with a startling statement—gets the audience thinking
- Start with a quotation—establishes credibility
- List a series of examples—makes material interesting and establishes credibility

### Start with a Quotation

It was Edmund Burke who said, "The only thing necessary for the triumph of evil is for good men to do nothing." Those words are as true today as they were in the eighteenth century. Many good Americans have sat passively by as this nation has continued its status as the world's leading exporter of weapons of destruction, exporting more missiles, aircraft, tanks, and ships than any other country. Rather than seeking peace, the United States has contributed to an arms race unparalleled in the history of the world. The world does not need more weapons of destruction. What is needed is an effective means for resolving conflict. Today I'd like to tell you about some specific things you can do to help stop this arms race.

### List a Series of Examples

On their way home from a family reunion, a young couple and their infant son are killed in a head-on collision with a pickup truck that crosses the center line. Two weeks later, an eight-year-old girl is crippled for life by a car that jumps the curb, crashes through a fence, and veers into the yard where she is playing. The next day, after leaving a party, a teenage girl and her drunken boyfriend are thrown from his motorcycle and killed when he fails to negotiate a dangerous curve. What do these accidents have in common? They were all caused by drivers who were intoxicated. They are typical stories that appear in newspapers day after day in cities throughout our nation. Yet, the greatest tragedy is that many of these kinds of accidents would never recur if we could do one thing: Find a way to get the drunk driver off the road.

## WWW *Working* WITH THE WEB

The following site may be helpful in finding an attention-getting introduction for your speech because it contains reference works such as *The American Heritage Dictionary* and *Roget's Thesaurus* as well as free online poetry, literature, and quotations:

www.bartleby.com

Another search engine for quotations or other catchy introductions and conclusions is Yahoo:

http://dir.yahoo.com/reference/quotations/

The list of suggestions given above for attention-getting introductions is by no means complete. Other methods include referring to a recent event or one that is soon to occur, a buildup of suspense, the use of a visual aid as part of the introduction, the use of novelty or the unusual, an introduction involving conflict, and establishing a common ground with the audience.

Choose your introduction carefully. It should be consistent with the purpose and the central idea of your speech. A humorous introduction to a serious speech would be a poor choice. Be aware that the introduction is the first thing your audience hears, and therefore it has much to do with the effectiveness of your speech.

## TYPES OF CONCLUSIONS

Some people believe that the **conclusion** is the most important part of the speech. It is your last chance to achieve your purpose, and it signals to your audience that your speech is ending. Plan your conclusion carefully. It is the final impression the audience will get of your speech, and it should leave them with a sense of completeness. It is no accident that many of the most memorable lines from speeches have occurred at or near the conclusion. Among them are the following:

**Conclusion:** A closing that signals to the audience that the speech is ending and reinforces your purpose.

> *I know not what course others may take, but as for me, give me liberty, or give me death!*
>
> —PATRICK HENRY

> *That we here highly resolve that these dead shall not have died in vain—that this nation, under God, shall have a new birth of freedom—and that the government of the people, by the people, and for the people shall not perish from the earth.*
>
> —ABRAHAM LINCOLN

> *Ask not what your country can do for you; ask what you can do for your country.*
>
> —JOHN F. KENNEDY

Finally, remember never to introduce new material in your conclusion. To do so will leave your audience with the impression that you failed to plan your speech carefully and added the new material as an afterthought, or that you left something out of your talk and remembered it just as you were about to close. Either way, you wind up with egg on your face. Following are six suggestions for effectively concluding your speech.

## END WITH A CALL TO ACTION

A speech that has as its central idea "After the devastating events of September 11, we need to help restore faith in the United States by unselfishly doing something for others" might end this way:

> By engaging in volunteer service in your neighborhoods and local communities and giving what you can financially to those organizations that are providing aid to the many victims and their families, you are helping to keep our nation strong. Helping an elderly neighbor, providing a meal for a shut in, shopping for someone who is disabled, ringing a bell for the Salvation Army, working in a food pantry, serving a meal, or cleaning up at a meal site are just some of the things you can do in your community to give something back for all the benefits you have received as a citizen of this great country of ours. And while you are out there, helping to improve your communities and helping others, keep in your hearts and minds the words of President John Fitzgerald Kennedy: "Our most common bond is that we all inhabit this small planet. We all breathe the same air. We all cherish our children's future. And we are all mortal."

A strong conclusion, such as John F. Kennedy's famous "Ask not . . ." line from his Inaugural Address, leaves the audience with a lasting final impression.

## END WITH A RHETORICAL QUESTION

A speech with the central idea "We need foolproof safeguards for stockpiling and handling plutonium" might end this way:

> Can the United States afford to manufacture and store a substance so deadly that a few ounces of it could destroy every living creature on this continent? The answer is obvious. However, our government has not yet responded. Haven't we learned anything from the space shuttle tragedy? How many more will have to die before we set up fail-safe systems? Write your representatives in the House and Senate now and tell them that we need foolproof safeguards for stockpiling and handling plutonium.

## END WITH A POSITIVE VISION OF THE FUTURE

The vision of the future that you project can be either positive or negative. The choice is up to you. For instance, in a **problem–solution speech**, you can visualize for your audience what the future will be like once the problem is solved. The following excerpt is the positive view of the future envisioned by Dr. Martin Luther King, Jr., in his stirring speech "I Have a Dream."

**Problem–solution speech:** A speech that encourages the audience to take specific action to solve the problem identified in the speech.

> From every mountainside let freedom ring. And when this happens, and when we allow freedom to ring, when we let it ring from every village and every hamlet, from every state and every city, we will be able to speed up that day when all of God's children, black men and white men, Jews and gentiles, Protestants and Catholics, will be able to join hands and sing in the words of the old Negro spiritual: Free at last! Free at last! Thank God almighty, we are free at last!

## END WITH A RESTATEMENT OF YOUR CENTRAL IDEA

A speech that has as its central idea that hate crimes are on the rise in this country and that they threaten our security might end this way:

> The alarming increase of hate crimes in the United States has a direct connection to the increase in hate websites on the Internet and the increase in the minority population. There must be an immediate and concerted effort to address this bigotry— through education, communication, cooperation, and litigation. We must put hate crimes into the spotlight so that we can see them for the evil they are. Hate crimes are on the rise in this country, and they threaten our security.

## END WITH A SUMMARY OF THE MAIN IDEAS DEVELOPED IN YOUR SPEECH

A speech with the central idea that mental illness can be devastating, but that for many recovery is possible, might conclude this way:

> As I stand here speaking to you today, there are researchers working on new medications and treatments in universities and medical research institutions throughout the

world. New psychotropic drugs are being tested. The cure for mental illness is out there. Someone has to find it and someone will. You can count on it. Remember, first, mental illness can affect anyone at any age—no one is immune. Second, most people have little knowledge or understanding of mental illness. Third, there is a lot of stigma attached to this biological brain disorder. Fourth, there are organizations that help those who are affected deal with mental illness. And, fifth, new discoveries in research and treatment offer greater hope for recovery. We start the twenty-first century with better treatment for mental illness and more help available. Remember, mental illness affects one out of four families, but there is hope. Mental illness can be devastating, but for many recovery is possible.

## END WITH A NEGATIVE VISION OF THE FUTURE

There may be times when you will want to leave your audience with the feeling that the problem must be solved before it is too late. In these cases, you might want to paint a picture of what the future will be like if something is not done to solve the problem as soon as possible. The speech that has as its central idea that sports utility vehicles, minivans, and light trucks pose a significant threat to our environment might end this way:

> The technology exists to make sports utility vehicles, minivans, and light trucks as clean as passenger cars, ensuring cleaner air and reducing the threat of global warming. According to the Union of Concerned Scientists, which was the 1999 Nobel peace prize winner, pollution from the tailpipes of these vehicles can be cut to passenger car levels for as little as a few hundred dollars. However, Detroit automakers are stonewalling. They refuse to spend a few hundred dollars to manufacture cleaner vehicles on which they make up to $15,000 profit. I am asking each of you as you leave

## ✔ *Checklist* FOR SUCCESS

Tips for Creating Effective Conclusions

- End with a call to action—motivates and makes a personal appeal
- End with a rhetorical question—leaves the audience with a thought-provoking and memorable impression
- End with a positive vision of the future—visualizes solving the problem presented in the speech
- End with a restatement of your central idea—reinforces the purpose of your speech
- End with a summary of your main ideas—also reinforces important points
- End with a negative vision of the future—conveys a sense of urgency about solving the problem presented

class today to sign three petitions, which will be sent to Ford, General Motors, and Chrysler, urging them to make their SUVs, minivans, and pickups meet the same fuel economy and pollution standards as passenger cars.

Other suggestions for concluding your speech are to end with a quotation, a poem, a story, a startling statement, a visual aid, a combination of methods, or an epigram.

# SAMPLE FULL SENTENCE OUTLINE FOR A SPEECH TO INSTRUCT

The following is a sample full sentence outline of a speech to instruct on the contributions African Americans have made to their country.

## BLACK IS BEAUTIFUL

### INTRODUCTION

    **I.** Did you know that there were more than 5,000 African American cowboys in the Old West, and that an African American named Bill Pickett invented the technique of "bulldogging"? Are you aware that African American participation in the development of this country began in the early 1600s? (Attention-getters)

    **II.** I learned quite a few interesting facts such as these when I attended a series of lectures on campus during Black History week last semester. Since then, I've been reading a lot and browsing the Internet learning about African American heroes. (Indicate qualifications)

A commencement speaker will often give the audience a positive vision of the future and a charge to make a difference in the world.

**III.** I learned that African Americans have contributed significantly to this nation's development. (Central idea statement) I was amazed, although somewhat disappointed, that I hadn't heard these things before.

**IV.** The record shows that African American men and women have been in the forefront of our progress as a nation throughout the years. These are things everyone should know about U.S. history. (Reason for listening)

**V.** That's why I'm going to tell you about some famous African Americans and also about some lesser-known African Americans who have contributed to our growth, have dedicated themselves to our welfare, and have added to the quality of life here in this land of ours. (Preview statement)

### BODY

**I.** Throughout our history, African American men and women have contributed significantly to the growth of the United States.

**A.** African Americans were instrumental in developing this country.

   **1.** African Americans sailed with Columbus on his voyages to the New World.

   **2.** African Americans were with Coronado in New Mexico and de Soto in Alabama.

   **3.** York, an African American slave, traveled with Lewis and Clark on their Northwest Passage to the Pacific.

   **4.** Jean Baptise Dusable, an African American, founded Chicago.

**B.** African Americans have furthered industrial expansion in the United States. Four significant contributions were:

   **1.** Lewis Latimer invented the first long-lasting light bulb and the safety elevator.

   **2.** Granville T. Woods invented the third rail.

   **3.** Garrett Augustus Morgen invented the gas mask.

   **4.** Shelby J. Davidson invented the adding machine.

**II.** Over the years, African Americans have been dedicated to the welfare of the United States.

**A.** African Americans have served illustriously in defending our country.

   **1.** More than 5,000 African Americans served in the Continental Army.

   **2.** African Americans fought with valor in the War of 1812.

   **3.** In World War I, 370,000 African Americans served their country with valor.

      **a.** The 369th received more citations than any other regiment.

      **b.** The 369th, 370th, and 371st were awarded France's highest honor.

   **4.** More than 1 million African Americans enlisted in World War II.

      **a.** The all-African American Panther tank battalion overwhelmed the Nazis.

      **b.** Benjamin O. Davis became the nation's first African American general.

**B.** African American religious and political leaders have enriched our values.

   **1.** Frederick Douglass worked with and influenced eight presidents.

   **2.** Reverend Martin Luther King, Jr., stirred the soul of United States with his dream of equality for all.

   **3.** Shirley Chisolm, the first African American woman to be elected to Congress, fought tirelessly for the rights of the disenfranchised.

      4. Reverend Jesse Jackson has been an outspoken advocate of social, political, and economic justice for all.

   **C.** African Americans have contributed significantly in the field of medicine.

      1. Dr. Daniel Hale Williams performed America's first open heart operation.

      2. George Washington Carver found more than 400 uses for the peanut and sweet potato.

      3. Dr. Benjamin Carsen was the first neurosurgeon to separate Siamese twins joined at the head.

      4. Dr. Charles Drew, an expert on blood plasma, set up the first blood bank.

**III.** From the outset, African Americans have contributed to the quality of life in our country.

   **A.** African American contributions to the cultural arts have been impressive.

      1. Marion Anderson, the first African American to sing at the Metropolitan Opera, won the National Medal of Arts.

      2. Alex Haley was awarded the Pulitzer Prize for his novel, *Roots*.

      3. Sydney Poitier won the Academy Award for his performance in *Lilies of the Field*.

      4. Maya Angelou, author of *I Know Why the Caged Bird Sings*, was awarded the National Book Award.

   **B.** African Americans have excelled in the area of sports.

      1. Jack Johnson won the world heavyweight boxing championship in 1903.

      2. Jesse Owens was the first athlete to win four gold medals in the Olympics.

      3. Hank Aaron set a new world record with 755 home runs.

      4. Jackie Joyner-Kersee was declared world's greatest female athlete after winning six medals at the 1988 Olympics.

   **C.** African American entertainers have shown remarkable talent.

      1. Harry Belafonte—world renowned singer—has won two Emmy Awards.

      2. Cicely Tyson won Best Actress of the Year for her role in *The Autobiography of Miss Jane Pittman*.

      3. Bill Cosby was named the *entertainer of the twentieth century*.

      4. Denzel Washington, a matinee idol of the 1990s, won an Academy Award for his performance in the Civil War film *Glory*.

## CONCLUSION

  **I.** This nation owes a debt of gratitude to African Americans who have helped develop and defend this country, have been dedicated to its welfare, and have added to the quality of life of its citizens. (Summary of main points)

 **II.** African Americans have made significant inroads in the field of medicine; impressive contributions in fine arts, sports, and entertainment; and have enriched our values.

**III.** Many African American actors, musicians, and writers are world renowned. It is easy to see why the words *black* and *beautiful* are synonymous.

**IV.** I hope I have introduced you to some African American heroes you hadn't heard of and that you now have a better understanding of how different people in this country have worked together for the common good. The Reverend Martin Luther King, Jr., said that understanding and creative goodwill for all comes from the love of God operating in the human heart. "We love men," he said, "not because we like them, nor because their ways appeal to us, nor even because they possess some type of divine spark; we love every man because God loves him."

**BIBLIOGRAPHY**

Abdul-Jabbar, Kareem. *Black Profiles in Courage*. New York: William Morrow, 1996.

Brodie, James. *Created Equal: The Lives and Ideas of Black American Innovators*. New York: William Morrow, 1993.

Haber, Louis. *Black Pioneers of Science and Invention*. New York: Harcourt Brace and World, 1970.

Harrison, Paul C. *Black Light: The African-American Hero*. New York: Thunder's Mouth Press, 1993.

Lee, George L. *Interesting People: Black American History Makers*. New York: Ballantine Books, 1989.

Potter, Joan. *African-American Firsts*. Elizabethtown, NY: Pinto Press, 1994.

Stewart, Jeffery C. *1001 Things Everyone Should Know About African-American History*. New York: Doubleday, 1996.

Although an outline for your speech similar to the one above involves a great deal of preparation, it is important for a number of reasons. First, it provides a logical arrangement of your main points and subpoints along with an idea of the supporting materials you are going to use. This will enable you to determine whether your ideas flow smoothly from one to another, and whether you have included a well-balanced and sufficient number of the six kinds of supporting materials. Second, it will provide a framework from which you can prepare note cards or a phrase outline, or from which you can write out a speech to be delivered from manuscript or from memory.

This outline includes a bibliography. Although many of the speeches you deliver will involve your own experience, there are times when you will want to include materials you have gathered through research. In these cases, or whenever your instructor so directs, attach a bibliography to your preparation outline.

## Chapter Review

After reading this chapter, you should be able to

- Explain the five objectives of an introduction to a speech.
- Describe the ten different methods for capturing the audience's attention with your introduction.
- Determine the most effective attention-getting method, depending on the specific purpose and central idea of your speech.
- Explain the six methods of creating an effective conclusion to your speech.
- Write a strong introduction and conclusion for your next speech, using the suggestions given.

## Key Terms

Introduction (p. 57)                     Conclusion (p. 63)

Preview statement (p. 58)                Problem–solution speech (p. 65)

Rhetorical question (p. 59)

# Exercises

1. Develop alternative introductions for an upcoming speech using the suggestions given in this chapter for getting and holding the attention of your audience.

2. Develop alternative conclusions for an upcoming speech using the suggestions given in this chapter for successfully concluding your speech.

3. Select several of the following topics and write an introduction that would capture your classmates' attention, choosing from among the ten methods discussed in the chapter. When would it be most effective to tell a story as an introduction, to begin with statistics or a startling statement, or to open with a quotation? Explain why each device would be the most appropriate given the topic.

   | | |
   |---|---|
   | Steroid use in sports | Binge drinking |
   | Third World poverty | Finding a cure for cancer |
   | Racial tension after Hurricane Katrina | Frat reform |
   | Changes at the vending machine (the dangers of fast food) | |
   | Where to go on spring break? | |
   | Credit card fraud | |

4. Describe a speech that you enjoyed recently. What did the speaker do to capture your attention? Was there a memorable conclusion?

# Speech Assignments

1. *Reading A Commercial*

   Read a one-to-two-minute radio or TV commercial that you have written yourself or picked up from a local broadcaster. Study it carefully to decide how best to indicate meaning and emphasis. Practice it so you can deliver it easily and naturally.

   *Delivery.* It is important that you communicate sincerity to your audience. You can do this best by using a conversational style. Be yourself. Try to inject color and feelings into your words and phrases by being enthuslastic about the product. Smile when you speak. Handle only one main point in the body, and restate your central idea at the conclusion.

2. *Reading Prose*

   Select a piece of prose that falls within a one-to-two-minute time limit. Pick something you think your listeners will like and that you can handle intelligently. Study it carefully in regard to mood and purpose. Practice it so you can read it effectively.

   *Delivery.* Speak clearly and distinctly using variations in pitch, volume, rate, and inflection to make your reading interesting. Know your selection well enough so you can maintain adequate eye contact.

# *Gathering*
# SUPPORTING MATERIAL

CHAPTER 3 SUGGESTS that you choose a subject that suits the purpose of your speech and that is interesting to you. This is wise because if you are going to be collecting facts and gathering ideas for your speech, you will be spending some time on it. Start collecting information on your subject immediately, and try to examine as wide a variety of resources as possible.

You can gather information for your speech in a number of ways: (1) develop it from your own knowledge and experience, (2) access it from written sources primarily through a library, (3) gather it through electronic resources, and (4) acquire it through interviews.

# PERSONAL EXPERIENCE AND KNOWLEDGE

If the subject you have chosen is from your own experience or knowledge, then this is the first place to start when gathering supporting material for your speech. Keep in mind that your experiences include not only your personal involvement with, or observation of, events as they occurred, but also those things you have experienced vicariously by reading or hearing about them. There are a number of ways to use personal experience when planning your speech. First, you can develop a speech to entertain in which you tell a story about something exciting, suspenseful, fascinating, unusual, or humorous that has happened to you.

Second, you can develop a persuasive speech to make a point in which you tell your audience about an experience you had that taught you a lesson. In the speech of personal experience there are two possible approaches to make a point: (1) the main idea (the point) is stated at the beginning of the speech followed by a story that reinforces it, and (2) the story is told first, and the point is made at the conclusion of the speech. Thus, you might say, "I learned at an early age never to trust strangers," and tell your audience about an experience you had that taught you this lesson, or you might relate the experience first and end by saying, "and that's how I learned never to trust strangers."

Finally, you can use your own experience and knowledge to compile a list of ideas on a particular topic. If your own knowledge or experience qualifies you as somewhat of an expert in a particular area you might be the only resource needed to develop your speech. Even if you are not an expert, you may be amazed at the amount of information you can come up with when brainstorming a topic with which you are familiar. If your list of ideas comes entirely from your own knowledge or experience, you might be able to develop your speech without further research. In most cases, however, you will have to do some research to add to the materials you already have. Keep in mind that you may choose to do your speech on a topic you find interesting but know little about. In this case, before brainstorming, you will want to do preliminary research not only to gather ideas, but also to determine if there is sufficient material available to develop an effective speech on that topic.

## BRAINSTORMING

**Brainstorming:** A technique used to generate ideas for speech topics by spontaneously coming up with as many ideas as possible without pausing to evaluate them.

**Brainstorming** is an excellent technique for generating ideas on your subject. The principle is to come up with as many ideas as possible about your topic as fast as you can think of them. Write them all down. Pay no attention to their quality and don't evaluate them. Don't worry if some seem irrelevant; you can discard them later. After you have listed as many ideas as you can, you are ready for step two: **clustering**.

## CLUSTERING

**Clustering:** The second step in the brainstorming process that involves writing down all related ideas about a topic to provide a framework for the important points of a speech.

In step two, you list your topic and write down all the ideas you have come up with on your brainstorming list that relate to it. Analyze the list carefully. See if you can identify any ideas as main points, supporting

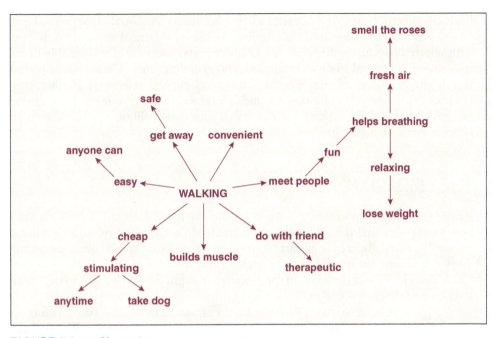

**FIGURE 5.1** ■ **Clustering**

In the clustering technique, you write down all the ideas that relate to your speech topic, in this case, "walking." The cluster of words around the subject, "walking," suggests various benefits of walking, some or all of which could be developed into main points of your speech.

points, or subpoints for your speech. Use arrows to indicate their relationships to each other as shown in Figure 5.1.

The cluster of words around the topic *walking* reflects your concept of the benefits of walking. You see walking as being healthy, inexpensive, convenient, and so on. Keep in mind that as you develop the cluster into a framework for your speech, not everything will be used. Some things will be left out and others will be changed. The important thing is that you have begun to gather ideas for your speech. Now you can consider ways to locate material other than through your own knowledge and experience. Consider interviewing someone you know who walks daily. How about your uncle Jeff? Your cousin Stacie? That old guy you see walking his dog around campus every morning? You jog every day. Isn't that a lot like walking? You might find material from these sources to contribute to a useful and interesting speech for your audience. And don't forget that you can add to this with information you get from your library and/or the Internet.

## THE LIBRARY

It is a mistake to think that because of the computer you no longer need to access the library. The Internet has significantly changed the way libraries operate. Using a computer to do a library search makes the search a lot easier and faster than it has ever been. To effectively use your library, link to your library's web-based catalog to locate books, periodicals, customized reading lists, and more. Many of these are in full text with selected backfiles going back ten or more years. You should also be able to link to many of your local library's reference center's online sites. These usually include search encyclopedias, biographies, literature, and general reference. Further, most libraries can access you to local, state, and federal web sites. If your local library does not have what you are looking for, check out your college library or the libraries of other colleges or high schools.

## THE LIBRARIAN

Perhaps the most important resource in any library is the librarian. Librarians know how to help you find the information you need. Most libraries have at least one reference librarian. Reference librarians are experts in locating obscure information. They are almost always experts in searching the Internet as well. If you just can't locate that elusive fact or detail on the Internet, it might be worth a trip to the library to talk to a reference librarian.

**Ready reference:** A phone service provided by many libraries that allows a caller to gain information from a reference librarian over the phone.

Also, many libraries have a phone service called **ready reference** that enables you to ask for information from a reference librarian over the phone. This service will save you a trip to the library when you're looking for the author of an obscure poem, the date of a particular event, a question involving usage or grammar, and so on. Most libraries have brochures listing the research services they provide. If they don't, ask them for a list.

## ELECTRONIC RESOURCES

### THE COMPUTERIZED CATALOG

A computerized catalog makes it easy to find the library materials you want because the program prompts you step by step. Even if you only know part of a subject title or author's name, key word searching will look for all occurrences of that word or words anywhere in the library's listing of materials.

Many libraries feature computerized card catalogs and have the ability to access the card catalogs of neighboring libraries.

Library computerized research services have expanded greatly in the last few years. Some offer those who have computers equipped with modems and telephone hookups the opportunity to access their catalog and research services from home or office practically twenty-four hours a day. As of 1994, DIALOG, the world's largest online databank of information, has grown to more than four hundred databases, which cover practically any topic imaginable from *aardvarks* to *zygotes*. Because of their popularity and usefulness, computerized research services are constantly improving. New programs are being developed, and existing programs are continually being updated and expanded.

Because these services are expensive, many libraries try to avoid duplicating one provided by another library in the same area. Consequently, if you fail to find a specific program in your school or local library, check the computer centers of neighboring libraries, particularly university, college, or well-equipped high school libraries in your area. Ask them which services they provide.

## THE INTERNET

The **Internet** is a system that provides an unlimited number of resources from all over the world. It was one of the most significant technological breakthroughs of the twentieth century, and it can be accessed twenty-four hours a day, 365 days a year. It was started in the

**Internet:** A system that provides an unlimited number of resources by connecting computers worldwide.

late 1960s by the U.S. Department of Defense as a military communications network. The network soon linked with others and, because it enabled scholars, researchers, and scientists to share information worldwide, the Internet grew with incredible speed. It now connects computers on a worldwide basis.

Over the years as programs have been developed for communicating and exchanging information over the Internet, academic research has improved significantly. The Internet provides the latest information from publications, educational institutions, and information centers worldwide. To use the Internet on your own personal computer, you have to have a computer software package, a modem connected to your computer and a way to connect, and an Internet service provider (ISP). These ISPs charge varying fees. However, most schools offer Internet access to their students free of charge. Internet offerings and databases continue to grow at a phenomenal rate. One of the few disadvantages of this rapid growth is that many users find its vastness overwhelming. You can follow information according to your research needs. However, because many links are not straightforward and you don't know where the link will take you, getting lost is a distinct possibility. You will need to allow yourself time to be able to explore the Internet to see what it has to offer. The Internet allows users to search for information on the World Wide Web, to exchange both national and international

Using Internet search engines such as Google to brainstorm speech topics as well as research information for your speech will provide quick and efficient access to a wealth of material.

e-mails, and to participate in *newsgroups*, a worldwide public facility for debate and the open exchange of information.

Another feature on the Internet is the **blog**, also called the *weblog*. Blogs have been called a Twenty-first Century Forum for Self-Expression. The content of a blog reflects the sender's agenda or personal opinion. Blogs are used by millions of people. Students, teachers, seniors, and young people all blog.

**Blog:** An Internet feature that allows a person to create a public, online forum that expresses his or her personal opinion or agenda.

## ETHICS IN USING THE INTERNET

Do not assume that the information you are accessing from the Internet is always credible. Because information on the Internet can be biased or inaccurate, it is your ethical responsibility to check the material you will be using in your speeches carefully. If it comes from a source that is unbiased and reputable, then most likely the material you are downloading is valid. However, anyone can launch a web site on the Internet. There are many thousands of new ones started each day. Because the Internet is not owned or regulated by anyone, there are no organizational rules to ensure accuracy or relevance. Unfortunately, in some cases web sites are filled with fallacious or useless content. Further, there is the issue of stability. A web site that was there one day may be gone or in a different location the next. This means you must be careful to investigate the credibility and relevance of the material you have found. Use common sense when evaluating the site you are accessing. Ask yourself these questions:

1. Is the information accurate? Who provided it? Is it documented or verifiable?
2. Is the information objective? Does the organization sponsoring the site have any interests or bias that would cause it to put misleading information on its web site?
3. Is the information reliable? What are the author's qualifications? If no author is listed, is the web site established by a reliable source such as a reputable organization, government agency, or university?
4. Is the information current? When was it published? Is there a more recent version? If no date is given, the information may be outdated.

If there is any question in your mind as to whether the information you will be using in your speech is accurate, objective, reliable, or up to date, don't use it. Above all, be suspicious of publications that have grammatical or typographical errors. If you have any misgivings and cannot verify your information, don't use it.

## THE WORLD WIDE WEB

**World Wide Web:** A global tool to help users access information on the Internet.

An incredible amount of educational material is becoming available on the **World Wide Web**, which was created in 1989. The web is by far the Internet's easiest tool for accessing information. It differs from previous Internet applications in its ability to project information on easy-to-read *screens* or *pages*. On the web page, you can click a graphic or an underlined name, fact, or concept that you want to know more about and your click takes you to another web page with

# Working WITH THE WEB

Most college libraries offer guidelines for checking the accuracy and reliability of web sites. To evaluate the web pages you have consulted, you might check the following resource, which guides you to critically evaluate Internet information sources:

www.library.cornell.edu/okuref/research/webeval.html

Newspapers can be a useful source of information on current and historical subjects. In searching for news stories as potential ideas for speech topics, you can browse more than 10,000 newspapers from around the world, with links to their home pages, by accessing this site:

www.OnlineNewspapers.com

For additional articles and information that may provide inspiration or useful supporting materials for your speech, you might visit

www.findarticles.com

for access to articles from a variety of magazines

www.pbs.org

for access to various Public Broadcasting System programs on a variety of subjects

Also, you may want to experiment with a new search engine, called *pixsy.com*, that compiles images and videos from the news feeds of a variety of sources, from the *New York Times* to YouTube to the BBC. You can search by category from 1 billion items or click on "Browse Recently Added" to get the latest links to new material.

information about that subject. With an Internet connection and a web browser on your computer, you can navigate a web site and read the web pages stored there. However, there are millions of web sites with millions of web pages on the Internet on a vast range of topics. Therefore, when searching for specific information on a web site, you must use one of the web's **search engines** to find the information you need. There are a vast number of search engines on the World Wide Web but only about a dozen major ones. Two of the most popular search engines are Alta Vista and Yahoo.

**Search engine:** A way of navigating the millions of web sites on the World Wide Web by quickly locating sources of information on a specific topic.

ALTA VISTA—www.altavista.digital.com
Alta Vista is fast and efficient and has a large listing of web pages.
YAHOO—www.yahoo.com
Yahoo searches for individual topics and also lists a broad variety of topics that can be especially helpful for the beginning researcher.
GOOGLE—www.google.com
The Google search engine is fast, accurate, and easy to use.

> ## ✔ *Checklist* FOR SUCCESS
>
> Tips for Searching the Web for Information:
>
> - As soon as you find an important site, bookmark the URL address on your browser.
> - Try several different search engines to get the best results because the results will vary with different engines.
> - Check your own college or university for valid web site listings.
> - Check publications such as *Harley Hahn's Internet Yellow Pages*, which is updated annually, for credible web sites.

## E-MAIL

Perhaps the most popular and practical feature of the Internet is electronic mail, known as e-mail. It can be sent anywhere in the world for a fraction of the cost of regular mail, and it will get there for sure as long as you use the correct e-mail address. Not only is e-mail a plus for educational purposes, it allows you to inexpensively keep in touch with relatives and friends.

### SOME TIPS FOR SENDING E-MAIL

Start by indicating to whom the letter is being sent and for what purpose.
Use an opening salutation and a complimentary closing.
Use correct grammar and spelling.
Avoid unusual type style or boldface.
Do not send junk mail (jokes, solicitations, appeals, etc.).
Avoid overusing exclamation points and capital letters.
Be polite.
Do not send e-mail when you are irritated or upset.
Although e-mail is faster than regular mail, it can be held up. If the message is urgent, call.

## TELNET

If you have your own personal computer with a modem or have access to one, you can use that computer as a terminal to link to your school's library. When you log on to a computer with Telnet software, your computer acts like a terminal. If your school library allows Telnet access to its computer, you can do at home what other students do on campus. Simply dial the library's phone number through your modem to access the Library Computer Catalog. In a typical university library the card catalog and other databases exist online. To find Telnet sites you must use an Internet search engine such as Webcrawler. Once you connect to a Telnet site, you must use the commands for the software at that site. Some useful Telnet sites include the following:

- **United States Library of Congress**—The Library of Congress lists nearly every book published in the United States. You can also gain access to other U.S. government services and other library databases.
- **Federal Information Exchange**—The Federal Information Exchange offers information for women and minorities about opportunities, grants, and programs within U.S. government bureaus.
- **Washington University Library**—This site offers access to research facilities and libraries around the world.

## USENET

Usenet is an interactive international magazine that covers a vast array of subjects in science and everyday life. Usenet consists of thousands of newsgroups. Each newsgroup is composed of a series of electronic articles on a particular topic. The topic can be anything from mud wrestling to voodoo to the latest news about AIDS research. In effect, Usenet is the Internet's open-discussion forum. Usenet allows you to take part in discussion with experts in a field in which you have an interest.

## INTERVIEWING

An interview can be an effective and interesting way to gather information. Up-to-date information from an expert in the field can often carry a lot of weight. Faculty members, clergy, community leaders, and local politicians are among those who would be pleased to provide you with speech material. Keep in mind, though, that regardless of the expertise of the person whom you are interviewing, you don't want to overload your speech with references to that interview. Unless you are an experienced note taker, you will want to tape-record your interview. Most subjects will gladly give you permission to tape-record them if you explain exactly how you want to use the material.

An interview can be an effective way to gather up-to-date or firsthand information for a speech.

You can also interview people electronically over Usenet. Add to the credibility of your speech with a statement supporting your plea for higher emission standards from a world-renowned environmentalist. Support your call for National Health Insurance with statements from Norwegian citizens who have had socialized medicine in their country for more than eighty-eight years.

Finally, you can engage in an e-mail interview to gather information from an expert in a particular area. A speech student at a college in Wisconsin recently interviewed a representative of the United Farm Workers of America on the plight of farm workers and their families after a citrus freeze in California. The interview provided a poignant, firsthand look at the plight of thousands of migrant farm workers who were left homeless and starving. You can locate experts on the Internet by accessing people finding or e-mail address finding services.

## TAKING NOTES

The more accurate your notes are, the less time you will have to spend rechecking your sources for dates, statistics, and exact wording.

Although you can record your material in notebooks or loose-leaf folders, I find that the use of note cards is best. There are a number of reasons for this: (1) Note cards are easy to handle. If a note card contains information that you decide not to use, you can throw it away. (2) Note cards can be shuffled and used to organize the speech. (3) Note cards can easily be used for reference during the delivery of the speech or during the question-and-answer period following it. (4) Note cards can more easily be grouped and classified. Here are some suggestions to follow when taking your notes:

1. Use uniform note cards. Whether you buy them or make them yourself, note cards that are uniform in size and stiffness are easier to work with and store.
2. Record the exact source of your information. When the source is written, indicate the call number, author(s), title, date, publisher, and page numbers in case you want to refer to the source again. If your information came from an interview, indicate the time and date of the interview along with the interviewed person's name and credentials.
3. Keep notes brief. Don't copy large selections of material at random. Be selective. Spend time deciding exactly what you want to say before writing.
4. Be accurate. If you are copying a direct quotation, make sure that the wording is exact. If you are paraphrasing, make sure the paraphrase accurately conveys the meaning of the original.
5. Indicate the subject of each note card. Then when you are ready to organize your speech, you can put the cards in piles according to the points they are supporting.
6. Take an ample number of notes. Don't be afraid of gathering too much information. It is much easier to select the best from an overabundance of information than to find you are short and have to go back and look for more.
7. Electronic note taking: Although taking notes on a computer has generally been thought of as too slow and laborious, new software has evolved that will help you develop and organize your ideas right on the computer. It will convert your ideas into an outline format, spell-check them, and move back and forth between text and outline view at any time.

## BIBLIOGRAPHY

It is sometimes necessary to include a bibliography with your speech outline to document the sources of your supporting material. A bibliography should be arranged alphabetically by the author's last name or the first important word in the title. When including a bibliography, type the first line flush with the left margin and indent subsequent lines. See Figures 5.2 to 5.4 for samples of bibliography entries.

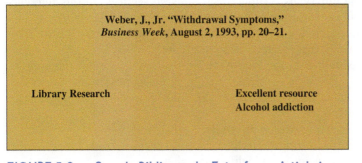

Weber, J., Jr. "Withdrawal Symptoms," *Business Week*, August 2, 1993, pp. 20–21.

Library Research                    Excellent resource
                                    Alcohol addiction

**FIGURE 5.2** ■ **Sample Bibliography Entry for an Article in a Periodical**

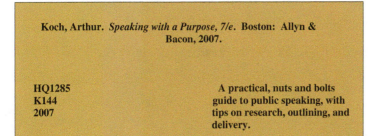

Koch, Arthur. *Speaking with a Purpose, 7/e.* Boston: Allyn & Bacon, 2007.

HQ1285                     A practical, nuts and bolts
K144                       guide to public speaking, with
2007                       tips on research, outlining, and
                           delivery.

**FIGURE 5.3** ■ **Sample Bibliography Entry for a Book**

Titus, James G., et al. "Greenhouse Effect and Sea Level Rise: The Cost of Holding Back the Sea," originally in "Coastal Management," Vol. 19, pp. 171–204 (1991).
http://yosemite.epa.gov/oar/globalwarming.nsf/content/ResourceCenter Publications.html

Article presents the first nationwide assessment of the impacts of rising sea levels. Discusses protecting developed areas and wetlands. Also, history of climate change and origin of term "greenhouse effect."

**FIGURE 5.4** ■ **Sample Bibliography Entry for a Web Site**

## Chapter Review

After reading this chapter, you should be able to

- Brainstorm a list of possible speech topics, drawing on your own personal experience and knowledge.
- Use the clustering technique to generate ideas about a selected topic and determine which of the related ideas can be used as points in your speech.
- Make use of the library, its computerized research services, and its reference librarians to find the information you need to develop your speech.
- Access the Internet and use the various search engines on the World Wide Web to gather supporting material for your speech.
- Evaluate the credibility and accuracy of the information you find on the Internet.
- Consult your personal networks of family, friends, neighbors, professors, coworkers, etc., and identify someone who could provide useful information about your speech topic.
- Conduct an interview in person or online.
- Take effective notes during your interviews, as well as from other sources you've located, following the guidelines provided.

## Key Terms

Brainstorming (p. 74)             Blog (p. 78)
Clustering (p. 74)                World Wide Web (p. 78)
Ready reference (p. 76)           Search engine (p. 79)
Internet (p. 77)

## Exercises

1. Brainstorm a list of topics that would be of potential interest or use to your intended audience. Select one or two of these topics and, using the clustering technique described in the chapter, brainstorm a "cluster" of ideas related to that topic. Analyze the list to determine if any of these ideas can be developed as points in your speech. Create a draft framework for your speech.
2. Set up and conduct an interview, in person or electronically, for your next classroom speech. Evaluate the interview and review the notes you took. How effective were you at gathering the information you needed? Did you find the interview a useful source of information? Explain.
3. Using a search engine you haven't used before, visit several web sites related to your speech topic. Ask yourself the questions on page 78. Are you able to determine the accuracy or credibility of the information? What are some of the factors that convince you either way?
4. Draft a sample bibliography from the sources you have located in exercise 3, including several different types of sources such as an article, a book, and an Internet source.

# Speech Assignments

1. *Speech to Inform*

   Choose a subject in which your main job to inform is to present information. Present your material in such a way as to hold and maintain the attention of your audience so they can easily understand and remember. Deliver the speech as your instructor directs.

   *Delivery.* This speech should be delivered extemporaneously. Keep the pattern of development simple so you can move from one idea to another smoothly.

   ### Sample Topics

   1. Creating a scrapbook
   2. Martin Luther King, Jr.
   3. Labor Day holiday
   4. History of the Olympics
   5. Finding a job
   6. Hurricane Katrina
   7. Organic food

2. *Special Occasion Speech*

   Deliver a two-to-three-minute special occasion speech to the class. Choose a type of special occasion speech that you can envision yourself having to give in the future. Explain the occasion to the class and indicate why you are involved.

   *Delivery.* Special occasion speeches are usually delivered as manuscript speeches. Practice delivering the speech enough so you can maintain adequate eye contact. You should sound as though you are talking to your listeners rather than reading to them.

   ### Types

   Toasts (weddings, banquets, dinners)
   Eulogies (funerals, memorial services)
   Acceptance (awards, honors, gifting)
   Introduction (banquets, ceremonies)

   ### Suggestions

   1. Try to establish a common bond with your audience.
   2. Keep the speech short and to the point.
   3. Make sure you pronounce all names correctly.
   4. Make sure your facts are accurate.

# *Supporting*
# YOUR IDEAS

ONE OF THE BEST ways to improve your effectiveness as a speaker is to learn how to select and use supporting materials. **Supporting materials** are necessary to make your ideas clear or persuasive to your listener. Although there are different lists of supporting materials, most experts in the speech field agree on these six: examples, explanation, statistics, testimony, comparison and contrast, and visual aids. You have most likely used each of these during your lifetime, perhaps without being aware that there was a specific name for each. Suppose, for example, that you want to convince your parents that your new boyfriend is the ideal male. You might use any of the six supporting devices to support your assertion:

**Supporting materials:** Materials used to support the points in a speech that make the ideas clear or persuasive to the audience.

Example: "Mom and Dad, you're going to love Chris. He's one of the kindest people I've ever met. He puts in eight hours of volunteer work a week at the Mayville Nursing Home, he's a big brother to an eleven-year-old boy from the inner city, and he supports a little Cambodian child through the Christian Children's Fund."

Explanation: "I see Chris as the perfect male. The consideration with which he treats me makes me feel special and loved, and his sensitivity to music, art, literature, and nature makes him a fascinating person to be with."

Statistics: "Chris is six feet tall, he weighs 180 pounds, and he makes over sixty thousand dollars a year."

Testimony: "Rabbi Silberg, who is on the board of directors of Mayville Nursing Home, says Chris is one of the hardest-working and best-liked volunteers they have."

Comparison and Contrast: "Chris isn't like any man I've ever met. The others have been interested in doing only what they want and in satisfying their own egos. Chris believes that love is sharing, and that's the way he acts."

Visual Aids: "Here are some snapshots of Chris. Doesn't he have a pleasant, open face? Did you notice how neatly he dresses?"

## EXAMPLES

**Example:** A specific, representative instance used to clarify and reinforce a point.

When wisely chosen, the **example** is without a doubt the most effective and versatile supporting device. You would be wise to use at least one example as a support for every main point in your speech. An example is actually a typical sample selected to show the nature or character of the rest. Examples can be brief or detailed, factual or hypothetical, and humorous or serious. If an example is factual and familiar to your audience, you need only to cite it briefly because they know the details. If the example is hypothetical or unfamiliar to your audience, you must develop it in enough detail so the point your story makes is clear to them. For instance, if you are talking about the problem of child abuse, and a highly publicized case has recently occurred in your community, you only need to mention the case briefly but clearly. If, however, the instance of abuse occurred in a different location or a number of years earlier, you might have to tell it as a short story with facts, names, and dates. Detailed examples are often called *illustrations*.

These illustrations or stories can take the form of anecdotes, personal experiences, allegories, or parables. Using illustrations in your speech can provide your audience with a clear mental picture of particular instances or events.

When selecting supporting materials for your speech, look for appropriate and interesting examples that are clear, concise, and to the point. Note how the following examples support the speaker's central idea: Every adult American should have an up-to-date will. A brief factual example, brief **hypothetical example**; detailed factual example, and detailed hypothetical example are provided.

**Hypothetical example:** An imaginary or fabricated situation or story used to illustrate a point.

## BRIEF FACTUAL EXAMPLE

Although a will can be made out by an individual or for as little as $100 by a lawyer, more than 50 percent of all Americans die without one. No doubt many of them planned to create one but just put it off. For example, Supreme Court Justice Fred Vinson died without a will, and Senator Robert Kerr was in the process of writing one when he died unexpectedly.

## BRIEF HYPOTHETICAL EXAMPLE

There are many reasons for keeping your will up to date. Suppose that you name your sister as executor, and she dies, moves away, or is too ill to serve? What if federal or state laws or court interpretations of them change? Suppose that you move to a state where inheritance tax laws differ? These are all reasons for reviewing your will whenever major changes occur.

## DETAILED FACTUAL EXAMPLE

Uncle George died about a year ago. He had never made a will, and this created some real problems for his wife, Aunt Edna, and their three minor children. The checking and savings accounts were in my uncle's name so the bank wouldn't let Aunt Edna withdraw any money. Because the deed for their house listed them as "tenants in common," the children were due to inherit two-thirds of the house. The result of this was that nobody would lend Aunt Edna money for a second mortgage on the house, and she could not sell it because, as minors, the children couldn't "sign off" ownership in favor of their mother. The whole matter had to be taken to probate court, where it is still being disputed. To date, Aunt Edna has yet to see a single penny of Uncle George's estate and has borrowed more than $10,000 from her relatives.

## DETAILED HYPOTHETICAL EXAMPLE

John Jones, a widower with four children, remarries. He registers everything he owns in joint ownership with the new Mrs. Jones knowing that she will provide for the children if he dies. A year later both are killed in an auto accident. To compound the tragedy, Mrs. Jones survives her husband by one hour, and his assets revert to her as co-owner. Unfortunately, Mrs. Jones had not made out a will, and the entire estate goes by law to her only blood relative, a cousin she doesn't even like. Because there was no will, none of Mr. Jones's assets went to his children because Mrs. Jones was related to them only as a stepmother.

## EXPLANATION

The purpose of explanation is to make an idea clear or understandable. Obviously then, explanation qualifies as an excellent supporting device. Explanation can involve a number of different forms. It can include exposition, analysis, definition, and description. A more comprehensive treatment of these supports is found on pages 153–158.

### EXPOSITION

**Exposition:** A precise statement that provides information or an explanation to the listener to increase understanding.

**Exposition** may be defined as communication that gives information to your listeners in order to increase their knowledge or their understanding of a situation or process. A speech on how to use a fly rod, bake a cake, lower a ceiling, or make a fortune in the stock market will in each case employ exposition. When a gas station attendant gives you directions on how to get to a nearby city, and you in turn pass his explanation on to the driver of the car in which you are traveling, both conversations have largely involved exposition.

### ANALYSIS

**Analysis:** The process of breaking a topic into parts and examining them.

**Analysis** is the process of explaining something by breaking it down into parts and examining them. You use analysis when you explain how something works. If, for example, you want to convince your listeners to install inexpensive, homemade burglar alarm systems in their cars, you would have to give them a clear idea of what is involved in this system and how it would work. Another form of evaluation with which you are all familiar is the critique, or review. Perhaps you have attended a movie, play, or concert and afterward totally disagreed with the review it received. Keep this in mind when you are using analysis as a supporting device so you might do so as objectively as possible.

### DEFINITION

When you use a term or concept that is unfamiliar to your audience, you must define it either in your own words or in the words of someone else. Be careful not to use words in your definition that are more difficult to understand than the term or concept you are defining. For the sake of imaginativeness and interest, avoid using dictionary definitions. They are often overly formal and complex. Keep your definitions clear and to the point, using wording that your listeners can readily understand.

Detailed explanation, often supported by visual aids, can make a complex idea, situation, or process clear and understandable to your audience.

## DESCRIPTION

Description makes use of the five sensory appeals (the five senses being taste, hearing, sight, touch, and smell) to make clear to your listener exactly what is being communicated. Although it isn't necessary to appeal to all five in each communication, the more of them to which you appeal, the more effective the communication. Effective description can create images or word pictures in the minds of your listeners.

# STATISTICS

When used correctly, **statistics** can be an effective means of support. However, unless your statistics are both valid and reliable, they should not be used.

**Statistics:** Numerical data that provide a representative sampling.

It was Benjamin Disraeli who said, "There are three kinds of lies: lies, damned lies, and statistics." His comment points up the fact that statistics can often be manipulated to support almost any assertion. For this reason, it is wise to document the statistics you are using. This means indicating when and by whom the statistics were compiled. It is quite likely that there are those in your audience who have been deceived by statistics in the past. Put them at ease by using statistics that are up to date and compiled by a reputable source.

Try to make the statistics you use as interesting and uncomplicated as possible. Remember, it is your job as the speaker to maintain your listener's attention. Here are some suggestions to follow when using statistics.

## DRAMATIZE YOUR STATISTICS

If you can present your statistics in a dramatic or vivid way, they are more likely to be understood and remembered by your audience. When stated unimaginatively, statistics can often be quite dry. When stated in terms that a listener can visualize, they can be quite thought provoking. Consider this example from a student speech called "America's Disadvantaged Minority":

> When we hear of the 200 million children in the world who suffer from malnutrition or the 50,000 children under the age of five who die each day from diarrhea, dehydration, or other preventable causes, or when we think of other young people in the world who are in peril, we usually think of those living in Third World countries torn by either war or famine. Yet, an October 8, 1990, article in *Time* magazine tells of America's most disadvantaged minority: its children. The article, written by Nancy Gibbs, reveals that nearly one-fourth of U.S. children under the age of six live in households struggling below the poverty level; that every eight seconds of the school day a child drops out; that every twenty-six seconds a child runs away from home; that every forty-seven seconds a child is abused; that every sixty-seven seconds an unwed teenager has a baby; that every seven minutes a child is busted for drug abuse; and that every thirty-six minutes one is killed or injured by a gun.

Statistics presented in this manner are dramatic and easy to visualize, and are therefore more likely to be remembered. To maintain credibility when presenting statistics as shocking as these, indicate the source of your information.

## ROUND OFF YOUR STATISTICS

Remember, unless you repeat your statistics, your listeners will hear them only once. For this reason it is a good idea to round off complex numbers. Although it may be more exacting, instead of saying that the medium income of police officers in this city is $35,167, round it off to "around $35,000" or "slightly more than $35,000." In the following excerpt, the student-speaker rounds off the statistics she uses to support her proposition that racism is still rampant in twenty-first-century America.

> Are you aware that although 76 percent of illegal drugs are consumed by white Americans and 14 percent are consumed by African Americans, 74 percent of all sentences for illegal drug use were meted out to African Americans? Did you know that although it has been stereotyped by politicians and the media as a black inner-city drug, 65 percent of those who use crack-cocaine are white? According to the U.S. Sentencing Commission, only 5 percent of those convicted for crack offenses were white, while 93 percent were African Americans. Even though white Americans and African Americans use drugs in proportion to their percentage in the overall population, African Americans go to jail at a far greater rate. Something must be done about the racism of the war on drugs in this country.

## DISPLAY YOUR STATISTICS VISUALLY

Complex statistical data should be presented on charts, tables, graphs, or diagrams in order to help your audience grasp what is being presented. A student used the example reproduced in Figure 6.1 (in a much larger form) to show that hypertension kills.

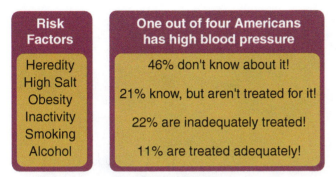

**FIGURE 6.1** ■ **Hypertension: The Silent Killer**
This chart is clear and simple, without too much text. It focuses on the dramatic statistics that support the main points of the speech.

# TESTIMONY

We live in a complex age, an age of specialization. For this reason it is often wise for nonexpert speakers to support their ideas with the **testimony** of experts. The testimony of an expert or authority on a particular subject carries the weight of that person's education and experience. Few of us would quarrel with an ophthalmologist who recommends that we switch to bifocals or an auto mechanic who tells us that we need a new vacuum advance. Unless we questioned their honesty or competency, we would have no reason to doubt their judgment. Consequently, when you are delivering a speech, support your opinions if need be with the opinions of others more expert than you to add credibility to your presentation.

*Testimony:* The words of an expert or authority on a particular subject, used to support a point.

When supporting your point of view with the testimony of others, you can either quote them verbatim or paraphrase what they have said in your own words. The decision is up to you. There are, however, two instances when it is better to quote directly than to paraphrase: (1) when the person you are quoting has said it so well you cannot possibly say it better, and (2) where the testimony is controversial and you want your audience to hear it straight from the source. Otherwise, it is perfectly acceptable to state the testimony in your own words. When doing so, be careful to paraphrase the testimony of another both fairly and accurately. As a speaker, you have a responsibility to be honest and straightforward.

If the experts you are citing are likely to be unfamiliar to those in your audience, give facts about them that will establish their credibility. Your listeners will give more heed to what Dr. Carl J. George, chairman of the department of psychology at the University of Wisconsin and author of *Knowing Your Child*, has to say about teenage suicide than they will to what Carl J. George or even Dr. Carl J. George has to say.

Although it is often important that the authority you are citing is up to date, this is not always necessary. It can often be effective to back up your point of view

Expert testimony, such as this cardiology expert speaking at a trial, carries the weight of that person's education and experience. Used in a speech, such testimony lends support and credibility to your ideas.

by citing an authority from the past whom most of your audience respects. For example, a reference to the Bible or other holy books can often be quite effective. These volumes contain a wealth of material on almost any subject of importance. Note how effectively Dr. Martin Luther King, Jr., challenges the conscience of America by citing those authorities who framed the Constitution and the Declaration of Independence:

> When the architects of our Republic wrote the magnificent words of the Constitution and the Declaration of Independence, they were signing a promissory note to which every American was to fall heir. . . . It is obvious today that America has defaulted on this promissory note, insofar as her citizens of color are concerned. Instead of honoring this sacred obligation, America has given the Negro people a bad check; a check which has come back marked insufficient funds. However, we refuse to believe that there are insufficient funds in the great vaults of opportunity of this nation. And so we've come to cash this check, a check that will give us on demand the riches of freedom and the security of justice.

The use of testimony as a support is often less effective when dealing with a controversial subject. Anyone who has had anything to do with debate is aware that when you are dealing with a controversial subject of significance, there is sure to be an unlimited number of experts who disagree with one another.

Provided you have some expertise in regard to your subject, one of the best forms of testimony you can use is your own personal experience. If you have some background or experience in regard to your subject that qualifies you as somewhat of an expert, mention it in the introduction to your speech. Let your listeners know immediately that you are backing up the information you are giving them with your own *expert* testimony. If you wait until the middle or end of your speech to tell them about your background, chances are that some in your audience will think, "I didn't know the speaker was an expert on the subject. I guess I should have listened more carefully."

## COMPARISON AND CONTRAST

One of the basic principles of education is that the only way you can learn anything new is to be able to relate it to something you already know. Therefore, the best way to teach the unknown is to compare it to the known. Jesus used comparison effectively when he preached to the different people he met. Depending on the backgrounds and occupations of those in his audience at the time, he variously revealed what the kingdom of heaven is like by comparing it to a fisherman throwing his net into the sea and pulling in both good fish and bad, a farmer harvesting his wheat along with weeds, a merchant selling all he had to buy a single pearl of great value, and ten bridesmaids who took their lamps and went to meet the bridegroom. This kind of comparison is called figurative comparison or **analogy**. It describes similarities between things that are otherwise different. Other examples are the comparison of a bargaining meeting to a barroom brawl and a major speech to a parachute jump without a parachute.

**Analogy:** A figurative comparison that describes similarities between things that are otherwise different, used to make a connection.

A **literal comparison** describes similarities between things that are physically alike. It can often give your listener a clear mental picture of what you are talking about. For instance, if you say that the new dean of men looks like a young Alec Baldwin or that a Trident submarine is half again as long as a football field, you are offering your listener a clear basis of comparison. Less visual examples would be comparisons between interest rates in the United States in 2004 and 2005, academic standards in private and public universities, and jazz versus rhythm and blues. Literal comparisons are often used to reinforce particular points of view. How many times have you heard or used an argument similar to the following: "Why can't I learn to drive? Sally already has her driver's license, and she's a year younger than I am"?

**Literal comparison:** Compares similarities between things that are physically alike.

Comparing differences is often called **contrast**. When you compare high school and college, living at home or living on your own, and apples and oranges, you are emphasizing differences rather than similarities between like things. Consider the comment, "Boy, you kids nowadays get away with murder. When I was your age I wouldn't dream of doing that." You are backing up your point of view by emphasizing differences rather than similarities.

**Contrast:** Compares differences between things that are physically different, as a means of emphasizing the differences.

## VISUAL AIDS

**Visual aid:** An instructional devise that appeals mainly to vision.

Often it is necessary to use **visual aids** when presenting your supporting material. Some material is almost impossible to present without using them. Try demonstrating how to use a slide rule without a slide rule or a facsimile of one. Try contrasting impressionism with surrealism without showing your audience examples of each. When used effectively, visual aids can be an effective means of reinforcing and clarifying your ideas. An audience will retain the information you give them longer if they are both told and shown something at the same time. The old adage "A picture is worth a thousand words" applies. Effectively used, audiovisual aids will enhance your audience's interest and understanding. Be mindful, however, that the aid should only reinforce or clarify your material. Showing your audience a good video, movie, or slide show would effectively hold their attention but would be an ineffective substitute for your speech. The word *aid* means to help or assist. That is what your visual aid should do. Some often used visual aids are listed as follows:

The item itself
Charts, graphs, and diagrams
Slides and filmstrips
Transparencies for overhead projectors

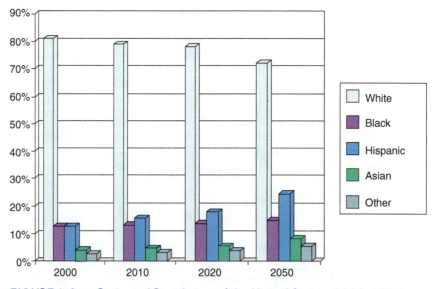

PROJECTED POPULATION OF THE UNITED STATES, 2000–2050

**FIGURE 6.2 ■ Projected Population of the United States, 2000–2050**
This bar graph showing projected population of the United States helps summarize data and present it in a clear, visual way that makes it accessible to the audience.

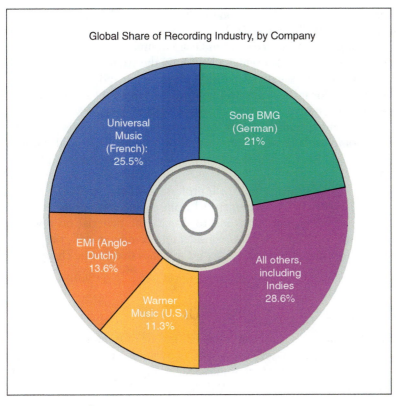

**Figure 6.3 ▪ Pie Chart**

This pie chart showing the distribution of the global recording business presents a clear visual image to the audience.

Flyers, pamphlets, and handouts
Paintings and posters
Chalkboards and flip charts
Photographs and drawings
CDs, audiotapes, videotapes, and DVDs
Records and movies
Yourself or others
Models and facsimiles
Computer-generated materials

## BENEFITS OF VISUAL AIDS

Visual aids help an audience remember what you say. An audience is far more likely to remember information when they are both told and shown something at the same time. For example, after seventy-two hours, most people can only remember 10 percent of what they have seen and 20 percent of what they have heard, but almost 65 percent of what they have both seen and heard.

Visual aids increase understanding. Models allow your audience to visualize things that are difficult to describe in words alone. Charts and graphs can make complex statistics and relationships easier for your audience to understand.

Visual aids add interest to your speech and help hold the attention of your audience. When effectively chosen, visual aids provide creativeness and variety to your presentation. The use of color in your aids will help you get and hold attention.

Visual aids reduce the amount of time you would have to spend giving lengthy explanations. The use of slides, transparencies, and computer display panels are helpful when a subject is complex. If these are impractical or unavailable, consider using handouts. Handouts should be distributed before you begin speaking and explained early in the speech.

Visual aids can give your speech a polished, professional look. An LCD (liquid crystal display) panel allows you to display material from your computer through an overhead projector. A converter will allow you to display the material on a wide-screen TV. Although this technique requires considerable computer skill, the effect can be quite impressive. Imagine presenting complex statistics that can be changed as your viewers watch.

## SPECIFIC SUGGESTIONS FOR USING VISUAL AIDS

When used effectively, visual aids can be an excellent means of reinforcing or clarifying your ideas. If, however, the visual aid is used incorrectly, it can detract from rather than improve your speech. Here are some specific suggestions for using visual aids:

1. A visual aid must be large enough to be seen by the entire audience. If you are using a poster or chart, make sure that your lettering or drawings are dark or vivid enough so those farthest away will get the information. Unless each member of your audience can see your visual aid clearly, don't use it.
2. Avoid visual aids that are overly complex. A complicated drawing or too many words or statistics will defeat your purpose. A listener must be able to grasp the meaning of your visual instantly.
3. Your visual aid should clarify or reinforce your point. Displaying a picture of yourself holding a string of bass during a demonstration on how to fillet fish might do something for your ego but will add nothing to your audience's understanding.
4. Make sure that you maintain good eye contact when referring to your visual aid. It is for the audience, not you, to look at. Besides, looking out at your audience will help you determine if you are displaying your visual aid in a way that can easily be seen by all.
5. Whenever possible, use poster board or a flip chart rather than a chalkboard during your presentation. If you must use a chalkboard, avoid turning your back to the audience for an extended period. Limit your use of the board to a simple drawing or a few words or phrases, or put what you need on the board before you begin the speech.
6. Keep your visual aid out of sight except when you are using it. Attention is intermittent. A person pays attention to something for a while, stops for a moment or

## Working WITH THE WEB

Using presentation software such as Microsoft's PowerPoint can be an effective way of enhancing your speech. The following sites, taken from the publisher's public-speaking web site, can provide digital audio and visual examples you can add to a software presentation:

www.hotbot.com/
www.lycos.com/lycosmedia.html
www.comlab.ox.ac.uk/archive/audio.html

Because PowerPoint is the most commonly used software program to create computerized visual aids, Microsoft does provide a tutorial to guide you through using the software. It would be useful to visit

www.microsoft.com/info

Additional sites that provide useful information on developing visual aids include

www.presentations.com
www.presentersuniversity.com/courses/cs_visualaids.cfm

so, and goes back to paying attention again. If you leave an interesting visual aid out to look at, chances are that some in your audience might find themselves paying attention to it rather than your speech.

7. Include your visual aid when practicing your speech. Become so familiar with your visual aid that you can refer to any part of it with little loss of eye contact. Know where your aids will be when you want them and where you will put them when they are not being used.

8. Never pass a visual aid around through the audience. If you do, you will lose the attention of at least three listeners—the one looking at the aid, the one who has just passed it on, and the one who will be getting it next. An exception would be if you were passing out an aid or handout to each member of your audience. There is less chance that this activity will be distracting if you pass the items out near the end of your speech, perhaps even at the conclusion.

9. Make sure that your visual aid does not take up too much time. Remember, you are using the visual aid to support a point you are making in your speech, not as a section of the speech itself. Running three minutes of a movie or slides during a five-minute speech is an overly long and inappropriate use of visual aids. However, make sure that everyone has enough time to see and understand your visual aid.

10. Do not let your visual aid interfere with the continuity of your speech. If, for example, you are going through the steps of mixing the ingredients of a cake or applying glaze to a ceramic during a speech to demonstrate, don't stop talking to

your audience while doing so. Your visual aid must support what you are saying, not substitute for it.

11. Be prepared to deliver your speech without your visual aid. No matter how careful you are when preparing and practicing with your visual aid, something can go wrong. Slide projectors can break, CDs or cassette players can malfunction, and markers or chalk can mysteriously disappear. Knowing that you can deliver your speech even if your visual aid fails will give you a sense of confidence and allow you to be more relaxed. Keep in mind, furthermore, that the ability to deliver a speech effectively when your visual aid fails will win you the admiration and respect of your audience.

12. Avoid presenting too much material on a visual aid. An overly complex visual aid may be worse than none at all. A visual aid should be clear, concise, and instantly intelligible.

## COMPUTER-GENERATED VISUAL AIDS

There are some excellent computer-generated graphic programs available, like Microsoft PowerPoint, that enable you to develop professional-looking visual aids (Figure 6.4). If your group is small enough, your visual can be viewed directly on a computer screen. For larger groups, you can format the content of your presentation on electronic slides that can be displayed on a screen from a projector. This is an effective way of enhancing and reinforcing your message.

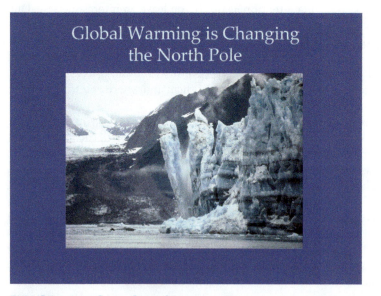

**FIGURE 6.4  ■  PowerPoint Slides**
PowerPoint slides such as this one on Global Warming can be developed to support the main points in your speech. They can include text and photos or statistics found online.

In addition to presenting specific content points of your message in an easy-to-read format, these programs allow you to incorporate your own photos or images from a scanner or digital camera. You can also access clip art, pictures, videos, and sounds. Most also include various chart types, animation features, and other tools to create visual stimulation. These programs will help you organize, illustrate, and deliver your ideas in a visually impactful way that will maintain your audience's attention.

## COMBINED SUPPORTS

Often, supporting materials are used in combination with one another. Thus, you might support a point of view with **combined supports** such as comparative statistics, a visual aid that has to be explained, an example that includes expert testimony, and so on. Tests, experiments, studies, surveys, polls, programs, and investigations often involve a combination of supporting devices. For example, the benefits of an exercise program might be stated in terms of comparison, testimony, and statistics. An investigation into the effects of budget cuts on transportation might involve examples, testimony, comparison, and statistics. Either subject might be explained to an audience with the help of a visual aid.

**Combined supports:** Supporting materials that are used in combination with one another.

## Chapter Review

After reading this chapter, you should be able to

- Explain the six most common types of supporting materials and when each would be most appropriate to use to support and clarify your ideas.
- Differentiate among various types of examples and explanation.
- Understand the importance of using current, reliable statistics to support the points in your speech.
- Determine how to present statistics in a vivid, understandable way that will capture your audience's attention.
- Assess who could provide expert testimony to support your ideas.
- Understand the differences among figurative comparison, literal comparison, and contrast, and when to use each most effectively.
- Name specific types of visual aids.
- Describe the benefits of visual aids and guidelines for using them effectively.

## Key Terms

Supporting materials (p. 87)
Example (p. 88)
Hypothetical example (p. 89)
Exposition (p. 90)
Analysis (p. 90)
Statistics (p. 91)

Testimony (p. 93)
Analogy (p. 95)
Literal comparison (p. 95)
Contrast (p. 95)
Visual aid (p. 96)
Combined supports (p. 101)

## Exercises

1. Choose one of the following statements or write one of your own, and support it with examples, explanation, statistics, testimony, and comparison and contrast.

   "Gambling should be legalized in the United States."
   "The United States should pass a law abolishing the death penalty."
   "The United States should restore friendly relations with Cuba."

2. Name at least one authority your classmates would respect in the following fields: science, education, energy, world affairs, terrorism, medicine, law, football, baseball, music, technology.

3. Find an ad that combines two or more supporting devices to sell its product. Do the supporting devices seem accurate and objective? Is the ad effective? Why or why not?

4. Consider an effective speech or presentation you've heard recently in your classroom, the community, or during a press conference. What types of supporting materials were used? Did the type of information used make a difference in your evaluation of the speech? Explain.

5. On the computer, create a chart or graph on a topic of interest to you, such as the trend in downloading music over the past ten years or hurricane activity over the past fifty years. Experiment with accessing the information you need and developing a professional-looking visual aid on the screen.

## Speech Assignments

1. *Speech to Instruct with Visual Aid*
   Prepare a four-to-six-minute speech to instruct using a visual aid. Choose a subject that you find interesting and whose effectiveness will be increased by the use of a visual aid. Organize your speech carefully, choosing visual aids that will effectively add to the listeners' understanding.

   *Delivery.* This speech should be delivered extemporaneously. You must be able to move around freely when using an aid. Follow the suggestions an how to use visual aids effectively on pp. 98–100.

   ### Sample Topics
   1. The hemispheres of the brain
   2. The vampire bat
   3. The principle of radar
   4. Wall Street reform
   5. The Vikings

2. *Demonstration Speech*
   Deliver a three-to-five-minute speech in which you demonstrate a technique or procedure. Choose something you enjoy doing and do well. Consider whether your audience will see the usefulness of your information. Topics that offer little utility to an audience must be made interesting to hold attention.

*Delivery*. This speech should be delivered extemporaneously. Demonstration speeches require freedom of movement. Practice this speech thoroughly so you can deliver it easily and naturally. The less dependent on your outline or notes you are, the better.

### Sample Topics

1. How to remove spots inexpensively
2. How to make a quilt
3. How to wrap a turban
4. How to make a Greek salad
5. How to perform a magic trick

# *Preparing*
# THE CONTENT
# OF YOUR SPEECH

NOW THAT you have gathered the supporting materials you will need to reinforce or clarify your central idea and main points, you are ready to begin preparing the content of your speech. The content should be developed around the central idea statement, which is the controlling idea of the speech. With a basic speech pattern you might simply state and support the central idea. Speeches of personal experience to entertain or to make a point are often developed in this generalization example pattern.

In the speech of personal experience to make a point, there are two possible approaches: (1) the central idea (the point) is stated at the beginning of the speech followed by a story that reinforces it; and (2) the story is told first, and the point is made at the conclusion of the speech. Thus, you might say, "I learned at an early age never to trust strangers," and tell your audience about an experience you had that taught you this lesson, or you might relate the experience first and end by saying, "And that's how I learned never to trust strangers."

In most cases, however, the central idea of a speech quite naturally breaks up into two or three main points. For example, consider a speech with the topic *Our Cafeteria*. In developing a speech about *Our Cafeteria*, which is a clean, inexpensive, good place to meet people, and so on, you could quite likely come up with the central idea, "Our school cafeteria is an excellent place to eat." You might support it with these three main points: (1) the prices are reasonable, (2) the food is well prepared, and (3) the surroundings are neat and clean. The basic format for this speech would be as follows:

Introduction: The introduction of a speech should capture the audience's attention, give them a reason for listening, present the central idea of the speech—in this case, our school cafeteria is an excellent place to eat—indicate your qualifications for giving the speech, and preview the main points of the speech.

Body: First main point—the prices are reasonable (supporting material).

Second main point—the food is well prepared (supporting material).

Third main point—the surroundings are neat and clean (supporting material).

Conclusion: The conclusion of a speech should end with a summary, a restatement of the central idea, a question, a call to action, or a vision of the future.

Although some central ideas can be logically broken down into five or more main points, it is advisable to limit your speech to no more than four. Keep in mind that you are speaking to listeners who must assimilate and remember the information you are giving them. Few, if any, will be taking notes. If you have too many points, the chances are great that you will confuse and perhaps even lose some of your audience.

# ORGANIZING YOUR SPEECH

## INTRODUCTION

An introduction should capture the attention of the audience, give them a reason for listening, present the central idea, indicate your qualifications, and preview the main ideas to be given. As a rule of thumb, the introduction should comprise 10 to 15 percent of the total speech time and should lead smoothly into the body of the speech.

## BODY

The **body** should comprise 75 to 85 percent of the speech. That is where the speaker's message is presented. The body consists of the main points of the speech, along with the supporting materials necessary to develop each point, and clear transitions from each point to the next.

> **Body:** The main points and supporting materials of a speech that develop the speaker's purpose and message.

## CONCLUSION

A conclusion should be short and to the point. It should comprise 5 to 10 percent of the total speech and include one or any combination of the following: a summary of the main points, a restatement of the central idea, a question, a call to action, a vision of the future, and so on.

# PLANNING THE BODY

The body is the most important part of the speech. It contains the development of the central idea, the major points, and the supporting material that proves or clarifies the central idea and main points. Therefore, it is wise to develop the body of the speech first. Follow these four steps as you plan the body of your speech:

1. Decide on the main points that will support or clarify your central idea.
2. Write these main points as complete sentences.
3. Arrange the central idea and main points in a logical organizational pattern.
4. Add appropriate supporting material to clarify and reinforce your central idea and main points.

## DECIDING ON MAIN POINTS

The central idea statement you have chosen should determine the main points you select. The number of main points you need to put your ideas across is up to you. In some speeches, as you remember, the body may consist simply of the support you are using for your central idea. In others, you might choose two to four main points around which to build your speech. Keep in mind during this stage that you are trying to get your audience to accept and remember your ideas. As I pointed out earlier, if you develop any more than four main points, chances are that some of your audience will be unable to remember them.

## WRITE YOUR MAIN POINTS AS COMPLETE SENTENCES

Writing your main points as complete sentences will help you determine whether they reinforce or clarify your central ideas effectively and whether they cover your subject adequately. Each main point should be stated clearly and succinctly so there is no doubt in your listeners' minds as to what your point is and what you are trying to accomplish. Following are four suggestions for developing main points for your speech:

1. They should clarify or reinforce your central idea.
2. They should cover your subject adequately.
3. They should be equal in importance.
4. They should be worded in a similar way.

THEY SHOULD CLARIFY OR REINFORCE YOUR CENTRAL IDEA.    To be effective, your main points must make your central idea clearer or more forceful. These main points will in turn be clarified or reinforced by your supporting materials: examples, illustrations, statistics, explanation, testimony, comparison and contrast, and visual aids. Main points that do not clearly reinforce or clarify your central idea are confusing. Consider the following example:

> *Central idea:* Iguanas make great pets.
> *Main point:* They are inexpensive.
> *Main point:* They are clean.
> *Main point:* They are easy to care for.
> *Main point:* They are reptiles.

Note that although the first three main points reinforce the central idea that iguanas make great pets, the fourth point, that they are reptiles, does not. Even though it can be argued that many reptiles make excellent pets, most would agree that others, like cobras or crocodiles, do not.

THEY SHOULD COVER YOUR SUBJECT ADEQUATELY.    To achieve your purpose in speaking, you must be sure to provide your listeners with the information they need to respond correctly. Choose your main points carefully so they fully develop your central idea. It is always better to have too much material than to fail to cover a subject adequately. Remember, your success or failure as a speaker is largely dependent on audience response.

THEY SHOULD BE SIMILAR IN IMPORTANCE AND PARALLEL IN PHRASING.    Besides reinforcing and clarifying your central idea, your main points should be similar in importance to each other. Supporting your central idea with two strong points and one weak one will lessen the effectiveness. Also, wording your main points in a parallel manner will emphasize the fact that they are coordinate. One way to achieve parallelism of main points is to repeat key words. Compare these two sets of main points for a speech on swimming:

### Nonparallel

*Central idea:* Swimming is beneficial to your health.
*Main point:* It conditions your mind and your body.

*Main point:* You exercise most of your muscles.
*Main point:* The capacity of your lungs is increased.

### Parallel

*Central idea:* Swimming is beneficial to your health.
*Main point:* It conditions your mind and your body.
*Main point:* It exercises most of your muscles.
*Main point:* It increases your lung capacity.

## ARRANGING THE CENTRAL IDEA AND MAIN POINTS

The information that you are presenting to your audience must be organized in such a way that it makes sense to them and can be easily followed. You can organize the central idea and main points that you present in your speech a number of ways. The seven most basic organizational patterns follow:

1. **General to Specific.** In a sense, a general-to-specific pattern is found in most speeches. The central idea, usually given in the introduction, is a general statement, and it is followed by a statement of the main points in less general terms. Finally, each main point is supported by specific details. The opposite of this would be a specific-to-general pattern, where the main points are given first and the central idea is stated in the conclusion.

**EXAMPLE A.** *Central idea:* Betty White is an excellent speech teacher.

   a. She has established an excellent rapport with her students and made them enthusiastic about speech.
   b. She has demonstrated her thorough knowledge of the subject along with sound teaching techniques.
   c. She has been able to communicate her understanding of speech to the students and has helped them improve.

**EXAMPLE B**

   a. Betty White has established an excellent rapport with her students and made them enthusiastic about speech.
   b. Betty White has demonstrated that she has a thorough knowledge of her subject along with sound teaching techniques.
   c. Betty White has been able to communicate her understanding of speech to the students and has helped them improve.

*Concluding central idea:* Therefore, Betty White is an excellent speech teacher.

2. **Chronological Order.** Many speeches lend themselves to development in chronological order. In this pattern, you relate a series of incidents or explain a process according to the order in which the incidents or steps in the process occur or have occurred—from first to last. You might analyze the development of rock and roll or demonstrate how to make lasagna.

Some speech topics, such as the recent rehabilitation of the Statue of Liberty, lend themselves to development in a chronological order. In this case, you would relate a series of steps in the process, from finding funding for the project to its completion.

**EXAMPLE.** *Central idea:* You must follow four steps when making lasagna.

    **a.** Step 1 involves preparing the meat sauce.
    **b.** Step 2 includes making and cooking the pasta.
    **c.** Step 3 involves preparing the three cheeses.
    **d.** Step 4 is layering the ingredients into baking dishes and baking the lasagna.

**3. Topical.** Sometimes a pattern of arrangement is suggested by the topic itself. For instance, a discussion of music history might logically divide itself into four areas: preclassical, classical, romantic, and contemporary. Similarly, a discussion of a college or university might involve the board of directors, the administration, the faculty, and the student body.

**EXAMPLE.** *Central idea:* The development of music can be roughly divided into four broad areas.

    **a.** The first is preclassical.
    **b.** The second is classical.
    **c.** The third is romantic.
    **d.** The fourth is contemporary.

4. **Space Order.** A subject might fall quite naturally into a spatial arrangement. An analysis of education in different parts of the country, a demonstration on how to landscape the front of a house, and an explanation of how the body digests food would lend themselves to this pattern of development.

**EXAMPLE.** *Central idea:* Digestion, the process by which the body absorbs and uses food, occurs in three areas of the body.

    **a.** Digestion begins in the mouth, where the food is ground into a semisolid mass.
    **b.** Digestion continues in the stomach, where food becomes a mixed liquid.
    **c.** Digestion is completed in the small intestines, where the final stage occurs.

5. **Cause and Effect.** Although it can be used as an organizational pattern for speeches to entertain or inform, the cause-and-effect pattern is most often used for persuasive speeches. A typical example is that of a salesperson trying to convince a prospective customer that buying the product (cause) will result in all sorts of advantages (effect). Following is an outline of a student speech that uses the cause-and-effect pattern to describe the beneficial effects of jogging.

**EXAMPLE.** *Central idea:* Jogging is the ideal exercise.

    **a.** It conditions the body.
    **b.** It removes unwanted fat.
    **c.** It provides emotional balance.

6. **Problem–Solution.** Another organizational pattern most often employed in speeches to persuade is the problem–solution order. This speech usually begins with an introduction that states a problem as the central idea of the speech. The body of the speech is organized around the solution or solutions to the problem. Following is a sample outline of a typical problem–solution speech.

**EXAMPLE.** *Central idea:* The amount of money that our student government will receive from outside sources this year has been cut in half, eliminating funding for many of our programs.

The solution to this problem is to hold a two-day bratwurst festival during the month of October, which will raise enough money to make up the difference.

**Motivated sequence:** An organizational pattern involving a five-step plan of action, developed specifically for persuasive speaking.

7. **Motivated Sequence.** Monroe's **motivated sequence** is yet another organizational pattern. It was developed in the 1930s by

A cause and effect organizational pattern could be used to describe the beneficial effects of jogging.

the late Alan H. Monroe, a speech professor at Purdue University. It lists a five-step plan of action.*

a. Capture the attention of the audience.
b. Indicate a need for the audience to listen.
c. Show how your proposal will satisfy that need.
d. Visualize what will occur if the plan is put into operation.
e. Indicate the action you want your audience to take.

---

*From Douglas Ehninger, Bruce Gronbeck, Ray McKerrow, and Alan Monroe, *Principles and Types of Speech Communication*, 10th ed. (Glenview, IL: Scott Foresman, 1986), p. 153.

# Working WITH THE WEB

You can get help organizing your speech by going to the following location on the publisher's web site:

www.abacon.com/pubspeak/organize/patterns.html

The Internet public library site also has a location that can help you outline your speech:

www.ipl.org/teen/aplus/linksorganizing.htm

In addition, there are a number of outlining tools available on the Internet that can help you map your ideas much as you would by arranging index cards to organize your ideas. You might visit

www.mindjet.com
www.inspiration.com/general_biz.html

**EXAMPLE.** *Central idea:* Congress must pass a federal law requiring stiffer penalties for drunken driving.

    **a.** Show pictures of fatal crashes involving drunk drivers.
    **b.** Cite statistics that emphasize the problem.
    **c.** Show how tougher laws have worked in other countries.
    **d.** Describe life without the menace of the drunken driver on the road.
    **e.** Tell those in your audience to sign your petition.

Speeches that are well organized are clearer and therefore more effective. Using one of the organizational patterns given here will make it easier for those in your audience to understand and remember the information in your speech. You have undoubtedly come in contact with many of these organizational patterns before. That is because the mind is conditioned to organize chronologically, spatially, topically, logically, and from general to specific. Your chances of communicating effectively with your audience will be much greater if you use an organizational pattern that can easily be followed.

## ADD APPROPRIATE SUPPORTING MATERIAL

Supporting materials are necessary for clarifying or proving the points you make in the body of your speech. By themselves the major and subordinate points are really only the structure or skeleton of your speech. It is the quality and relevancy of the supports you choose that make your ideas clear, interesting, and acceptable to your audience.

# OUTLINING YOUR SPEECH

Although outlining your speech involves extra work, the rewards are worth it. The major benefit of an outline is that it allows you to check your speech for potential mistakes. A speech outline is essentially a plan of what you want to say. Carefully examining your outline will help ensure that the main points of your speech clarify or reinforce your central idea, cover your subject adequately, are equal in importance, and are worded in a similar way. In addition, an outline will enable you to assess whether your subpoints and supporting materials are adequate and sufficiently varied, and whether your introduction and conclusion are appropriate to the body of your speech. Finally, an outline will help you determine where transitions might be needed. There are two types of outlines that may be helpful for developing and delivering your speech: (1) a planning outline and (2) a delivery outline. This section deals with the planning outline from which a delivery outline, as given in Chapter 8, can be developed.

## PLANNING OUTLINE

**Planning outline:** A tentative plan of what the speaker wants to say, allowing for review and changes.

Keep in mind, what you put down in a **planning outline** is only tentative. It can always be changed. You can't expect to come up with a finished product on your first try. You will probably wind up with a number of rough drafts before you decide on one you like. When your outline is complete, you will have the skeleton for your speech.

**DIVIDE OUTLINE INTO THREE PARTS: INTRODUCTION, BODY, AND CONCLUSION.** A speech should be divided into three parts: the introduction, the body, and the conclusion. Each part has a specific function. The introduction should get your audience's attention, give them a reason for listening, indicate your central idea and qualifications, and preview your subject. The body should communicate your ideas clearly and meaningfully, and the conclusion should restate your central ideas and main points and tie them together in a neat package. "In other words," as a wag once said, "in your intro, you tell the people what you're going to tell 'em; in the body, you tell 'em what you said you'd tell 'em, and in the conclusion, you tell 'em what you've told 'em."

**USE STANDARD OUTLINE FORM.** Standard outline form requires that you write your outline in complete sentences and follow the rules of coordination and subordination. Coordination means that all statements at the same level in your outline are equal in importance. Subordination means that each statement in your outline supports the statement in the level directly above it.

Outline numbering follows this order:

  **I.** Main Point Number 1 (Roman numerals)
    **A.** Supporting Point (Capital letter)
      **1.** Supporting Material (Arabic numeral)
        **a.** Evidence (small letter)
        **b.** Evidence
    **B.** Supporting Point
  **II.** Main Point Number 2
    **A.** Supporting Point
      **1.** Supporting Material
        **a.** Evidence
        **b.** Evidence

---

### ✔ *Checklist* FOR SUCCESS

Tips for developing a planning outline:

- Divide the outline into three parts.
- Use standard outline format.
- Write out your main points.
- Support each main point.
- Develop your conclusion.
- Develop your introduction.
- Add transitions.

---

Indent all headings in the outline. Place numbers and letters of all headings directly under the first word of the heading above. Roman numerals for main points are placed closest to the left margin. Note that the periods following the roman numerals line up directly below each other. Putting your ideas into this outline form allows you to see the relationship between main points, supporting points, subpoints, and supporting materials in your speech. Thus, you can judge whether main points are worded similarly and are approximately equal in importance, whether all points at a given level have about the same amount of support, and whether each level in the outline is related to the level above it.

**WRITE OUT YOUR MAIN POINTS.**    The main points should be written as complete sentences and should clarify or reinforce your central idea. Combined, they should cover your subject adequately. They should be equal in importance and worded in a similar way. Your main points should be numbered in standard outline form. A speech with the central idea "Rocks Make Great Pets" might be supported with these four main points:

  **I.** They are inexpensive.
 **II.** They are easy to care for.
**III.** They are fun to watch.
**IV.** They're great to throw when you want to let off steam.

**SUPPORT EACH MAIN POINT.**    Each main point in your speech requires specific supporting material. Supporting materials are necessary to make your ideas clear or convincing to your audience. As a rule of thumb, the more controversial your main point is, the more supporting material you will need to back it up. In any event, each main point should be supported by at least two supporting points. If you can't find at least two supports for a main point, it probably should be omitted. Supporting points should be supported by subpoints and so on.

Keep in mind that some speeches may have only one main point. A short speech to persuade with the central idea "Never buy anything sight unseen" might involve you telling your audience about an experience you had that taught a lesson that was the single main point of your speech: "I learned at an early age never to buy anything I hadn't seen first." You might deliver a speech of personal experience to entertain with a central idea that is also the main point: "Camping can be fun, for bears!"

**DEVELOP YOUR INTRODUCTION.** The minimum purpose of any introduction should be to get the audience's attention and reveal your subject. However, most introductions should have five objectives: (1) to capture the audience's attention, (2) to present the central idea of the speech, (3) to indicate your qualifications for giving the speech, (4) to give the audience a reason for listening, and (5) to preview the ideas to be covered in the speech. As a rule of thumb, the introduction should comprise only 10 to 15 percent of the total speech time.

**DEVELOP YOUR CONCLUSION.** A conclusion should be short and to the point. It should comprise 5 to 10 percent of the total speech and include one or any combination of the following: a summary of the main points, a restatement of the central idea, a question, a call to action, a vision of the future, and so on.

Following is an outline of the body of the speech whose central idea is "walking is the ideal exercise," to which supporting materials have been added.

## BODY OF SPEECH

I. Walking strengthens the heart.
   A. Walking improves collateral circulation.
      1. (*Testimony*) Dr. Samuel Fox, president of the American College of Cardiology, says walking increases the number and size of your blood vessels and the efficiency of the heart.
      2. (*Example*) Steve McKanic was told at the age of forty-six that his heart condition was incurable and that there was no hope. He started walking, and five years later he's healthy and happy again.
      3. (*Statistic*) It is estimated that 12 million people in this country are being treated for heart disease that could be improved by walking and 12 million have heart disease but don't know it.
   B. Walking lowers blood pressure.
      1. (*Explanation visual aid*) Muscles in your feet, calves, thighs, buttocks, and abdomen help push seventy-two thousand quarts of blood through your system every twenty-four hours. These muscles are exercised by walking, making them more efficient in lowering your blood pressure.
      2. (*Example*) Eula Weaver suffered her first high blood pressure heart attack at the age of seventy-eight. Today at eighty-nine, she walks regularly and her blood pressure is normal.
      3. (*Testimony*) A recent study by Dr. Kenneth Cooper, author of *Aerobics*, demonstrates the relationship between walking and a person's fitness level.
II. Walking conditions a person mentally.
   A. Walking reduces stress.

1. (*Testimony*) Dr. Herbert DeVries, University of California physiologist, stated that a university study showed that a fifteen-minute walk reduced neurotransmitter tension more effectively than a standard dose of tranquilizers.
2. (*Example*) Albert Einstein, Harry Truman, and Abraham Lincoln walked daily to escape from the tension of their jobs.
3. (*Testimony*) Dr. Paul D. White, dean of American cardiologists, said a minimum of an hour a day of fast walking is absolutely necessary for one's optimum health.

B. Walking improves self-image.
1. (*Testimony*) "Walking," says psychologist John Martin, "helps you function more efficiently because you know you are doing things that are positive and constructive which give you satisfaction."
2. (*Example*) Aunt Rose, who had tried to lose weight for years, began walking and in six months went from a size 22 to 14.
3. (*Explanation*) Walking improves circulation, sending more oxygen to the brain and creating a euphoria that improves self-concept.

III. Walking conditions a person physically.
A. Walking removes unwanted fat.
1. (*Visual aid*) This chart indicates the number of calories a person of particular weight will expend each hour by walking at various speeds.
2. (*Statistical testimony*) Dr. Charles Kunzleman, national fitness consultant for the YMCA, estimates that there are presently more than 60 million Americans who are seriously obese.
3. (*Example*) Three-hundred-pound Molly Ryan, who felt her glandular problem kept her fat, began walking after a heart attack and lost 100 pounds the first year.

B. Walking improves a person's fitness.
1. (*Comparison*) A study of the health records of 30,000 double-decker bus workers in London found that the fare collectors who climbed the stairs regularly had a much lower mortality rate and faster recovery from heart attacks than the inactive bus drivers.
2. (*Example*) Scrambling over the slopes of their mountainous homeland has given the long-lived citizens of Hunza in the Himalayas such a high degree of physical fitness that even when they suffer a heart attack it does little harm.
3. (*Testimony*) Dr. Lawrence Golding conducted a controlled experiment at Kent State University that showed that walking combined with dieting was far superior to dieting alone in improving physical fitness.

## TRANSITIONS

The body of the speech outlined above consists of main and supporting points, along with supporting material for each. However, to move your listeners smoothly from one point to the next, you must include **transitions** or links between each point. Transitions act like guideposts for your listeners. When you use words like *also* and *in addition* you

**Transitions:** Words or phrases that act as guideposts for listeners to connect ideas in the speech and move from one point to the next.

indicate that your thinking is moving forward. Words like *on the other hand* and *conversely* indicate a reversal of direction. Imagine the following situation: An instructor walks into class and says to her students, "As you all know, you are scheduled to take your midsemester exam in this course today. However . . ." The instructor pauses. An audible sigh of relief is heard throughout the room. The word *however* has caused the students to reverse their thinking. There will be no exam today.

Transitions will help provide coherence to your speech so your ideas flow smoothly from one point to the next. Following are a number of suggestions for providing coherence to your speech:

1. Use transitional words: also, again, as a result, besides, but, conversely, however, in addition, in contrast, likewise, moreover, nevertheless, similarly, then, therefore, thus, yet.

Martin Luther King, Jr.'s extensive use of signposts, such as the repetition of the phrases "I have a dream" and "Let freedom ring," made his "I Have a Dream" speech one of the most memorable of all time.

2. Use enumerative signposts. "There are three main reasons: first . . . second . . . third . . ."
   "Point A is this: . . ."
3. Repeat key words. "Our nuclear buildup isn't defense. Our nuclear buildup is suicide."
4. Conclude your discussion of one point by introducing the next point. "This concludes the discussion of step two, stripping. Next we will consider step three, sanding."
5. Begin your discussion of a new point with a reference to the point you just finished discussing. "Now that we have finished our discussion of step three, sanding, we are ready to move on to step four, refinishing."

Keep in mind that as a speaker you are obliged to do whatever you can to make your ideas as clear and interesting to your listeners as possible. Using effective transitions in your speeches will help you achieve this goal.

## Chapter Review

After reading this chapter, you should be able to

- Identify the goals of the three main parts of a speech: introduction, body, and conclusion.
- List and describe the seven organizational patterns and determine which would be most appropriate for your speech topic.
- Create a planning outline for your next classroom speech, following the specific guidelines provided.
- Identify the type of supporting materials that would most effectively illustrate each main point in the speech.
- Understand where to insert transitions so ideas flow smoothly.

## Key Terms

Body (p. 107)                      Planning outline (p. 114)
Motivated sequence (p. 111)        Transitions (p. 117)

## Exercises

1. Write a general purpose, specific purpose, central idea, and two or more *main points* for one or more of the following subjects:
   a. Restaurants
   b. Hobbies
   c. Sports
   d. Mass media

   e. Politics
   f. International news
   g. Health and fitness
2. Use your library's resources or log on to a web site that provides historical archives and find the text of a famous speech, such as Martin Luther King, Jr.'s "I Have a Dream," and determine what organizational pattern it uses. Identify the main points and supporting points. Is there an attention-getting introduction? Conclusion? What does the speaker do to relate to the audience? Find several examples of transitional words and phrases. Prepare your findings to share with the class.
3. Using the brainstorming and clustering techniques discussed earlier in the book, select a topic and write at least ten ideas related to that topic. Rearrange the ideas in outline form so they follow a logical sequence. Develop the body of the speech, determining the main points and supporting points and identifying any areas you need to fill in.
4. Expand the outline you have just created, adding an introduction, conclusion, and appropriate transitions. Indicate what type of supporting material each main point in your speech should have and where you might find the information.

## Speech Assignments

1. *Relating a Personal Experience to Make a Point*
   Develop a three-to-four-minute speech in which you describe an experience you had that taught-you a lesson. The story may be true, partly true, or fictitious. Develop your material informally with emphasis on details of action.

   *Delivery*. This speech should be delivered extemporaneously. Use no more than one note card. An audience will expect you to have almost total eye contact when talking about your own experiences.

   ### Sample Central Ideas
   1. Taking a chance can pay off.
   2. A first aid course can save someone.
   3. Seat belts save lives.
   4. Don't judge a person on the basis of your first meeting.

2. *Relate a Personal Experience that Taught a Lesson*
   Deliver a two-to-four-minute speech in which you relate a personal experience that taught you something about yourself. (1) You can begin by stating what you learned, followed by a story that reinforces it, or (2) you can tell the story first and then state what you learned at the conclusion.

   *Model*. I found out at an early age that I was an honest person. One hot summer day, two friends and I went to the beach for a swim. While we were putting on our swimsuits in the bathhouse, I noticed a wallet under one of the benches. I picked it up and found that there was more than $100 in it. "Wow!" I said. "Look what I found." "Way to go," said one of my friends. "Let's split it." "No," I said. "It has a name and address in it. I'm giving it back." "You're nuts," my friends said, but when I got home I called the owner and he came to the house, got his wallet and money back, and we both were happy.

# CHAPTER 8

# *Delivering* YOUR SPEECH

ONCE YOU HAVE determined your purpose and subject, analyzed your audience, and developed the content of your speech, you have completed the hardest part of your job. However, all the work you have done will be wasted if you fail to deliver your speech effectively.

The method of delivery you choose may vary, depending on a number of variables such as the purpose of your speech, the subject, the occasion, and your audience. Most of the time you will want to deliver your speeches extemporaneously. This is usually the best and most effective method for most speakers on most occasions. However, in some instances, you might be required to deal with so many facts, statistics, and other data that you will want to write your speech out completely and deliver it verbatim so as not to run the risk of forgetting anything. Or, you might be one of those gifted few who have the kind of retention and acting ability needed for delivering an effective memorized speech. Even then, it would be wise to take along a written copy of what you memorized if you're speaking at an occasion involving stress such as a funeral or memorial service. If you are lucky, you will not be required at some future date to deliver an impromptu speech with practically no time for preparation at all. In case that occurs, however, a number of suggestions are offered in this chapter to help you manage more effectively in a difficult situation.

The manner in which you prepare your speech for delivery will depend on the type of delivery you choose. Impromptu speeches (those delivered on the spur of the moment) are either not prepared at all or prepared very hastily. Manuscript speeches are written out completely and read. Memorized speeches are usually written out first and then committed to memory and delivered. Extemporaneous speeches are carefully prepared but delivered from note cards or a written or memorized outline rather than from a manuscript or memory. In most cases, the extemporaneous method is by far the best method of delivery. It provides spontaneity and will enable you to adapt your message to your audience while you are speaking to them and to modify it when necessary in response to their feedback. Let's consider these four methods of delivery in more detail.

## IMPROMPTU SPEECHES

**Impromptu speech:** A speech that is developed on the spur of the moment, with little or no preparation.

An **impromptu speech** is one that is developed on the spur of the moment. It demands a lot of the speaker because it seldom gives time for advanced thought or preparation. When delivering an impromptu speech, you have little time, if any, to analyze the subject, audience, or occasion. You must think on your feet to choose and organize your material. Although this can impart spontaneity and directness to your delivery, it can also result in inappropriate statements, unexpressed thoughts, and repetitiveness. Consider your own experience. How many times have you looked back at a situation and thought "Why didn't I say that?" or realized that you had put your foot in your mouth and said the wrong thing?

There are times, however, when it is necessary to deliver an impromptu speech. If that situation arises, consider the following advice: (1) keep your speech short and to the point, (2) try to use illustrations for supporting material (from personal experience

Extemporaneous speakers, such as the one pictured here, often use note cards or an outline to help them move smoothly through the speech. This method allows for directness and eye contact, which conveys a high degree of spontaneity.

if possible), (3) handle only one main point, and (4) make sure your central idea and purpose are absolutely clear to your audience. Experience in the planning, preparation, and delivery of extemporaneous speeches will provide further guidelines for greater effectiveness in impromptu situations.

## MANUSCRIPT SPEECHES

A **manuscript speech** is one that is completely written out in advance. It is used in situations where the presentation must be precise. You would probably choose a manuscript speech if you were reporting to

**Manuscript speech:** A speech that is completely written out in advance and read.

a group on a convention that you attended as their delegate or explaining a complicated statistical procedure. Although the manuscript speech offers security to speakers afraid that they will forget what they want to say or say it badly, it has a number of disadvantages: (1) it reduces eye contact with the audience, (2) reading a speech in a spontaneous and convincing manner takes skill and practice, and (3) the speaker has difficulty in changing the language or content of a manuscript speech to adapt to the mood or reaction of the audience.

Even though you may be willing to accept these disadvantages in return for the security of a manuscript speech, the best advice is to deliver a manuscript speech only when time does not permit you to prepare and practice an extemporaneous speech or when exact word order is crucial to the success of the presentation. To deliver a manuscript speech effectively, consider the following suggestions:

1. Type your manuscript speech in capital letters, triple spaced, and underlined to ensure easy reading. Type on only one side of the paper and number the pages.
2. Edit your speech by reading each sentence aloud. Avoid overly long or complex sentences. No matter how involved or technical your material is, it must be communicated clearly.
3. Indicate places of emphasis and pauses.
4. Practice your manuscript by reading it aloud at least three or four times. Become familiar enough with it so you can maintain adequate eye contact. When possible, tape or videotape your delivery. You should sound as though you are talking to people, not reading to them.
5. Use appropriate facial expression and body action to enliven your delivery.

## MEMORIZED SPEECHES

**Memorized speech:** A speech that is written out first, committed to memory, and then delivered.

A **memorized speech** is written out as a manuscript speech and then committed to memory. Although it appears to offer the advantages of a manuscript speech along with total eye contact, it has a number of weaknesses: (1) it takes an inordinate amount of time to memorize a speech, particularly a long one; (2) it takes a skillful actor to deliver memorized material in a natural, spontaneous way; (3) the speaker who delivers a memorized speech runs the risk of forgetting; and (4) as with the manuscript speech, it is difficult to change a memorized speech to adapt to feedback from the audience. However, for the right person, the memorized speech can be an excellent method, especially for someone who plans to give the same speech a number of times.

There are times when it would be desirable to commit part of a speech to memory. You might want to memorize the first few lines of the introduction to your extemporaneous speech in order to start positively and with total eye contact. Memorizing particularly suitable words or phrases can often produce positive results. Actually, most effective speakers use a combination of different delivery methods.

## EXTEMPORANEOUS SPEECHES

**Extemporaneous speech:** A speech that is carefully planned in advance and includes a complete sentence outline, but the not the exact wording of the speech.

Like the manuscript and memorized speech, the **extemporaneous speech** is carefully prepared in advance. The difference is that the speaker does not deliver the speech in a predetermined word order. Effective extemporaneous speakers usually develop their speeches in a complete sentence outline form as shown in Chapter 7. They know what they are going to say in the introduction, body, and conclusion of the speech but decide on the wording of the speech at the moment of delivery. You

## ✔ *Checklist* FOR SUCCESS

### Advantages and Disadvantages of Speech Delivery Methods

| | Advantages | Disadvantages |
|---|---|---|
| *Impromptu—given spur of the moment* | Spontaneity<br>Directness | No advance preparation<br>Must think on feet<br>No time to analyze audience<br>Inappropriate statements<br>Repetition |
| *Manuscript—written* | Speaker security<br>Speaker confidence<br>Opportunity to be precise and detailed (good for complex data, facts, or procedures)<br>Nothing left out or forgotten | Reduces eye contact<br>Speech seems read<br>Lacks spontaneity<br>Difficulty changing language or content in response to audience |
| *Memorized—written out as a manuscript speech and committed to memory* | Speaker security<br>Opportunity for eye contact<br>Nothing is left out or forgotten | Takes a long time to memorize speech<br>Takes skill to make delivery natural and spontaneous<br>Difficult to change material to adapt to audience |
| *Extemporaneous— carefully prepared in advance but not written word for word* | Complete sentence outline: security for speaker<br>Completely planned introduction, body, conclusion<br>Relaxed, spontaneous style | Takes time to prepare |

Adapted from Seiler Beall, *Communication: Making Connections,* 6/e, Allyn & Bacon, 2005.

might compare extemporaneous speech delivery with the telling of a funny story. Most people tell a funny story extemporaneously. They are aware of the important details of the story and know how the story is going to unfold, but they haven't memorized the word order. As long as they include those details necessary to make the humor clear, they can tailor the story for any occasion. The result is a relaxed, spontaneous style, which is the main advantage of extemporaneous delivery.

Extemporaneous speakers often use note cards or an outline to help them move smoothly from one idea to the next. However, these cover the main and supporting ideas of the speech, rather than the words used to express them. The extemporaneous method offers the same directness and spontaneity as the impromptu method without the danger of your rambling off the point or repeating yourself unnecessarily. For most situations, it is the most effective method of delivery.

# NONVERBAL COMMUNICATION

Much of what we communicate to others is communicated nonverbally, through our bodily movement, facial expression, personal appearance, voice, and so on. Obviously, it is important that these nonverbals reinforce the words that we use when communicating something to others.

Have you ever had a person tell you something when you could tell by her tone of voice, gesture, or facial expression that she did not mean what she said or meant just the opposite? We say a lot to others by the way we look and sound when we say it. In fact, most listeners will give more credence to what we say nonverbally than what we say verbally.

**Nonverbal communication:** Behaviors, including body movement, facial expression, voice, and personal appearance, that are part of our communication.

Given the importance of **nonverbal communication** in delivering the speech, it should be a prime consideration when choosing a method of delivery. As indicated previously, although a manuscript speech offers the security of having everything written out so there is no danger of forgetting, it presents a challenge in communicating, enthusiasm, interest, and sincerity. A manuscript speech locks you into reading what you have previously written, rather than allowing you the flexibility of being able to modify your ideas in response to feedback from your audience, and it requires a lot of practice if you intend to have adequate eye contact with your audience.

The memorized speech requires even more practice than the manuscript, and there is always the danger of forgetting. Furthermore, unless you are an excellent actor, the memorized speech, like the manuscript speech, can also lack enthusiasm and sincerity. Also, with the memorized speech, although you do not have to look at a manuscript or note cards, it is difficult to look directly into the eyes of your listeners while trying to remember what you're going to say next.

The impromptu speech is an exercise in thinking on your feet. The difficulty is in organizing and presenting your ideas in a logical, interesting manner when you have had little chance to prepare.

By far the best method for delivering your speech both verbally and nonverbally is the extemporaneous method. With this method, you speak from notes or an outline that is written out or memorized. You know what you are going to say but are not restricted to exact wording. This offers you the ability to be enthusiastic, interesting, and sincere without having to worry about forgetting, losing your place, or not being able to respond to audience feedback. With the extemporaneous method, you will be free to communicate to your audience nonverbally with your bodily movement, facial expression, and your voice, as well as with the words that you use.

In the broadest sense, nonverbal communication includes almost everything about you that communicates something to others except for the language you use. This would include the car you drive, the clothes you wear, your hairstyle, the organizations to which you belong, the friends with whom you associate, and whatever else there is about you that communicates who you are and what you stand for. However, for the purpose of analysis, we examine only two broad areas of nonverbal communication: kinesics and paralanguage.

# KINESICS

**Kinesics** is the study of how the body, face, and eyes communicate. The way you walk, your manner of gesturing, your posture, your facial expression, and the way you look at people or avoid looking at them, all say something about you to others. Whether they are interpreted by others correctly or incorrectly, these nonverbal elements communicate to others who you are.

> **Kinesics:** The study of how the body, face, and eyes communicate; also known as "body language."

**BODILY MOVEMENT.** Consider the speaker who seemingly can't stand still, who paces back and forth in front of the audience. Does that speaker seem to be communicating nervousness? Or, consider the speaker who shuffles slowly up to the front of the room and hunches over the lectern when delivering the speech. Does that speaker's movement indicate weakness in confidence or preparation? In contrast, consider the speaker who strides briskly up to the front of the room and stands in front of the audience with good posture. Isn't that speaker saying, "Pay attention. I've got something to say to you that you will find interesting"? These three examples show the importance of positive bodily movement. It is all right to move around occasionally as long as the movement seems motivated by what you are saying. You might move to indicate the beginning of a new idea or a change of direction in your speech. You might move closer to an audience to share something personal or indicate a positive feeling toward your audience. The key is that your movement should seem motivated by what you are saying and not detract from it.

Your listeners begin forming opinions of you the moment they see you. Therefore, when you go up to deliver your speech, walk up to the podium briskly with a friendly expression on your face. Then, when you finish your speech, smile at the audience (when appropriate) and return to your seat as briskly and enthusiastically as you came.

The bodily movements of your listeners can also be helpful in predicting how well you are doing in communicating. The speaker who sees audience members leaning forward in their seats knows she is doing a good job. Feedback is highly important to the communicator. You don't have to have people turn their backs to know they are not interested in what you're saying. If they lower their heads or shrug their shoulders, you soon get the idea, and if you can react to these signals and say it in another way, you will have become more aware of nonverbal audience feedback, which will improve your ability to communicate.

Another kind of bodily movement is the gesture. You can gesture with almost any part of the body. A shrug of the shoulders can communicate many things, depending on the situation. A shake of the head can indicate agreement or disagreement, depending on the direction. Toe tapping can indicate nervousness or irritation. Or, when combined with music, it can also indicate that the toe tapper is synchronized with the music. It is apparent, then, that most bodily gestures can communicate a variety of things and must be evaluated according to the situation.

Hand gestures are particularly important to the speaker. Hand gestures can be divided into two types: descriptive gestures and emphatic gestures.

Emphatic gestures, such as this speaker's strong arm movement, emphasize and reinforce what you are saying.

**Descriptive gestures:** Hand gestures, including signs that communicate information about what you are discussing, such as the size or shape of objects.

*Descriptive Gestures.* If you are describing to your listeners how large the tomatoes you grew were or how high your fence is, you can use your hands to give them an idea of shape or height. You can also use your hands to describe a winding staircase, a circle, or a square.

Another form of descriptive gesture is called the *sign*. Some signs are usually instantly understandable to your audience, such as the black power sign, the "we're number one" sign, and the peace sign.

**Emphatic gestures:** Gestures that emphasize or reinforce what you are saying.

*Emphatic Gestures.* Emphatic gestures emphasize what you are saying. The straight arm salute accompanying "Heil Hitler" indicated the fervor the Nazis had in support of *Der Fuhrer*. The synchronized gestures of cheerleaders at a pep rally emphasize the importance of the team getting out there and winning. Emphatic gestures are necessary nonverbal messages that support our concern or enthusiasm for our message. When we fail to reinforce our words with appropriate gestures, we risk sending a confusing message to those with whom we are trying to communicate.

THE FACE AND EYES.     One reason to avoid manuscript speeches or any speech where you are too dependent on your notes is to avoid obscuring your face and eyes. If your head is bent forward when you speak, your audience cannot see your eyes or read your facial expressions, which can communicate a wide range of emotions, including sadness, compassion, concern, anger, annoyance, fear, joy, and happiness.

Maintaining eye contact with your audience is important for a number of reasons. First, you communicate to your audience both verbally and nonverbally. You say a lot to them with your facial expressions, especially with your eyes. An audience will have difficulty seeing your facial expressions if you have your head buried in your notes.

Second, you indicate your interest in others by looking at them. It is a way of saying to each of them, "You are important." It is desirable to get each listener to believe that he or she is being addressed personally. Although you might not be able to look directly at each individual in a large group, be careful to focus on the eyes of as many individuals as possible in all parts of the room. Be sure to include those in the front and back rows and those on the extreme right and left.

Third, eye contact is often thought of as an indication of honesty and sincerity. If your parents asked you how things are going at school and you looked down or averted your eyes when you tell them things were great, would they be likely to believe you? Whether true or not, we often believe that if people don't look at us when they are telling us something important, they either have something to hide or are stretching the truth.

A final, important reason for maintaining eye contact is to obtain feedback from the audience. We look at those to whom we are communicating in order to get their reactions to what we are saying. We can tell through changes in their facial expressions, postures, and gestures whether they are interested or bored, understanding or confused, supportive or opposed, and, hopefully, we react accordingly.

PERSONAL APPEARANCE.     The way you dress is often interpreted by others as communicating a lot about who and what you are. Although perceptions based solely on personal appearance can often be wrong, personal appearance is often a powerful nonverbal communicator. When deciding what to wear, a good rule of thumb is to take your cue from your audience. People are most comfortable with those who dress the way they do. You should dress in something you are comfortable wearing that is clean and neatly pressed. Of course, you should dress for the occasion. In some instances, this might mean slacks and sport coat or a suit and tie for men and a dress or suit for women. When in doubt about what to wear, the safest thing to do is dress conservatively. For a classroom speech, wear clothing that is clean, pressed, and in good repair. For a more formal occasion, or if you want to put your best foot forward in class, wear an appropriate dress or suit. In any event, clothing that does not call attention to itself is always the best choice.

## PARALANGUAGE

**Paralanguage** refers to how you say something. There are many ways that the voice can communicate. Vocal elements like rate, pause, volume, pitch, intensity, force, vocal quality, and nonfluency can either reinforce or contradict the verbal messages you are sending. Emphasizing different words within the same sentence can change the meaning of the sentence significantly. The tone of voice you use can communicate different types of emotions: anger, sadness, elation, boredom, sincerity, excitement, sarcasm, affection, fear, and so on. Like the other nonverbal elements listed above, paralanguage is of the utmost importance in communicating your meaning to others. In fact, when your voice contradicts the verbal message you are sending, most people are inclined to believe what the voice is communicating.

### VOCAL ELEMENTS

*Rate.*    Rate, the speed at which a person speaks, can vary depending on the situation and the emotional attitude of the speaker. Most communication texts list the average speaking rate as between 125 and 150 words per minute. However, people who are excited, enthusiastic, or angry often speak at a much faster rate, whereas those who are lethargic, bored, or depressed speak more slowly. Because of the nonverbal connection between a faster rate and enthusiasm, announcers read hard-sell commercials considerably faster than 150 words per minute.

*Pause.*    Pause in speech can be either filled (vocalized) or unfilled (silent). A person who pauses continuously during a speech and who fills those pauses with *ahs* and *ums* is either thought of as being nonfluent or poorly prepared. Other interpretations of this type of "filled" pause might be seen in the following examples:

1. John asks his girlfriend why she didn't call last night when she promised she would, and her explanation is replete with filled-in pauses. Rather than accepting her answer as fact, John believes that she is being evasive.
2. An English professor asks one of her students to explain the difference between a restrictive and nonrestrictive clause, and the student's response is filled with *ahs* and *ums*. Consequently, the professor feels the student is stalling for time or just doesn't know the answer.

Pause, however, can also be effective. Dramatic pause, when used before an important point, can alert the listener to be especially attentive because something important is coming. When used at the end of an idea, it can give listeners time to think about what has been said and relate to the idea from their own experience. Effectively used, pause adds meaning and variety to a speaker's delivery.

*Volume.*    An essential element to any communication is adequate volume—the loudness or softness of your voice. If people cannot hear you adequately, they will soon stop listening. One of the nonverbal aspects of volume is that it tends to communicate positiveness and confidence. If you asked two people the same question and one responded in a barely audible voice, while the other answered with sufficient volume, whom would you believe? Probably the second one who sounded both confident and positive—if, of course, that person did not speak too loudly. Adequate volume is essential to effective communication. However, most people view those who speak too loudly as being aggressive or boorish. Your volume will be effective if your voice can be easily heard without being offensive.

*Pitch.*    Pitch refers to the highness or lowness of a person's voice as related to a musical scale. The length and thickness of your vocal folds determines whether your voice will be high or low. The ideal pitch level to speak at is called *optimum pitch*, which should be the pitch level most comfortable for you for speaking. One way of determining optimum pitch is to determine how low and how high you can sing, and then find the note that is one-third above your lowest note. That note would be your optimum pitch. Speaking at a pitch level higher or lower than your optimum pitch can cause unpleasant quality, inadequate volume, and monotony in your speech patterns. So, if you want to avoid problems with your voice, speak at your optimum pitch level.

Inflection is the upward and downward movement of pitch. A natural conversational style is characterized by a variety of inflectional patterns. A voice without these inflectional patterns sounds monotonous and tedious. Nonverbally, upward inflectional patterns are believed to communicate enthusiasm, sincerity, and excitement, while downward patterns communicate boredom, sarcasm, and dejection. To communicate enthusiasm and sincerity and to add interest to your speech, use a variety of inflectional patterns. Be aware, of course, that an overuse of upward inflection is inappropriate to serious subjects.

*Quality.*    Your voice quality is determined by a number of things, some of which you cannot control. Two of these—timbre and resonance—are greatly influenced by the size and shape of your head and body. It is no accident that most famous opera singers have similar bodily features: wide cheekbones, large mouths, and ample lung capacity. These provide both timbre (the distinctive sound that characterizes one voice from another) and resonance (fullness and richness of sound) to their voices. However, that is not to say that without these bodily features you cannot make improvements in your vocal quality. Two well-known speech authorities, Jeffrey and Peterson, make the following suggestions for improving your vocal quality*:

1. The speaker should learn to hear his voice as others hear it. An almost universal reaction of persons upon hearing a recording of their voice for the first time is, "That's not me. There must be something wrong with the recorder." But, of course, there is nothing wrong with the recorder and the recording, as classmates or friends will verify, is a faithful reproduction of the individual's speech. The speaker's initial reaction reveals that most people do not hear themselves as others hear them. This is in part because some of the sound is carried from the voice box to his ears through the cheek and neck bones. But it is also in part because most

---

*Robert C. Jeffrey and Owen Peterson, *Speech: A Text with Adapted Readings* (New York: Harper & Row, Publishers, 1971), pp. 385–86.

people have become so accustomed to hearing their own voice that they really do not listen to themselves carefully or analytically.

Quite clearly, the first step in learning to hear one's voice as others hear it is for the speaker to record and listen to his speech frequently. The second step is to develop an awareness at all times of how it sounds.

2. To avoid strain, one should speak at a comfortable pitch level.
3. The speaker should maintain adequate breath support.
4. The speaker should remain relaxed while speaking.
5. If strain or hoarseness occurs regularly, the speaker should consult a speech correctionist.

**Articulation:** The physical process of forming the consonant and vowel sounds of words.

ARTICULATION. **Articulation** is the process of forming the consonant and vowel sounds of words. These sounds are molded into language by the five articulators: lips, teeth, tongue, hard palate, and soft palate. Improper articulation results in indistinct speech. If you articulate your words poorly, you will be difficult to understand.

Sometimes speakers are unaware that they have problems with articulation. We learn to speak by imitating the speech of those around us. Consequently, our speech habits resemble the speech habits of those we have imitated. If, for example, someone grew up in a household or neighborhood where the *d* sound was substituted for the *th* sound, that person would undoubtedly say *dis* for *this*, *doze* for *those*, and so on, and perhaps not even be aware of it.

The three most common errors in articulation are running words together, substituting one sound for another, and omitting necessary sounds. For example, *did you* becomes *di ja*, *student* becomes *stoont*, *asked* becomes *ast*, and so on. This kind of careless articulation is distracting to an audience. To deliver your speech effectively, you must make sure that your articulation is precise.

One of the best ways to become aware of any articulation problems you might have is to record your voice with a tape recorder. Tape yourself not only while practicing your speech, but also during ordinary conversation as well. Listen to your articulation carefully. What are your problems? Substituting sounds? Running words together? Omitting necessary sounds? Once you have determined your problems, you can begin working to correct them. Keep in mind, though, it took you a long time to form your bad habits, so it will take time and effort to eliminate them. But rest assured, it will be time and effort well spent.

**Pronunciation:** Articulating the accepted consonant and vowel sounds with the proper accent.

PRONUNCIATION. While articulation is the process of forming the consonant and vowel sounds of words, **pronunciation** is much more complex. It involves articulating the correct consonant and vowel sounds of a word and accenting that word in a proper manner. Or put in simpler terms, pronunciation means saying a word the way it should be said. Owing to the makeup of the English language, that is not always an easy task. Several characteristics of our language make the task even harder.

First, sometimes a letter in a word is silent and should not be articulated; for instance, the *w* in *sword* and the *t* in *often*. Remember, you cannot always tell how to pronounce a word just by looking at it. When you are not sure you are saying a word correctly, consult a standard dictionary.

Second, there are an inordinate number of ways to pronounce the same vowel in our language. People who study English as a second language are often frustrated by the fact that the same vowel is often pronounced differently in different words. For example, consider the six pronunciations of the letter *o* for the following words: *do, no, dot, oar, woman,* and *women*. Even some words that are spelled alike can require different pronunciations depending on the form they take. For instance, the word *read* as in "Read the same passage you read yesterday."

Third, correct pronunciation requires knowing how to accent words of more than one syllable. This is more difficult in some cases than in others. While the word *contact* is accented the same regardless of whether it is used as a noun, verb, adverb, or adjective, the similar word *contract* has the accent on the first syllable when used as a noun but on the second syllable when used as a verb. The word *rebel* is even more irregular. Not only does the accent change depending on whether the word is used as a noun or a verb, but the vowel sounds also change. Thus, the phonetic pronunciation is indicated as [reb'l] for the noun and [ri bel'] for the verb.

## EFFECTIVE WORD CHOICE

To deliver your speech effectively, you must use language that is clear, interesting, and appropriate. An audience cannot respond to a message that is unclear to them, will not pay attention to a message that is uninteresting to them, and will reject a message they believe is inappropriate. Below are suggestions for making your language more effective.

### CLARITY

Although clarity is important in all communication, it is indispensable to speech. A reader can reread a passage as many times as necessary to understand it. For the listener, it must be instantly understood or it is gone. If too much of what you say is missed or misinterpreted, your communication will fail. You can achieve clarity in speaking by (1) using an oral style, (2) choosing concrete rather than abstract words, and (3) using specific rather than general words.

ORAL STYLE.    Beginning speakers often phrase main ideas and subpoints in a stilted, unnatural way, usually because they have composed their ideas in a written rather than an oral style. Although similarities exist between the two styles, there are also significant differences. For this reason, whenever you write a central idea, scope statement, main point or subpoint, and so on, always read it aloud to make sure it sounds like you are talking in a conversational way. Following are some of the most common characteristics of an oral style:

1. An oral style is replete with contractions. Although in writing, *will not* and *it is* are often preferred to the contractions *won't* and *it's*, contractions are common to an oral style.

2. Oral sentences are usually shorter and less complex than written sentences. Your English teachers insisted that you use longer and more complex sentences in your writing to achieve variety. However, variety can be achieved nonverbally in speech, and overly long sentences cause problems for both speakers and listeners.

3. Oral sentences usually employ a subject–verb order. A common method for achieving variety in writing is to combine normal, periodic, parallel, and balanced sentences. In speaking, the normal sentence (subject–verb pattern) occurs far more frequently than any other type.

4. An oral style uses many familiar words. Always remember that when you are communicating your ideas, you must choose words that mean the same things to your listeners as they do to you. In most cases, the best language to use in speaking is the simplest and most familiar.

5. An oral style makes frequent use of personal pronouns. The use of *us, we, our, you,* and *I* is typical of what is called a *conversational speech style.* They give the speech an air of familiarity, as if the speaker is talking *with* the audience rather than *to* it.

CONCRETE WORDS. Concrete words refer to specific objects or particular instances, things that are relatively easy to visualize or define. They differ from abstract words, which refer to concepts, ideas, or emotions and often mean different things to different people. *Dog, book, rose, World War II,* and *Easter* are concrete words. *Democracy, communism, love,* and *hate* are abstract words. Obviously, a concrete word will always be clearer to your audience than an abstract one. Whenever possible, choose concrete rather than abstract words for your speech. When you must use abstract terms, define them as clearly and as completely as you can.

SPECIFIC WORDS. Another way to achieve clarity in your speaking is to choose specific rather than general words. General words refer to a group or class of things. Specific words refer to a particular part of that group. Specific words are always clearer. Imagine going to your favorite butcher shop and asking for two pounds of meat. How can the butcher fill your order without knowing what kind of meat you want? Two pounds of beef is better but still not specific enough. Do you want hamburger, ground chuck, rib roast, pot roast, or eye of round? Even if you say steak, you leave the butcher wondering which one of a dozen or more kinds of steak you mean. When wording your speech, do your audience and yourself a favor and be as specific as you can.

## VIVIDNESS

An effective way to make your speeches more interesting is to use words that appeal to any of the five senses: sight, hearing, taste, touch, and smell. For example, although it might be perfectly accurate to tell your listeners that a man came toward you, it would be much more visual and therefore more interesting to them if you told them that he staggered, lurched, inched, or crawled. In the same manner, the *eager buzz* of excited fans at a homecoming game and the spicy red chili that heats the mouth and

Descriptive language paints a clear word picture to support your ideas and makes them come alive for the audience. Imagine the vivid, sensory details you could use to describe the excitement of hang gliding.

causes perspiration to rise from the pores of the brow present vivid images to those listeners who can relate to them through one or more of their senses.

A second way of adding interest to your speeches is to use descriptive language to present a clear and definite word picture of what is taking place. Note the following two statements: (1) I sat next to a pretty blonde. (2) I sat next to a tall, slender, tanned blonde with a round and radiant face and dark, inviting eyes. Which statement is more likely to hold attention and establish a clear mental picture?

A third way to make your speeches interesting is to use an attention-getting technique called the *real*—talking in terms of actual people and places. This technique involves giving names to the characters you describe in your stories. For example, it is easier to imagine yourself sitting next to *Sheldon* or *Juanita* than next to your *friend*. One can more easily picture your being attacked by the neighbor's vicious boxer, Cruncher, than by the "dog next door."

Finally, you can make your speeches interesting by using the active rather than the passive voice. An added benefit is that besides being more vigorous, the active voice is usually less wordy. Note the following examples:

Passive: *First, the water was boiled by Jane, and then the eggs were added.* (13 words)
Active: *Jane boiled the water first and then added the eggs.* (10 words)
Passive: *The rapist was shot by the intended victim.* (8 words)
Active: *The intended victim shot the rapist.* (6 words)

## APPROPRIATENESS

When presenting your speech, you must always use language appropriate to your audience and the occasion. It would obviously be inappropriate to use sophisticated scientific terminology in explaining the problems faced in rocket liftoff to a group of laypeople. Not so obvious would be the use of electrical terms (even though simple) in a demonstration speech to a general audience on how to install a 220 outlet.

Unless you know your audience extremely well and the occasion warrants it, it is best to avoid off-color stories or profanity. Always keep in mind that you are speaking to a captive audience. Although you might capture the attention of some in your audience with the startling use of a four-letter word or ribald story, any advantage you gain will be negated if you make others uncomfortable or antagonized.

Finally, except in cases where you make it obvious that you are deviating for a special effect, always observe the rules of correct grammar. An audience will forgive or even miss an occasional slip, but if your speech contains too many errors it will affect your credibility. Like it or not, one variable by which an audience tends to judge the competence of speakers is by their correct or incorrect use of language.

## EXTEMPORANEOUS METHOD

By far the most effective method of delivering a speech is the extemporaneous method. You know what it is you are going to say, but you haven't written it out or memorized it word for word.

**Delivery outline:** A speaking outline that contains key words and phrases from your complete sentence outline, used to deliver an extemporaneous speech.

You have a number of options available when you choose to speak extemporaneously. The two most common of these are: (1) develop a **delivery outline** of key words and phrases from your complete sentence outline and deliver the speech from it, or (2) formulate note cards containing key words from your complete sentence outline and deliver the speech from them.

A third option depends on the confidence and memory of the speaker. If you can remember the important details of your speech and there is no chance that you might forget them, you can deliver your extemporaneous speech without notes or a speaking outline. Understandably, most speakers feel more comfortable having one of these along just in case. Because you cannot pick out more than four or five words at a time when glancing at your notes or speaking outline, when preparing either of them be careful not to write down too much. Effective notes and speaking outlines for extemporaneous speaking should consist of key words or phrases instead of complete sentences. The extemporaneous method offers the same directness and spontaneity as the impromptu method without the danger of rambling off the point or repeating yourself awkwardly. For most situations, it is by far the most effective method of delivery. It offers the following advantages:

1. Directness
2. Spontaneity
3. Ability to adapt to audience

4. Conversational style
5. Total eye contact
6. Relaxed bodily movement

Following is a sample delivery outline made from the full sentence outline on pages 67–70. At first glance, it may appear to have little meaning. Keep in mind, however, that it is meaningful to the speaker and provides signals as to the structure, the ideas, and the direction of the speech.

# SAMPLE DELIVERY OUTLINE

## INTRODUCTION

I. More than 5,000 A-A cowboys—Bill Pickett "bulldogging"—A-A involved since 1600
II. Black History lectures—last semester—reading—browsing Internet
III. A-A contributed significantly—disappointed I'd not heard before
IV. A-A men/women in forefront of progress—everyone should know
V. Tell about famous and less known contributors—growth—welfare—quality of life

## BODY

I. Throughout history—A-A men/women—contributed significantly—U.S. growth
  A. Developed country
    1. with Columbus
    2. Coronado NM—deSoto AL
    3. York—Lewis/Clark NW Passage
    4. J. B. Dusable—Chicago
  B. Furthered industrial expansion
    1. L. Latimer—light bulb/safety elevator
    2. G. T. Woods—3rd rail
    3. G. A. Morgen—gas mask
    4. S. J. Davidson—adding machine
II. Dedicated to U.S. welfare
  A. Defended our country
    1. Continental Army—5,000
    2. War of 1812
    3. WWI—1,400
    4. WWII—more than 1 million
  B. Religious/political leaders enrich values
    1. F. Douglass influenced eight presidents
    2. MLK Jr.—stirred our souls
    3. S. Chisolm—first A-A woman in Congress fought tirelessly for all women
    4. Jesse Jackson—voice of justice for all

    **C.** Significant in medicine
        **1.** Dr. Daniel Hale Williams—of the United States first open heart surgery
        **2.** George Washington Carver—more than 400 uses for peanuts and s. potatoes
        **3.** Dr. Benjamin Carsen—first neurosurgeon—Siamese twins joined at head
        **4.** Dr. Charles Drew—first blood bank
**III.** Quality of life
    **A.** Cultural arts impressive
        **1.** Marion Anderson—first at Metropolitan Opera—won National Medal of Art
        **2.** Alex Haley—Pulitzer—*Roots*
        **3.** Sydney Poitier—Academy Award—*Lilies of the Field*
        **4.** Maya Angelou—"Caged Bird"—National Book Award
    **B.** Excelled in sports
        **1.** J. Johnson—heavyweight champ in 1903
        **2.** J. Owens—first to win four gold medals in Olympics
        **3.** H. Aaron—world record 755 home runs
        **4.** J. Joiner-Kersee—six medals at 1988 Olympics
    **C.** Entertainers shown remarkable talent
        **1.** H. Belafonte—two Emmys
        **2.** C. Tyson—Best Actress of Year—Miss Jane Pitman
        **3.** B. Cosby—named entertainer of twentieth century
        **4.** D. Washington—Academy Award for the film *Glory*

## CONCLUSION

  **I.** Nation owes to A-As who developed—defended—added to quality of life
 **II.** A-As have excelled in medicine—fine arts—sports—entertainment—values
**III.** Many A-A musicians—actors—writers are world renowned
**IV.** Hope you found some new heroes who worked for the common good of all

## USING NOTE CARDS

Many effective extemporaneous speakers choose to deliver their speeches from note cards rather than from a delivery outline because they offer several advantages. Note cards are easier to handle than a sheet of paper and are less noticeable. They won't waver if your hand trembles slightly. Note cards are especially helpful if you must deliver your speech without a lectern because you can hold the cards in one hand and still be able to gesture freely. Here are a number of suggestions to follow when using note cards for an extemporaneous speech:

1. Use standard three-by-five-, four-by-six-, or five-by-eight-inch note cards. The number of cards you use will depend on the length and complexity of your speech. If you choose to make your own cards rather than buy them, use rigid paper or cardboard.

2. Always use note cards as unobtrusively as possible except when reading a direct quotation or complicated statistics. In these cases, hold your notes up so your audience can see you are taking special care to be accurate.

3. Make sure your notes are legible. Note cards are easy to read when they are typed or printed in capital letters and double or triple spaced.
4. Number multiple note cards. That way you will be able to put them in order quickly if you drop them or find they are disarranged.
5. Write on only one side of your note card. Even though your audience will expect you to use notes when delivering your speech, turning the cards over is distracting and time consuming.
6. Avoid writing your notes in too much detail. Note cards should serve only as a guide when delivering your speech. The extemporaneous method requires good eye contact and spontaneity. Overly detailed notes might tempt you to read your speech.
7. Avoid putting too much down on each card. Except for cards on which you have written full quotations or a set of statistics, limit to five the number of lines you put on a card. That way you'll be able to find your place in an instant. Remember, except for direct quotations and complicated statistics, the notes are there to jog your memory. Longer speeches will just require more cards.
8. Highlight ideas you want to stress. Circle or underline key words so you will remember to emphasize them while delivering your speech. It is often helpful to make notations on your note cards to *pause* or *slow down* at different times during your speech.

Figure 8.1 is a sample note card that could be used to substitute for a section of the delivery outline above. It begins with the transition from the introduction to the body of the speech. Note that although the wording is similar to the key word outline, the symbols of outlining, roman numerals, capital letters, and so on are left out.

When you deliver a speech in class, you are communicating in a friendly atmosphere. You are speaking to fellow students who can empathize with you because they are in the same situation. Under these circumstances, a speaker should feel relaxed and at ease—but many don't. Why? Many beginning speakers see the situation as threatening rather than friendly. They worry that their classmates will see their shortcomings and imperfections, real or imaginary. Worrying too much about what other people will think of you can cause nervousness.

This is not to say, however, that you should not be concerned with what your listeners will think of your speech. You have good reason to be nervous if you deliver a

---

Developed—with Columb—Coronado—NM—de Soto AL

York—L & Clark—NW Pass = J. Dusable Chicago

Industrial expan—Latimer—bulb/safe el—Woods 3rd

Morgan gas msk—Davidson add mach—U.S. welfare

---

**FIGURE 8.1 ■ Sample Note Card**

This sample note card could be used to substitute for a section of the delivery outline. It leaves out the roman numerals and other outlining symbols, but otherwise contains the same key words to prompt the speaker.

## Working WITH THE WEB

One way of improving your delivery is to listen to effective speakers and emulate them. You can listen to clips of some effective speakers such as Martin Luther King, Jr., John F. Kennedy, or Franklin Roosevelt via these web sites:

www.historychannel.com/speeches
www.library.www.edu/ref/howtoguides/speeches.htm

Notice some of the distinctive nonverbal qualities of these speakers, such as JFK's accent, Hitler's emphatic gestures, or the richness of FDR's voice.

If you are interested in continuing to work on giving speeches and presentations, you might consider joining Toastmasters International, an organization for professional speakers with members around the world. You can learn more about the organization if you visit its web site:

www.toastmasters.org

speech for which you have done little to prepare or practice. Although most listeners will expect you to make mistakes while delivering your speech, especially if you are a beginning speaker, few will react favorably to your presentation if they believe it has involved little effort on your part. It is not hard to understand why those who are poorly prepared suffer from nervousness.

## PRACTICING THE SPEECH

Regardless of whether you deliver your speech extemporaneously, from manuscript, or from memory, the key to doing so effectively is practice. Here are some suggestions for practicing your speeches:

1. Allow ample time for practice. Practice delivering your speech from two to five times. The idea is to practice enough to develop an easy and natural delivery but not to the extent that you unintentionally memorize an extemporaneous or manuscript speech.
2. Always practice with the same key word outline, note cards, or manuscript that you plan to use when delivering your speech. If you retype something, run it through a practice session to make sure you haven't typed in an error or left something out.
3. Always practice your speech as if you were delivering it to your intended audience. After you have practiced alone a few times, try to find a person or two to serve as your audience.
4. Go through the entire speech during each practice. If you hit a trouble spot or two during practice, don't stop and start over. Chances are that if you do, you might do this while delivering your speech. Like it or not, the actual delivery of the speech is more stressful than practice. Don't give yourself any unnecessary disabilities.

5. Do not try to deliver your speech the same way each time you practice it. Whether your speech is extemporaneous, manuscript, or memorized, an important characteristic is spontaneity. Delivering an extemporaneous speech the same way each time might cause you to unintentionally memorize the words. Delivering a manuscript or memorized speech the same way each time could inhibit your vocal variety.

6. Do not coordinate specific gestures with the exact wording of your speech. To be effective, gestures must be spontaneous. Although you should practice your speech with the kinds of emphatic and descriptive gestures you will be using in its delivery, don't pinpoint the exact moment to raise your index finger or dust off your shoulder during a speech. A planned or stilted gesture is worse than no gesture at all.

7. Practice your speech aloud with the same volume you plan to use in delivering it. Don't go over the speech in your head or say it so softly that no one can hear you.

8. However, some find it helpful to practice their speech mentally as well as aloud. If this method works for you, use it.

9. Practice your speech each time with whatever visual aids you plan to use. If you plan to mix some ingredients together during your speech, mix them during at least one practice session. This will help prevent slipups.

10. Time your speech in practice. No one appreciates a speech that goes on and on interminably. If you have been given a specific time limit for your speech, conform to it while practicing. As a safeguard, arrange for a friend in the audience to signal you when you have only one minute or so left.

11. Practice the way you will approach the speaker's stand at the beginning of the speech and leave it at the conclusion.

12. If you have access to a tape or video recorder, use it. Recorders are excellent aids. The best audience you can have is you, provided you have learned to listen to yourself critically and objectively.

13. If possible, try to practice at least once in the room where you will be delivering your speech or a similar room. Anything you can do in practice to approximate the real thing is worth the effort.

## ✔ *Checklist* FOR SUCCESS

Delivery Distractions: Tips on behaviors to avoid when delivering your speech:

- Slouching
- Rigid posture
- Rattling keys or coins in pocket
- Fiddling with jewelry
- Fingering hair
- Pulling on ears
- Clenching lectern
- Drumming fingers on lectern
- Adjusting glasses
- Twisting rings

# DELIVERY PITFALLS

Here are some common pitfalls to delivery that you should avoid:

1. *Mispronunciation*—Make sure that you pronounce words correctly.
2. *Not being heard*—When you are competing with external noise or some other distraction, stop speaking until the audience can easily hear you.
3. *Equipment not working*—Check your equipment. Avoid the embarassment of equipment not working or your not being able to operate it.
4. *Nonfluency*—Nonfluencies must not occur too frequently. Filling in pauses with *ahs*, *uhs*, and *mms* sends a negative message. Avoid other nonfluencies such as the frequent use of "you know" or "right?"
5. *Conflicting messages*—A significant delivery pitfall occurs when your verbal message says one thing and your nonverbal says another; for example, saying to an audience "I'm really happy to be here!" when your posture, gestures, and facial expression are telling them that you're not. Remember, nonverbals communicate a lot to the audience, and in most cases the audience will believe nonverbals over verbals.
6. *Ineffective gesturing*—If the gestures you use do not reinforce your message, they interfere with it. Don't plan gestures. They should be spontaneous.
7. *Using visual aids incorrectly*—Check the proper use of visual aids in Chapter 6.
8. *Uninteresting voice*—Enthusiasm and variety are important in maintaining your audience's attention.
9. *Inappropriate dress*—Gaudy, provocative, or untidy clothing can ruin your presentation.
10. *Poor eye contact*—Eye contact indicates honesty, sincerity, and interest to an audience. Avoid overdependence on your notes.
11. *Inappropriate humor*—If you are not positive the humor is appropriate, don't use it! Offensive or inappropriate humor can ruin your presentation.
12. *Ineffective transitions*—Without effective transitions in your speech, it will be hard for your audience to follow the movement from one idea to another.
13. *Weak introduction*—An effective introduction is imperative for gaining the audience's attention and letting them know what they're going to hear and why they should listen.
14. *Weak conclusion*—The conclusion is the last thing your audience hears. Some believe it is the most important part of the speech. An ineffective conclusion can spoil an otherwise good effort.

## Chapter Review

After reading this chapter, you should be able to

- Identify the four methods of speech delivery, and explain the advantages and disadvantages of each.
- Explain in what situations each type of delivery method might be used.
- Describe the preparation process for delivering the most effective speech.

- Explain the significance of nonverbal communication in conveying a message effectively.
- Identify different types of nonverbal communication.
- Describe vocal elements that could be a factor in how well your message is communicated.
- List and explain guidelines for practicing your speech.

## Key Terms

Impromptu speech (p. 124)
Manuscript speech (p. 125)
Memorized speech (p. 126)
Extemporaneous speech (p. 126)
Nonverbal communication (p. 128)
Kinesics (p. 129)

Descriptive gestures (p. 130)
Emphatic gestures (p. 130)
Paralanguage (p. 132)
Articulation (p. 134)
Pronunciation (p. 134)
Delivery outline (p. 138)

## Exercises

1. Pay close attention to the next conversations you have with friends, family, teachers, coworkers, and so forth. Take note of vocal elements in their communication: Do they use fillers? Do they pause frequently? Do they articulate clearly and pronounce words correctly? What other qualities do you notice, such as how loudly or softly they speak or an unusual accent? Do these vocal factors affect how well they communicate, and/or how well you receive their messages? Had you noticed these factors before? Share your observations in class.

2. In your next class, listen to the speakers. Make a list of what is being communicated nonverbally through movements, gestures, facial expression, personal appearance, and vocal qualities. Do the speakers communicate confidence nonverbally? Do they appear nervous? What do you observe that leads you to these conclusions? Do the speakers make eye contact with the audience? Do they appear to be engaging with the audience? Do the nonverbal factors affect the overall communication?

3. Make two lists—one with concrete words such as objects or events and the other with abstract words such as ideas or emotions. Choose several of the words and try writing down as many different meanings as you can. For example, *dog* might include different breeds, as well as characteristics such as aggressive, docile, or barker. Is it easier to come up with meanings for the concrete words? Are the abstract words harder to define? Is it easier to picture something specific based on the concrete words? How might these observations influence the language choices for your next speech?

4. Select several pieces of poetry from a poetry anthology and try reading each aloud, varying your pitch, volume, rate, and inflection. Notice how you might read each differently, depending on the mood of the poem. Try stressing different aspects of each piece: Does that change the meaning of the poem? If possible, try tape-recording your reading so you can hear how you sound.

## Speech Assignments

1. *The Impromptu Speech*
   Deliver a one-to-two-minute impromptu speech as your instructor directs. You will either be assigned a subject or be allowed to choose one of two drawn from a hat.

   *Delivery.* Keep your speech short and to the point. Make sure your purpose and central idea are clear to your audience.

   ### Sample Topics
   1. The perfect age
   2. My favorite teacher
   3. The ideal husband (wife)
   4. What I like (hate) about my job
   5. Why _____ should be legalized
   6. How to bounce a meatball

2. *Relate a Personal Experience to Entertain*
   Deliver a two-to-four-minute speech in which you relate a personal experience to entertain. The story you tell can be humorous, suspenseful, exciting, or memorable. It may be true, partly true, or fictitious.

   *Delivery.* This speech must be delivered extemporaneously. Your audience will expect you to have total eye contact when telling a story about something that happened to you. The more spontaneous and relaxed you are, the more your audience will enjoy your presentation.

   *Model.* I was having a drink with a few friends the other night, when a little guy came in and sat across from us. He was about five foot six and slender. He ordered a beer, and while he was drinking it a bunch of bikers pulled up outside and came in. A couple of them started spinning the little guy around on his bar stool and tipped over his drink. "Cut that out," he yelled. "What's wrong with you guys?" "If you don't like it, do something about it," one of them said. Well, the little guy went to the door and walked out without a word. "Not much of a man, is he?" one of them asked the bartender. "Not much of a driver either," said the bartender. "He just ran over your motorcycles."

   The speech evaluation form shown in Figure 8.2 is designed for both student and instructor evaluation. It lists those characteristics of content and delivery that should be considered when evaluating a speaker.

| | Poor -- | 1 | 2 | 3 | 4 | --Excellent | Comments |
|---|---|---|---|---|---|---|---|
| A. | Delivery | | | | | | |
| | 1. Appearance | | | | | | |
| | 2. Bodily movement | | | | | | |
| | 3. Directness | | | | | | |
| | 4. Gesture | | | | | | |
| B. | Voice | | | | | | |
| | 1. Rate/pause | | | | | | |
| | 2. Volume/tone | | | | | | |
| | 3. Pitch/inflection | | | | | | |
| | 4. Articulation/ pronunciation | | | | | | |
| C. | Content | | | | | | |
| | 1. Subject | | | | | | |
| | 2. Preparation | | | | | | |
| | 3. Supports | | | | | | |
| | 4. Language | | | | | | |
| D. | Organization | | | | | | |
| | 1. Introduction | | | | | | |
| | 2. Transitions | | | | | | |
| | 3. Body | | | | | | |
| | 4. Conclusion | | | | | | |

**FIGURE 8.2 ■ Speech Evaluation Form**
This form can be used by students and instructors to evaluate a speaker's content and delivery.

# *Informing*

WE LIVE in an increasingly complex age—one of new technology, endless research, and specialization. Each year, more and more new information is added to the total of human knowledge in our world. It was estimated that by the year 2000 there would be 1,000 times more knowledge in the world than there was in 1900. It is obvious, then, how important it is for us to be able to send and receive informative communication accurately and effectively.

All too often we take **informative communication** for granted. We listen to weather forecasts, news stories, stock market updates, and traffic reports with only half an ear and then wonder why we didn't get things straight. We give vague instructions as to where and when we're going to meet someone or exactly how we'd like our hair done and then become irritated when

**Informative communication:** Communication that adds to a listener's knowledge and understanding of a subject.

things go wrong. The purpose of informative communication is to add to a listener's understanding. To achieve this goal, a speaker must communicate information clearly and interestingly.

There are many different ways to categorize informative speeches. This chapter deals with three of the most popular categories: demonstration speeches, description speeches, and exposition speeches.

## DEMONSTRATION SPEECHES

**Demonstration speech:** A speech to show an audience how to do something.

The informative **demonstration speech** is designed to show your audience how to do something so they will be able to do it on their own or have a better understanding of how it is done. Thus, you might deliver a demonstration speech to teach your audience how to make Swedish pancakes or to show them how various mathematical problems can be solved with a slide rule. As with most speeches, the key to delivering a demonstration speech successfully is effective audience analysis. You must ask the question, "What response can I reasonably expect from my listeners?" You could teach an audience to make Swedish pancakes in a reasonable amount of time; however, unless those in your audience are familiar with a slide rule, it seems unlikely that you could do much more than give them an understanding of how a slide rule can be used.

To show someone how to perform a card trick, prepare a salad, carve a turkey, or read palms, you will want to use the technique of demonstration. Demonstration speeches can either involve participation from the audience or can be nonparticipative. In demonstrating the card trick, for example, you might ask one or two members of the audience to try the trick to show how easily it can be learned. When demonstrating palm reading, you might have members of your audience read the lines and marks on their own palms to identify their life lines, their character, and so on. When members of your audience are observers rather than participants in your demonstration, you must be careful to present your material clearly and interestingly enough so you achieve your purpose: audience understanding.

Following are examples of demonstration speeches:

| *Demonstrations to Teach* | *Demonstrations for Understanding* |
|---|---|
| How to: | How: |
| wrap a gift | a parachute is packed |
| recognize cuts of beef | a head is shrunk |
| apply a tourniquet | belly dancing is done |
| remove a stain | a lute is played |
| cover a book | a person is hypnotized |
| give a facial | fires get started |
| take good snapshots | an abacus is used |
| toss a salad | ballet is danced |

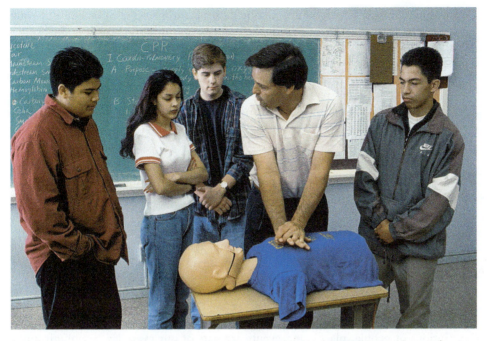

An informative demonstration speech shows your audience how to do something, such as performing CPR, as this photo illustrates. This type of speech may or may not involve audience participation.

Listed next are eight suggestions for making your demonstration speeches clear and interesting:

1. Practice your speech exactly as you plan to deliver it. If you are showing how to make a tossed salad, mix the ingredients in practice just as you would in front of an audience. This will enable you to time your speech accurately. (It might take you longer to prepare and toss the ingredients than you thought it would.)

2. Determine whether the audience will see the usefulness of your demonstration. If it is not obvious to your audience that they have something to gain from paying attention to your demonstration, tell why your information will be useful to them during your introduction.

3. Break your speech down into units or steps so it can be more easily followed by your audience.

4. Preview the steps you are going to follow in your introduction and summarize them in your conclusion. If your demonstration is long or complicated, consider a review of what has been said during the body of your speech.

5. Provide continuity to your discussion by talking throughout. Don't be like one young student who began her speech by saying, "Today I'm going to show you how to make Swedish meatballs," and then proceeded to make them without saying another word for the next three minutes. Her meatballs were excellent; her speech was not.

6. Make sure that what you are showing the audience can easily be seen by all. Keep in mind that you must reach the entire audience, not just those in front. If you are

not sure your demonstration can easily be seen, estimate the distance from your farthest listener and have a friend take a similar position to check visibility.

7. Maintain your cool. If you make a mistake, acknowledge it and go on. Your audience will appreciate the fact that you admitted your error.

8. Conform to a predetermined time limit for your speech. Before your speech, you decide what you want to show your audience and how much time you want to spend doing it. Don't change that during your delivery.

## DESCRIPTION SPEECHES

**Description speech:** A speech that makes use of sensory appeals to give the listener a clear picture of what is being described.

A second method of communicating information, description, makes use of sensory appeals to give the listener a clear picture of what is being communicated. In a **description speech**, you describe an object, person, place, event, or experience. You might give your listeners information about an object's appearance, what it sounds like, what it tastes like, what it feels like, or what it smells like. You might describe a major event that you witnessed and what it felt like to be there.

### TYPES OF DESCRIPTION SPEECHES

Descriptions of people, places, and events are part of our everyday communication. We insist on an in-depth description of our roommate's cousin before agreeing to a blind date. We talk to a number of people who have vacationed at that new island paradise before we agree to go. We listen to a description of the events that took place at last year's homecoming game before buying our tickets for this year's game. Five types of descriptive speeches are described next.

INTRODUCING YOURSELF.    Perhaps one of the first speeches you will be asked to deliver is one in which you introduce yourself to the rest of the class. Because you should be an authority on yourself, the content of this speech should pose no problem for you. Include those things that you believe will be of interest to the class.

INTRODUCING A CLASSMATE.    Another type of introductory speech involves describing a classmate to your audience. Describe his or her accomplishments, talents, hobbies, goals, likes and dislikes, or anything you think will be of interest to the class.

DESCRIBING A PLACE.    A vivid description of your hometown or favorite place can make an effective speech. This can be a particularly effective presentation when the speaker is describing a location with which most of the audience is unfamiliar.

DESCRIBING AN EVENT.    The description of an event can be an effective informatory speech. An eyewitness account of the Olympic Games, a rocket launching, a bank robbery, or other such topics could be developed into exciting, attention-holding presentations.

DESCRIBING HISTORICAL EVENTS.    The historical events speech involves describing an episode or sequence of events in history. A vivid description of the scene, characters, and setting of the battle of the Alamo would effectively hold an audience's attention. Following are samples of historical events speeches:

| | |
|---|---|
| The Battle of Bunker Hill | Custer's Last Stand |
| Watergate | September 11 |
| D-Day | The Valentine's Day Massacre |

Although description is a technique that can be used in any of the other kinds of speeches, sometimes it is necessary to develop an entire speech of description. If you want your listeners to have a greater appreciation for a classmate, for example, you might describe their accomplishments, talents, goals, hobbies, and likes and dislikes. Listed next are samples of speeches of description:

1. Summerfest in Milwaukee
2. Super Bowl 2006: The Perfect Matchup
3. Joyce Jackson: The Ideal Classmate
4. Copenhagen: The Perfect Vacation Spot
5. Abraham Lincoln: Our Greatest President
6. The Duckbill Platypus
7. Life in a Dormitory
8. Las Vegas: City of Dreams

# EXPOSITORY SPEECHES

The primary purpose of exposition is to inform. It is communication that explains a concept, process, idea, or belief. It can include explanation, analysis, explication, evaluation, comparison and contrast, and example.

## TYPES OF EXPOSITORY SPEECHES

**Expository speeches** are those that explain a process, concept, idea, or belief. They include speeches to explain a process, to instruct, and to review.

> **Expository speech:** A speech that explains a concept, process, idea, or belief, the primary purpose of which is to inform.

**SPEECHES TO EXPLAIN A PROCESS.**    Speeches to explain a process inform an audience how something works. Although they are often organized similarly to demonstration speeches, they differ in purpose. A student studying photography might deliver a demonstration speech on how to take an effective snapshot. If he or she is asked to deliver an explain-a-process speech, an appropriate choice would be to demonstrate how a camera works. Following are examples of explain-a-process speeches:

How:

| | |
|---|---|
| a generator works | a microlaser operates |
| food is digested | a steam engine works |
| photosynthesis occurs | Project Elf functions |
| the eye functions | kidneys clean your blood |

SPEECHES TO INSTRUCT.    Instructive speeches are presentations in which the speaker gives facts and information about concepts or ideas. The topic of a typical instructive speech would be what makes the sky blue? These speeches can be thought of as informal class lectures. To deliver an instructive speech effectively, you should choose a subject that will be either useful or interesting to your listeners. Following are samples of instructive speeches:

| | |
|---|---|
| Ideas of Thoreau | Solar energy |
| The chromatic scale | What controls the tide? |
| Nuclear submarines | Supply-side economics |

SPEECHES TO REVIEW.    Reviews of current novels, television shows, short stories, or plays can provide effective material for an informative speech. Choose one that you believe you are qualified to analyze and that will be interesting to your listeners.

Speeches of exposition may include elements of demonstration, definition, or description speeches. For example, in speaking of solar energy, you will need to define exactly what it is and describe how it works. However, expository speeches rely largely on explanation, analysis, explication, evaluation, comparison and contrast, and example.

## EXPLANATION

**Explanation:** The process of explaining something to make it clear and understandable.

A significant form of exposition is the **explanation**. The primary purpose of explanation is to make things clear or understandable. As a student, you are constantly involved with explanations. The school bulletin explains what courses your school offers and which ones you have to take to satisfy the requirements for your degree. Your instructors and advisors are primarily explainers. The syllabi you get at the beginning of the semester are explanations of what you will be studying in each course and what you are expected to accomplish.

The first rule to follow when you are going to use explanation is that you must thoroughly understand something before you can explain it to someone else. A second rule is always to use words in your explanation that will be clear to your audience. To use technical terms to explain a process or concept with which your audience is unfamiliar will be self-defeating. Note how the writer uses references common to the experience of his audience to explain what narration is:

Can you imagine one of your ancestors attempting to relate a personal experience to a friend? Perhaps he was stung by a bee as he walked through the forest seeking food or shelter. Later, when the pain subsided, he re-created this experience for his companion by imitating the buzzing of the bee, gesturing to depict its flight, and uttering a sound that articulated the pain he suffered when he was stung. A baby's early attempts to communicate follow a similar pattern. The baby frequently imitates the sound associated with a particular animal or object, and this sound becomes a word in his limited vocabulary. The cat is a *meow*, the dog a *bow-wow*, and the train a *choo-choo*.

An expository speech, such as a speech to instruct, provides the audience with important facts and information. In this photo, the speaker provides detailed explanation of weather patterns, supported by effective visual aids.

An exclamation of joy—*Ah!*—or pain—*Ow!*—accompanied by an occasional gesture help it to tell its story. Narration or storytelling is our oldest form of communicating experiences.*

## ANALYSIS

**Analysis** involves breaking down a situation or concept into its parts in order to examine each part separately. It often asks such questions as who? what? why? when? where? and how? It is used frequently in speeches to inform. When organizing a speech titled "How Our Government Operates," you might divide your speech into three parts: (1) the legislative, (2) the executive, and (3) the judicial, and examine each branch separately.

**Analysis:** The process of breaking down a situation or concept in order to examine each part separately, to determine who, what, why, when, where, and how.

---

*Used with permission from Arthur Koch and Stanley B. Felber, *What Did You Say?* 3rd ed. (Englewood Cliffs, NJ: Prentice Hall,1985).

The following excerpt from a TV speech delivered by President John F. Kennedy on October 22, 1962, uses analysis to show how our country was threatened by the Cuban missile sites:

> This government as promised has maintained the closest surveillance of the Soviet military build-up on the island of Cuba. Within the past week unmistakable evidence has established the fact that a series of offensive missile sites is now in preparation on that imprisoned island. The purpose of these bases can be none other than to provide a nuclear strike capability against the Western Hemisphere.
>
> The characteristics of these new missile sites indicate two distinct types of installations. Several of them include medium-range ballistic missiles capable of carrying a nuclear warhead for a distance of more than 1,000 nautical miles. Each of these missiles, in short, is capable of striking Washington, D.C., the Panama Canal, Cape Canaveral, Mexico City, or any other city in the southeastern part of the United States, in Central America, or in the Caribbean area.
>
> Additional sites not yet completed appear to be designed for intermediate-range missiles capable of traveling more than twice as far, and thus capable of striking most of the major cities in the Western Hemisphere. This urgent transformation of Cuba into an important strategic base by the presence of these large long-range and clearly offensive weapons of sudden mass destruction constitutes an explicit threat to the peace and security of all the Americas.*

## EXPLICATION

**Explication:** A form of analysis that clarifies what is not clear or only implied.

**Explication** is a form of analysis that makes clear what is obscure or implied. In the following statement, the writer Rev. Paul P. Kuenning, points out that happiness is depicted by some as owning an expensive car or home, winning the lottery, or making a lot of money. This is not true. The following excerpt uses explication to show that happiness cannot be defined in materialistic terms:

> We often attempt to motivate young people to take their education seriously, to attend classes regularly and to study harder, by assuring them that doing these things will eventually enable them to make more money and obtain a higher standard of living. What is promised may or may not be true. But what is implied is that these things will also make for greater happiness in their lives, and that is not necessarily true at all. Unless learning itself becomes a joy, unless the knowledge and the skills acquired are directed in some way to serve their fellow human beings, unless our children learn not only to be mercenary, but merciful, not only to make money but to make peace, not only hunger for riches but for righteousness, then the fire which drives them toward materialistic reward, may turn to ashes once it has been acquired.†

---

*Quoted in George Breitman, ed., *Malcolm X Speaks*, p. 50; copyright © 1965 by Merit Publishers and Betty Shabazz. Reprinted by permission of Pathfinder Press.

†From Paul P. Kuenning, *A Worldly Christianity* (Lima, Ohio: Fairway Press, 1995), pp. 48–49.

## EVALUATION

**Evaluation** is another form of analysis. Perhaps, as a student, you have already been asked to give an end-of-the-course evaluation, or in the future you will have to evaluate a teacher, the school, or yourself. When you use this technique, keep in mind that in order to be informative, evaluations must be objective. That is not always easy.

**Evaluation:** Another form of analysis that reviews and assesses material or performance.

Reviews are a form of evaluation. Many of us listen to reviews on the radio or TV to decide which movies or programs we will watch or at which restaurants we will dine. The following is a student newspaper review of four special editions of Earth, Wind & Fire albums:

> The best reissue campaign of the summer belongs to **Sony Legacy's** work with the **Earth, Wind & Fire** catalog. A great rhythm section, a killer horn section, augmented by serious songwriting and producing, they dominated record, radio, and concert sales and crossed over to all audiences. They've released four special editions of their classic albums.
>
> **That's the Way of the World** brought the band to the forefront with the title track "Shining Star," as well as the romantic classic "Reasons." This reissue includes five demo bonus tracks, including the first vocal take of "All about Love."
>
> **Gratitude**, a two-LP set, caught the band still growing, evolving, and finding each other musically. The live stuff gives listeners a taste of the energy the band displayed at every concert.
>
> **Gratitude** proved **EW&F** is not a one-hit wonder and demonstrates both studio and concert growth. The lone bonus track is a live medley of their hits "Serpentine Fire," "Saturday Nite," "Can't Hide Love," and "Reasons."
>
> Both the **All 'n' All** (with the hits "Fantasy" and "I'll Write a Song") and **The Best of Earth, Wind & Fire, Volume I** CDs feature three and two bonus tracks, respectively, and round out the campaign. All are digitally remastered to CD and are the best reissues any label has done so far in 1999.*

## COMPARISON AND CONTRAST

As you have seen above, comparison and contrast is the act of examining two or more things in order to determine differences or similarities. A fundamental principle of education is that the only way you can teach anything to students is to relate it to what they already know. Comparing the ideas that you are presenting to concepts that your listeners can relate to from their own experiences will improve your chances of success. In the following excerpt the author gives his reader a clearer understanding of the writing process by comparing it to building a wall:

> In northern New England, where I live, stone walls mark boundaries, border meadows, and march through the woods that grew up around them long ago. Flank-high, the walls are made of granite rocks stripped from fields when pastures were cleared and

---

*Duane Rodriguez, *The MATC Times*, Milwaukee Area Technical College.

used to fence in cattle. These are dry walls made without mortar, and the stones in them, all shapes and sizes, are fitted to one another with such care that a wall, built a hundred years ago, still runs as straight and solid as it did when people cleared the land.

Writing is much like wall-building. The writer fits together separate chunks of meaning to make an understandable statement. Like the Old Yankee wall-builders, anyone who wants to write well must learn some basic skills, one at a time, to build soundly.*

## EXAMPLE

The use of detailed or undetailed examples can be a clear and interesting way to present information. Biographies and autobiographies are written to give us information about a person's life. When your grandparents tell you what life was like when they were your age, they are using examples to inform. A series of examples can be an excellent way of introducing a speech. The amount of detail to include in your examples depends on your listeners. If you believe that your listeners are unfamiliar with your example, you must develop it in detail. If the example you are using is familiar to your listener, you need only cite it briefly. Examples that are both interesting and relevant are bound to ensure both attention and understanding.

For example, in an 1866 speech to a group of English workingmen, Thomas Huxley, a renowned biologist, explained the process of induction in terms that were familiar to those in his audience. Here is an updated paraphrase of the speech Huxley delivered more than 130 years ago:

Suppose you go into a fruit shop wanting an apple—you take one up and upon biting it you find that it is sour. You look at it and see that it is hard and green. You take another one and that too is hard, green, and sour. The shopkeeper offers you a third, but before biting it you examine it and find that it is hard and green, and you immediately say that you don't want it since it must be sour like those you have already tried.

Nothing can be more simple than that, you think; but if you will take the trouble to analyze and trace out into its logical elements what has been done by the mind, you will be greatly surprised. In the first place, you will have performed the process of induction. You found that in two experiences, hardness and greenness in apples went together with sourness. You found a general law, that all hard and green apples are sour; and that, as far as it goes, is a perfect induction.

## GUIDELINES FOR INFORMATIVE SPEAKING

To communicate effectively, you must have the attention of your audience. In fact, without attention, communication does not exist. Listeners will not pay attention for long to a speech that is neither clear nor interesting. The following are specific suggestions.

---

*Roger Garrison, *How a Writer Works* (New York: Harper & Row, 1981), p. 4.

## (WWW) *Working* WITH THE WEB

For examples of speeches to inform, go to

Homepage.powerup.com.au/~mamalade/TMspeeches.htm

As discussed earlier in the book, you will want to access the Internet Public Library's subject collection of ideas and material for informative speech topics. You can visit

www.ipl.org/div/subject

Also, as previously recommended, an excellent source of reference works to give you ideas for informative speeches can be found at

www.bartleby.com

## MAKE YOUR MATERIAL CLEAR

The purpose of informative speaking is to add to a listener's understanding. To do this, a speaker must communicate clearly. You can help make your material clear by using words that are familiar and specific and by using descriptive gestures.

USE FAMILIAR WORDS.   Be assured, unless your listener understands the message, communication will not take place. Sometimes speakers are so concerned with impressing their audience with their vocabularies that they actually fail to communicate. This can be a serious mistake. Unlike the reader who can reread an unclear passage or look up unfamiliar words, the listener misses part of the message unless the words the speaker uses are understood instantly. Therefore, when you choose your words as a speaker, always choose those that are the most familiar. For example, why say fecund instead of fertile, efficacious rather than effective, and so on? If you want everyone in your audience to understand you, use terms that are familiar to them.

In situations, however, where you must use words that are unfamiliar to your audience, be sure to define the words before using them. This is especially important when using technical terms that you will be repeating in your speech. Don't avoid using an unfamiliar technical term—just explain the term the moment you use it.

USE SPECIFIC WORDS.   An effective way of making your ideas clear to others is to use specific language. To say that a person entered the room gives your listener little information. To say that they strutted, ambled, staggered, crept, or marched says it more clearly. The word *tree* is general. *Fruit tree* is more specific. But *Bartlett pear*, *Courtland apple*, and *Bing cherry* are much more specific and therefore much clearer.

Sometimes a difficult concept can be made clear by explaining it in specific terms. Many people, for example, are unaware of the danger involved in improper disposal of nuclear waste. The student who began her speech, "Even though the dosages would be microscopic so you couldn't even see them, if two pounds of plutonium could be evenly distributed among the world's population, each person on earth would receive a lethal dosage," used the specific to give her audience a better understanding as to the magnitude of the problem.

USE DESCRIPTIVE GESTURES.    Descriptive gestures aid by giving your audience a clearer picture of something. You might gesture to show your audience a proper golf swing or to give them an idea of the size of the tomatoes you grew. Or you might give your audience a clear picture of how effective karate can be for self-defense by demonstrating different karate techniques with a volunteer. Descriptive gestures not only make your ideas clearer, but they also aid in maintaining audience interest.

## MAKE YOUR DELIVERY INTERESTING

You must have the attention of your listeners if you want to communicate anything to them. Emphasis and variety will help hold their attention by making your material as interesting as possible.

EMPHASIS.    We emphasize our ideas in speech nonverbally and verbally. An upward inflection and an increase in volume often indicate great enthusiasm. You can tell when people are concerned by the intensity with which they say things. Tone of voice can emphasize, as can pause. Used before an important idea, pause says to an audience, "Pay close attention to what is coming next." A pause after an idea sets the idea apart and gives each listener a chance to reflect on what was said.

Besides being descriptive, gestures also emphasize. A positive movement of the hands or arms or a nod of the head may emphasize an idea or a point you are making. Leaning or moving toward your audience suggests interest or emphasis. Remember, gestures must be seen to be effective. A good rule of thumb is "the larger the audience, the broader the gesture."

Another way to emphasize your ideas is to preview and summarize them. List the points you are going to make or steps you are going to follow in your introduction and summarize them in your conclusion.

VARIETY.    Most of us prefer to listen to a speaker with a pleasant, conversational style, one who seems to talk with you rather than to you. The key to the conversational style is speaking in a natural manner. In everyday conversation, people speak with various vocal patterns to indicate the meanings they want to convey. Their voices rise and fall as they inflect from one pitch to another, their volume increases or decreases depending on their subject and how they feel about it, and their rate varies anywhere from 90 words a minute to more than 180.

However, put many of these same people in a public speaking situation and they become overly aware that some are forming opinions about what they say and the way they are saying it. They become conscious of how they look and sound and what they are saying. The result is that they lose their naturalness and spontaneity. They convey words rather than meaning in a flat, colorless way.

The next time you are engaged in enthusiastic conversation with your friends, make note of their speech patterns, gestures, and facial expressions. If you can transfer

U.S. Senator John McCain is a polished speaker. His careful preparation allows him to use a conversational style and maintain eye contact with his audience. He also uses decisive gestures to give emphasis to his ideas.

your animation and physical expression in informal conversation to public speaking, you will be more interesting and enjoyable to listen to and watch.

# SAMPLE SPEECH TO INFORM

Here is a sample speech to inform on the impact of mental illness on a victim and her family.

### Mental Illness Can Be Devastating

**INTRODUCTION**     After working for nine months as a clerk in a shoe store, my sister, Ellen, told her boss that she had a mental illness. The new medication she was taking was causing nausea, and although her doctor assured her that this would soon pass, she felt she should explain why she was losing time from work. She thought she had a good relationship with her boss, who seemed sympathetic when she told him, but four days later, at the end of the week, she was laid off. In the three years since that incident, Ellen has worked successfully as a waitress and a secretary, but she no longer speaks of her illness to anyone except her family and closest friends. (attention step)

During the last four years, because of my sister, Ellen, I've learned a lot about mental illness. (indicates qualifications) I've learned how scary it is for both the victims and their loved ones. When Ellen was diagnosed with schizophrenia, neither she nor our family knew how to deal with it. It took time but we learned; we learned a lot—and we found out that mental illness can be devastating, but for many recovery is possible. (central idea)

Because mental illness can happen to anyone in this audience at any time and at any age, I'd like to share some of what I've learned with you. (gives reason for listening)

I've divided my speech into five main points that I believe will answer the following questions that most people ask about mental illness: (1) Who gets mental illness? (2) What do people know about it? (3) Why is there stigma attached to it? (4) Are there organizations that can help? (5) Is adequate research and treatment available? (preview main ideas to be covered)

**BODY**   The first question is: Who gets mental illness? Mental illness can happen to anyone at any age; no one is immune. One out of four families in this country is affected by it. Any one of you in this audience could be affected. My sister was diagnosed with schizophrenia when she was nineteen. Her psychiatrist has mentally ill patients who are as young as five. Mike Wallace, the newscaster, was stricken with a mental illness in his sixties. Mental illnesses are more common than cancer, diabetes, and heart disease. In any given year five million American adults suffer from an acute episode of one of five serious brain disorders: schizophrenia, bipolar disorder, major depression, obsessive–compulsive disorder, and panic disorder. More than three million of America's children suffer from these disorders. People with mental illness utilize more hospital beds than cancer, heart disease, and lung ailments combined.

Question two: What do people know about it? As I told you before, Ellen and the rest of us didn't know what to do because we knew nothing about mental illness. We talked to some mental health professionals, navigated through the Web, picked up some books and brochures on mental illness, and started to learn as much as we could. It soon became apparent to us that when our friends and relatives found out about Ellen they lacked knowledge and understanding about mental illness, too. However, that didn't stop them from giving advice. Some of them thought that Ellen's schizophrenia was a problem caused by bad parenting. Others thought that she might have gotten into mind-altering drugs. A few suggested that we try tough love to straighten her out. None of them understood that mental illness is a medical condition like diabetes or heart disease requiring treatment, love, and support. The fact is: Most people have little understanding or knowledge of mental illness.

Question three is: Why is a stigma attached to mental illness? Ignorance and misinformation are the main sources of the stigma about mental illness. Unfortunately, people incorrectly use terms such as psycho and mental to label those with biological brain disorders. Yet the treated mentally ill are no different than the rest of the population. According to the National Institute of Mental Health, eight out of ten mentally ill people can function productively if they receive proper treatment. How many of you in the audience know some people who are mentally ill and can function productively because of the medications they are taking? I'll bet that all of you do but are not aware of it.

For example, you might be surprised to find out that Dick Clark, Bette Midler, Kirk Douglas, Marlon Brando, Patty Duke, Dick Cavett, and Sting are a few of the celebrities who suffer from mental illness. While some of you didn't know that, I'll bet that many of you do know that John Wayne and Steve McQueen had cancer. Cancer is a horrible disease, but you don't have to be ashamed that you have it. People who have a mental illness often don't admit it because of the stigma attached to it. Kirk Douglas explains it this way: "Why is it that most of us can talk openly about the illnesses of our bodies, but when it comes to our brain and illnesses of the mind, we clam up? And because we clam up, people with emotional disorders feel ashamed and stigmatized, and don't seek the help that can make the difference." The answer to question three is: There is a great deal of stigma attached to mental illness. In the area of stigma, there is much work to be done.

Question four: Are there organizations that can help? There are organizations in every state that you can go to for help. The first months were very stressful for Ellen and the rest of the family, but things got better when we joined the National Alliance for the Mentally Ill. NAMI is a national organization with over 220,000 members and more than 1,200 county and local affiliates in every one of the fifty states and Canada. At NAMI meetings we learn a lot about mental illness, the latest advances in research and treatment, what is being done to fight stigma and discrimination, what help is available for victims and families, and so on. Ellen attended NAMI meetings, too, and the NAMI clubhouse where she met new friends and could hang out. At NAMI we can get together with others who have mentally ill loved ones and share our stories of successes and failures and give each other support. Quite a few other places offer help to the mentally ill and their loved ones. To help you find them, NAMI has a toll-free help line. I've put the number on the board. It is 1-800-950-6264. They will put a caller in touch with the closest NAMI affiliate or another organization that can help.

The last question: Is adequate research and treatment available? Research and treatment offer new hope for recovery from mental illness. They've learned a lot about mental illness in the last twelve years—much more than they learned in a thousand years before that. Research organizations like National Association for Research on Schizophrenia and Depression, NARSAD, have made dramatic breakthroughs in the areas of medication and treatment that offer significant hope to victims of this terrible brain disorder. NAMI was one of the founders of NARSAD. Because of organizations like NARSAD that fund research in universities and medical research institutions, giant strides have been made in both research and treatment of biological brain disorders. Newer classes of medications can better treat individuals with severe mental illnesses with far fewer side effects.

**CONCLUSION**    Well, I hope that you now have a better understanding of mental illness and what is being done in this country to deal with it. I hope that none of you will become members of the 25 percent of American families that are affected by it, but if it happens, at least you'll know what you're in store for and have some idea of where you can find help.

As I stand here speaking to you today, there are researchers working on new medications and treatments in universities and medical research institutions throughout the world. New psychotropic drugs are being tested right now. The cure for mental illness is out there. Someone has to find it and someone will. You can count on it. Remember, first, mental illness can happen to anyone at any age—no one is immune. Second, most people have little knowledge or understanding of mental illness. Third, there is a great deal of stigma attached to this biological brain disorder. Fourth, there are organizations that help those who are affected to deal with mental illness. And, fifth, new discoveries in research and treatment offer greater hope for recovery. We start the twenty-first century with better treatment for mental illness and more help available. Remember, mental illness affects one out of four families, but there is hope. Mental illness can be devastating, but for many recovery is possible.

## Chapter Review

After reading this chapter, you should be able to

- Define the three types of informative speeches.
- List and explain guidelines for preparing and giving a clear and interesting demonstration speech.
- Describe the five types of description speeches.
- Explain the three types of expository speeches and how they differ from demonstration and description speeches.
- Describe the different elements that can be used in an expository speech.
- Define different types of analysis and when each would be used.
- List and explain guidelines for informative speaking.

## Key Terms

Informative communication (p. 149)          Explanation (p. 154)
Demonstration speech (p. 150)                Analysis (p. 155)
Description speech (p. 152)                   Explication (p. 156)
Expository speech (p. 153)                    Evaluation (p. 157)

## Exercises

1. Select a topic for each type of speech discussed in the chapter: demonstration, description, and expository. Write a specific purpose statement for each.

*Sample Topics:*
* How to:  plant a garden
          make a pizza
          carve a pumpkin
          wash and wax a car
          perform a magic trick
* Hobbies/crafts
* Traditions
* Vacation spots
* Mass media
* Technological innovations
* World news

2. Describe which organizational pattern (as discussed in Chapter 7) you would use for each topic you've selected. Create a list of main points and supporting points for each, following the organizational structure you've chosen. What supporting materials would be most appropriate?

3. During different classes for the next few days, observe your professors and make note of how they present information. Do you detect a particular organizational pattern in how they present their material? Do you observe different styles, such as storytelling, use of detailed examples or comparisons, or straightforward explanation? Which styles are most effective at getting and holding your attention? Which are most effective at making the material understandable and increasing your knowledge?

## Speech Assignments

1. *A Letter to the Editor* (An expression of viewpoint; 2–3 minutes)
   Write to the "Letters to the Editor" column of one of your local newspapers expressing a point of view. It will be helpful if you familiarize yourself with these columns in order to be aware of the rules and format to follow. A reader will judge you on your style and grammatical correctness. A simple, to-the-point style must still be interesting. Or, find a Letter to the Editor with which you agree, that you think is timely and interesting.

   *Delivery.* This speech will be delivered in the manuscript method of presentation. Remember, the successful speaker reads as though he were speaking extemporaneously. Practice to deliver this speech in a spontaneous, convincing manner.

   ### Suggestions
   1. If you are writing in response to a published letter, read it so your audience is clear as to what you're disagreeing with.
   2. Write as if you were speaking—in an informal, direct way.
   3. Read the letter aloud to a friend or two.
   4. Become familiar enough with the letter to develop good eye contact.
   5. Proofread your letter to eliminate weaknesses in style and grammatical errors.

**2.** *Speech of Opinion* (An expression of viewpoint; 2–3 minutes)

The speech of opinion states your point of view to your audience. It uses a common ground approach to support your viewpoint. It tries to establish a common bond with the audience by referring to those values and principles with which the audience agrees. Below is a sample speech of opinion:

The events of September 11th were incredibly shocking. The human carnage, the thousands buried under mountains of debris, the suffering of so many innocent victims, their families and friends and the rescue workers who gave their lives will never be forgotten. But to retaliate with air strikes against cities in Afghanistan and Iraq that are killing thousands of innocent civilians is not the answer. The Afghan and Iraqi people have been suffering for centuries from war, famine, and political oppression. The best response would have been to go immediately to the United Nations Security Council asking that all members of the United Nations be enjoined to work together to find the terrorists whoever they are and wherever they may be hiding. Terrorism is an international problem affecting all of mankind which should be dealt with by the world community. By enlisting the aid of some of our allies, we have already acknowledged that the United States cannot go it alone. By enlisting the aid of all the member countries of the U.N. for this war on terrorism, we will be able to apprehend and punish those responsible for these heinous acts without this being seen as strictly an American response which would invite future acts of terrorism against us.

Let us follow the advice of Martin Luther King in his last Sunday sermon: "It is no longer a choice, my friends, between violence and nonviolence. It is either nonviolence or nonexistence. And the alternative to disarmament, the alternative to a greater suspension of nuclear tests, the alternative to strengthening the United Nations and thereby disarming the whole world may well be a civilization plunged into the abyss of annihilation, and our earthly habitat would be transformed into an inferno that even the mind of Dante could not imagine."

There is no doubt that the United States is a prime target for terrorism. However, unless we start dealing with terrorism as a world problem, further acts of terrorism directed specifically against our country will inevitably occur, and they will become increasingly deadly. With the widespread availability of biological and chemical weapons and the ability to make nuclear devices that can be carried, we will someday be faced with acts of indescribable destruction and death.

Ours is the richest and most powerful nation in the world. But our 300 billion dollar yearly military budget has not given us security over terrorism. Our military and nuclear superpower status has not given us security. And our immeasurable wealth has not given us security. Acts of terrorism are an assault on the entire human community. We need to work with the international community to deal with these crimes against humanity. I urge you to write or e-mail President Bush and tell him that the U.S. should not fight a unilateral war against terrorism but rather should turn to the United Nations for support.

**1.** Do you agree with the speaker's viewpoint? Why?

**2.** Deliver a two-to-four-minute speech expressing an opposite view.

**3.** Identify any fallacies you see in the speech.

# Appendix: Sample Informative Speech Topics

| | |
|---|---|
| The iPod | Democracy |
| Reality TV | The electronic book |
| Condoleezza Rice | Dr. Phil |
| Running a marathon | Third World poverty |
| Downloading music | Identity theft |
| Congressional elections 2006 | Alzheimer's disease |
| Rebuilding New Orleans | Fictional "memoirs" |
| Health care reform | The *Challenger* disaster |
| Drug use in the Tour de France | Cultural customs |
| The rise of Islam | Barry Bonds |
| Hybrid cars | Solar energy |
| Digital media | Xfire |
| Cinco de Mayo | Oscar winners |
| Vending machines | Amusement park safety |
| How do you like your latté? | Caring for your pet |
| "No Child Left Behind" Act | Scientology |
| How the stars were born | Community service |

# Persuasion

WHEN YOU think of the word *persuasion*, what mental picture appears? Do you visualize a TV commercial done by some slick multi-million-dollar advertising agency? Do you picture a political candidate who would promise almost anything if it meant getting elected? Do you envision someone selling condos, used cars, or magazines? Do you see yourself trying to get a few extra days to finish that term paper or pay off that loan? It might very well be that you see all these images and more because in this country persuasion is so much a part of our society and our lives.

We are involved with persuasion daily as both receivers and senders. We are constantly being bombarded with appeals to "get with it," to "enjoy life," and to give ourselves "the very best." We spend a lot of our time talking to others trying to get them to act a certain way, to agree with our point of view, or to just simply like us more.

The two main differences between this one-to-one persuasion and delivering a persuasive speech are that the latter involves talking to more people and spending more time and effort in planning, preparation, and delivery. Otherwise, the methods are basically the same.

## PERSUASION DEFINED

**Persuasion:** A deliberate attempt to influence the thought and behavior of others through the use of personal, psychological, and logical appeals.

**Persuasion** can be defined as *a deliberate attempt to influence the thought and behavior of others through the use of personal, psychological, and logical appeals*. Let us examine this definition in detail.

First, consider the word *deliberate*. You must know that your purpose is to persuade. The more aware you are of exactly what you want to accomplish, the more likely you are to be successful. An informative speech may also persuade, but if its primary purpose is to inform, then the persuasion is accidental.

The second word to remember is *attempt*. Regardless of whether you are successful, you are still involved in persuasion. The vacuum cleaner salesperson can make a good living delivering the same sales pitch to ten customers a day, even though only two or three of them buy the product.

The third important word is *influence*. You don't have to sell the product immediately to be a successful persuader. Persuasion can be a long-range process, which influences thought or behavior a little at a time. Consider, for example, an attempt to improve the image that minority residents of a major city have of the police department. You can't expect to change overnight attitudes that for some it took years to develop. The best you might be able to expect from some of these citizens is to make them a little less antagonistic toward the police.

Finally, there are three appeals or types of proof in the definition that persuaders use to sell their products more effectively: personal, psychological, and logical.

### PERSONAL PROOF

**Personal proof:** The image the speaker presents to the audience, including competence, goodwill, integrity, and credibility.

More than 2,000 years ago, the Greek philosopher Aristotle stated that no other factor was more important to success in persuasion than the audience's perception of a persuader as having good sense, good moral character, and goodwill. Speech experts agree that the principle of **personal proof** is as true today as it was then. No factor is more important to your success as a persuader than the image your listener has of you as a person. Ideally, you want your audience to see you as a competent person who has integrity and goodwill toward them. If they do, your chances of being successful as a persuader are excellent.

COMPETENCE. Competence means being well qualified, having good sense, and knowing what you are talking about. Most of us are influenced by those who are capable. When we have problems with our electronic equipment, we take it to an expert to have it fixed. When our dentist tells us that we need a root canal, we set up an appointment. When our doctor tells us that our appendix must be removed immediately, we agree.

To be an effective persuader you must project an image of competence to your audience. To a great extent, this will depend on how much time and effort you put into preparing and delivering your speech. A carefully organized, clearly worded speech is the mark of a competent communicator. Following are five specific suggestions you can use to project an image of competence to your audience:

1. Articulate your words clearly and use correct grammar and pronunciation. A listener is likely to question your ideas if they are unclear or expressed incorrectly.
2. Be up to date. A competent person uses the most current information available.
3. Indicate your qualifications. If you have education or experience that provides you with special knowledge about your subject, indicate this during your introduction.
4. Speak with confidence. One of the characteristics of the competent person is a positive approach.
5. Be fluent. Practice your speech so you can deliver it easily and naturally. Regardless of whether justified, listeners often judge nonfluency as an indication of poor preparation or indecision.

INTEGRITY.    Have you ever had the feeling that a politician you were listening to was just a little too smooth, or that even though you couldn't put your finger on it, something made you wonder if you could trust a particular salesperson? In today's world, with its hypocrisy and credibility gaps, integrity is of major concern to an audience. Before an audience will accept your ideas, they must believe that you are worthy of their trust and respect. Following are specific suggestions that will help you indicate to your audience that you are sincere and honest:

1. Dress appropriately. Your chances of achieving a desired response will be greater if you dress according to the expectations of your audience.
2. Establish a common bond. Listeners are more inclined to respond positively to a speaker they see as having similar attitudes, values, and experiences.
3. Be objective. To be effective, you must show your audience that you are presenting your views fairly and fully.
4. Indicate your motives. If you have strong motives for presenting your viewpoint, indicate these to your audience. Even if they don't agree with you, they will admire your convictions.
5. Be sincere. You are more likely to project an image of sincerity if your tone of voice and facial expression are appropriate to what you are saying.

GOODWILL.    "The key to success for a salesman is to be well liked," says Willie Loman in Arthur Miller's play *Death of a Salesman*. Although this is an oversimplification, being well liked is an important qualification for a salesperson. People are much more apt to buy something from someone they like than from someone they are indifferent to or don't like. Therefore, one of your most important jobs as a persuader is to get your audience to like you. The best way to do this is to

Former South African President Nelson Mandela, here speaking about AIDS, has developed great credibility as a speaker. He is perceived as a person of sincerity and compassion due to his battle against apartheid and subsequent imprisonment.

show that you like them. Here are some specific suggestions you can use to enhance your image as a person of goodwill:

1. Show enthusiasm. Greeting your audience in a lively, energetic way will show them that you are interested in them and happy to be there.
2. Use tact. You can project an image of goodwill by being diplomatic and flexible, especially when dealing with an issue to which some of your listeners are opposed.

3. Be respectful. Treat your listeners with courtesy. Give them credit for having ability, uniqueness, and intelligence.
4. Use humor. An attitude of friendliness is projected by a speaker's use of humor. When used effectively, humor causes both the speaker and the audience to relax.
5. Establish rapport. *Rapport* is a French word meaning "to bring harmony." You can establish rapport with your audience by showing that you like them. Whenever you can, make reference to those in your audience. If you are on a first-name basis with some, refer to them whenever it suits the occasion.

IMAGE.    In persuasion, the term *image* refers to a mental picture that a customer has of the product that the persuader is selling. That product can be political candidates, a company, a brand of wine, and so on. When you deliver a persuasive speech, the *product* you are selling is you. As you have seen, you want your listeners to have a mental picture of you as a person of competence, integrity, and goodwill. If they do, your personal proof will be strengthened, and the chances that they will believe you will increase.

CREDIBILITY.    There is a positive relationship between image and **credibility**: the better the image, the better the credibility. Conversely, a person with a poor image has low credibility. The strength of personal proof can clearly be demonstrated by examining the image–credibility relationship of Dr. Martin Luther King, Jr. As a highly educated, renowned speaker and writer, this national figure projected an image of competence. As a Baptist minister, civil rights leader, and winner of the Nobel Peace Prize, he projected an image of integrity. As a leader who was so close to his followers that he marched with them, slept with them, and went to jail with them, he projected an image of goodwill. Among his supporters, King's credibility was so high that many of them risked harassment, jail, personal injury, and even their lives to follow him.

> **Credibility:** The speaker's ability to be believable to the audience and worthy of its confidence and trust.

## PSYCHOLOGICAL PROOF

The second appeal used by persuaders to sell their products is **psychological proof**. Psychological proof appeals to the attitudes and motives of the audience. We tend to act in certain ways because of two factors: attitude and motive. Attitude often determines the way we are going to act, and motive supplies the impulse or desire to act.

> **Psychological proof:** An appeal to the attitudes and motives of the listeners.

ATTITUDES.    Attitudes are learned. We form them from our education, experience, and interaction with others. For example, we form favorable or unfavorable attitudes about government, religion, abortion, communism, sex, and so on. These attitudes give direction to our behavior, causing us to act in predisposed ways in different situations.

MOTIVES.    The inner drive or impulse that stimulates behavior is called **motive**. If you consider attitude as the directive force of behavior, motive could be considered the driving force. There are two basic types of motives: physical motives and social motives.

> **Motive:** The inner drive or impulse that stimulates behavior.

*Physical Motives.*    Often referred to as basic human drives, physical motives are common to people of all societies. All of us are born with the same basic physiological needs. We want to eat when hungry, drink when thirsty, defend ourselves when threatened, seek safety from the weather, and so on. For many of us in the United States, these basic needs are being abundantly satisfied. The more money we have, the more we spend to achieve the greatest possible comfort. We buy central air conditioning, contour furniture, and heated swimming pools to pamper our most priceless possession, ourselves. We are, to a great extent, creatures of the body. Although it is unlikely that you will encounter a situation where your listeners have not satisfied their physical needs, making them aware of those who have not can often be quite effective.

*Social Motives.*    A baby is born with a set of physical motives but without social motives. These are learned. No doubt the first social motive the infant develops is the security motive. This motive is primary to the newborn baby and continues as a powerful need at least until the child goes off to school. The tendency of little children to cuddle up; carry a doll, teddy bear, or security blanket around; or hide behind mother when a stranger comes to the door are all examples of the strength of this motive in the small child.

Another motive that develops during this period of closeness to the mother is the approval motive. The baby soon learns that cooing, smiling, laughing, and the like win approval. The child also soon finds that although some things win a pat on the back, others result in a pat on the backside. Approval becomes an important need for the child. For some children the need for approval is so strong that isolation becomes a significant punishment. Banishing a child to his or her room with the comment "Go to your room. I don't want to see you any more today" can be devastating for some. During this time, children also develop their own attitudes of approval or disapproval toward themselves.

### SPECIFIC MOTIVE APPEALS

*Sex.*    Perhaps no motive is appealed to more often in persuasion than the sex motive. Advertising in this country is supersaturated with sex to sell everything from shock absorbers to perfume. For example, CDs are sold with covers featuring attractive women or handsome men who have absolutely no relationship to the music inside. Automobiles, cigarettes, toothpaste, and diet sodas are all used by young, vibrant, *beautiful* people, and if you use these products, somehow you will be beautiful, too. Be assured, the sex motive plays an important role in all areas of persuasion.

*Security.*    Another appeal often used in advertising is the security motive. The effect that this motive has on us and our loved ones is clearly evident in today's society. We have banks to protect our money, unions to protect our jobs, and insurance companies to provide for our health care, and when the time comes, for our survivors.

We go to college to provide for a more secure future, we "go steady" to ensure a dependable date, and we put money aside for a "rainy day." In this age of violence and uncertainty, no generation has been as security minded as this one.

*Approval.*  Whether it be at home, at work, at school, or among friends, we are constantly seeking the approval of others. Any advertisement that features brand names is selling approval along with the product. A person might spend months landscaping a backyard or painting a picture for the satisfaction of being able to say, "I made this myself."

One effective technique in persuasion is to take the feeling of approval away from an individual, making the person feel uncomfortable. An example is the priest, rabbi, or minister making hell *hot* for the congregation. Another example is the ad that talks about the starving children of the world, pointing out that the average dog in the United States was eating better than many children in the rest of the world or that the average American citizen threw away enough garbage per day to feed a family of six in India. The idea is that the readers or listeners feel uncomfortable about the situation until they contribute their money in an effort to help.

*Conformity.*  Closely related to the approval motive is the motive to conform. Even in the most primitive societies, people have customs, mores, and rules to which they must conform in order to live in harmony with their peers. Most people tend to go along with the group rather than swim against the stream. Have you ever, for example, worn a style that was not particularly becoming to you because it was the thing to do? Or would you dare show up in jeans at a formal dance?

Early in life you learned to conform to the expectations of those around you. As you grew older and came in contact with more people, you found that conforming to these expectations became considerably more difficult. You could, for example, be labeled un-American for conforming to the expectations of a Christian *peace group* or un-Christian for advocating the nuclear destruction of Communist nations.

*Success.*  The desire to succeed can be a powerful motive. For some, it is so intense that it overshadows all others. Individuals have been so strongly motivated to succeed that they have lied, cheated, and even killed to further this ambition. Advertisers have used the success motive to sell products ranging from toothpaste to condominiums. The success motive has long been used to sell luxury cars. People who buy Mercedes, Cadillacs, Porsches, and Lexuses are buying success along with the automobile.

*Creativity.*  Creativity is one of the motives that can be unusually forceful. It is a form of self-actualization. Some have spent years of self-sacrifice and deprivation in an attempt to develop an artistic or musical ability. Who hasn't heard of a starving artist's sale or an author who could paper a room with rejection slips from publishers. The fact that these people continue creating testifies to the strength of this motive.

It should be pointed out that while a person may be more influenced by one motive than another at any given time, motives seldom operate individually. Sometimes two or more motives combine to affect a person's behavior. A person might be motivated to lift weights for a number of reasons. Weight lifting conditions the body, satisfying the good health motive. It develops muscles and a trim figure, satisfying both approval and popularity motives.

At other times, motives are in conflict with each other. Take, for example, the person who attends a party where drugs are being used. To refuse to go along with the group can threaten that person's popularity and peer approval, but to use the drugs can be a threat to security and parental approval. As you can see, motives have a significant impact on people's lives.

## LOGICAL PROOF

**Logical proof:** The use of evidence to appeal to the audience's ability to reason, used to support the speaker's argument.

**Reasoning:** The process of drawing conclusions from evidence.

**Argumentation:** The reasoning process used to attempt to influence others' beliefs.

**Logical proof** involves the use of evidence and reasoning. **Reasoning** is the process of drawing conclusions from evidence. There are two kinds of evidence: evidence of fact and evidence of opinion. The explanation of this reasoning process to others in an attempt to influence belief is called **argumentation**. A basic argument consists of two statements: a premise and a conclusion drawn from that premise. Here are two basic arguments:

1. Mark is a member of the Ku Klux Klan. Therefore, he is a troublemaker.
2. Mark has been arrested three times. Therefore, he is a troublemaker.

The use of evidence and reasoning is typical for an attorney seeking to persuade an audience of a defendant's guilt or innocence.

Both statements involve a premise–conclusion relationship. In the first example, the conclusion is drawn from the fact that Mark is a member of the K.K.K. "Mark is a member of the Ku Klux Klan. Therefore, he is a troublemaker." This argument is based on deductive reasoning. You have come to the conclusion that Mark is a troublemaker because he belongs to the Ku Klux Klan. You reason from a general premise (members of the K.K.K. are troublemakers) to a minor premise (Mark is a member of the K.K.K.) to the conclusion (therefore, Mark is a troublemaker). Whenever you reason from a general rule to a specific case, you are reasoning deductively.

The second statement, "Mark has been arrested three times. Therefore, he is a troublemaker," is an example of inductive reasoning. There is no rule to guide the reasoner, only the observation about Mark: He has been arrested three times. Therefore, he is a troublemaker. When you come to a conclusion as the result of observing or experiencing individual situations or cases, you are using inductive reasoning. Although you may not have been aware of it, you have used this form of reasoning throughout your life. Do you like pizza? Enjoy rock music? Think that you are a good student? Whether your answer to these questions is yes or no, it has undoubtedly been based on inductive reasoning. You probably decided whether you liked pizza after eating one, three, five, or more. The same was true about your attitude toward rock music and your status as a student. Your observation or experience with these involvements has determined your conclusion.

## DEDUCTIVE REASONING

As you can see, induction draws conclusions from specific experiences or observations, and deduction begins with the acceptance of a general rule (as stated in a major premise) and applies it to a specific case in the conclusion. In most cases, **deductive reasoning** is stated in a form called an *enthymeme*, where one of the premises or sometimes the conclusion is not expressed but implied. This was the case with the deductive statement above: Mark is a member of the K.K.K. Therefore, he is a troublemaker.

**Deductive reasoning:** A three-step process of reasoning from a general rule to a specific conclusion.

When formally stated, deduction is expressed in a three-step pattern called a **syllogism**. The reasoning moves from a major premise to a minor premise to a conclusion. In the example above, the major premise was not expressed but implied. The formally stated syllogism would appear this way:

**Syllogism:** A three-step pattern of deductive reasoning, which moves from a major premise to a minor premise to a conclusion.

*Major premise:* Members of the K.K.K. are troublemakers.
*Minor premise:* Mark is a member of the K.K.K.
*Conclusion:* Therefore, Mark is a troublemaker.

It is often useful to examine a syllogism by putting it in this formal, three-step form. This makes it easier to determine (1) whether the major and minor premises are true, and (2) whether the conclusion follows logically from them. A syllogism is like a framework for deductive logic.

Keep in mind that while inductive reasoning moves from specific instances to a general conclusion, deductive moves from a general rule (heavy smokers are likely to get lung cancer) to a minor premise (Helga is a heavy smoker) to a specific conclusion (therefore, Helga is likely to get lung cancer).

To use deductive reasoning effectively as a speaker, you must get your audience to agree with your major and minor premises, and present a conclusion that follows logically from the premises. To do this, you will need to support your premises with evidence.

Suppose, for instance, that you are delivering a speech on the undesirability of eating too many meals at fast-food restaurants, and one of your points is that much of the food served in fast-food restaurants is extremely high in cholesterol. Your deductive argument would be expressed in a syllogism similar to this one:

*Major premise:* High-cholesterol foods are dangerous to your health.
*Minor premise:* The food served at fast-food restaurants is mostly high in cholesterol.
*Conclusion:* Therefore, the food served at fast-food restaurants is dangerous to your health.

Now that you have constructed the syllogism, you need to get your audience to agree with your premises. If they accept your premises as true, and if the premises are set up properly, then they will agree with your conclusion if it follows logically from the premises. First you will have to present evidence to get your audience to agree with your major premise: High-cholesterol foods are dangerous to your health. You might quote the testimony of one or two experts on the subject. Choose people your audience will consider objective and well qualified. You could quote recent statistics or research studies. Perhaps an explanation of the effects of cholesterol on the body would be effective.

When you have supported your major premise adequately, you are ready to deal with the minor premise: The food served at fast-food restaurants is mostly high in cholesterol. Certainly, you would give examples of the kinds of high-cholesterol foods you are talking about: hamburgers, french fries, fish fried in animal fat, and the like. Following this you might use comparative statistics to show the contrast between these foods and the kinds you would eat in a well-balanced diet.

If you have succeeded in getting your listeners to agree with your premises, they will accept your conclusion: Therefore, the food served in fast-food restaurants is dangerous to your health. The test of a good conclusion must always be, "Does it follow logically from the evidence that has been presented?" If you have supplied your listeners with enough evidence to get them to accept your major and minor premises, they will accept your conclusion. When used correctly, deductive reasoning can be an effective form of persuasion.

## INDUCTIVE REASONING

**Inductive reasoning:** The process of reasoning from a specific observation or experience to a general conclusion.

As you have seen, deductive reasoning moves essentially from a general rule to a specific conclusion. **Inductive reasoning**, in contrast, reverses this process. When you reason inductively, you examine specific instances and, as a result of your observations, come to a general conclusion. For example, if you have had good service from three cars, a Pontiac, a Chevrolet, and a Buick, you might come to the conclusion that a General Motors product is a good car to own. If you have read statistics that show people with college degrees earn far more than those who are less educated, then you might have concluded that college is the place for you. Both of these forms of reasoning are primarily inductive. The first, generalization, examines individual cases—three GM automobiles—and concludes that what is true about these specific cars is also true about GM products in general. The second, statistics, involves drawing conclusions from numerical evidence. If the figures show that people with college degrees earn more, then the chances are that if you get a higher education, you will make more money, too. Let us look at these two forms of inductive reasoning in more detail.

## REASONING BY GENERALIZATION

This type of reasoning involves examining specific details or examples and coming to a general conclusion. If there are a limited number of instances involved, the more you cite, the more probable are the conclusions. For example, you might argue that Senator Jones is prolabor and Senator Smith antilabor by citing their voting records on legislation affecting labor.

When used well, **generalization** can be an effective argument in persuasion. Carefully controlled scientific experiments and studies can provide strong evidence for your speeches.

**Generalization:** A general conclusion based on examining specific examples or details.

## OTHER FORMS OF REASONING

Reasoning by generalization is primarily inductive. However, reasoning by comparison and by cause and effect mixes induction and deduction.

## REASONING BY COMPARISON

Argument by comparison involves the examination of two similar cases. If the two have enough similarities, it is possible to argue that what is true of one case will be true of the others as well. The comparisons may be either literal or figurative. Literal comparisons compare things that are within the same categories, such as U.S. inflation rates in 2001 and 2002 and a comparison of academic standards at different universities. If the similarities in the literal comparisons are significant, the conclusions often appear logical.

Figurative comparisons point out similarities between things in different categories. Comparisons between life and a pathway and between the kingdom of heaven and a sower of seeds are examples of figurative comparisons. Although figurative comparisons are often weak as arguments because they are based on only one major similarity, they are both popular and colorful and also useful in relating the unknown to the known.

## REASONING FROM CAUSE AND EFFECT

**Causal reasoning:** A process that links cause and effect.

**Causal reasoning** is based on the principle that every cause has an effect. When two things occur together with any frequency, we might naturally determine that one is caused by the other. For example, the person who complains, "Every time I eat pizza, I get heartburn," might logically assume that the pizza has triggered the heartburn. However, because cause-and-effect relationships can often be quite complicated, it could be that the heartburn is caused by a gallbladder disorder, which is aggravated by eating the pizza, so rather than giving up pizza, the person should see a doctor.

Causal relationships are most clearly demonstrated in carefully controlled situations. For example, a number of years ago researchers were interested in finding out what effect music had on the milk production of dairy cows. They used two experimental groups and a control group. Each group of cows was housed in the same size barn, fed the same food, and matched in every relevant way, except that after the first week, light classical music was piped into barn A, hard rock into barn B, and no music into barn C. The results of the experiment, which ended after week 2, were that group A produced half as much milk as they had during week 1, group B's production was reduced by one-third, and group C's production remained the same. The experiment showed clearly what effect the music had on the cows.

Keep in mind that causal relationships are more difficult to identify in less controlled situations. This is especially true in political, economic, and social situations, which frequently have multiple causes.

## FALLACIES

**Fallacies:** Arguments based on incorrect or flawed reasoning.

Fallacious reasoning can be the result of faulty induction or deduction, or the acceptance of misleading argumentation. Some of these **fallacies** occur so often that they have been isolated and labeled. The most common of these are treated next.*

### UNWARRANTED OR HASTY GENERALIZATION

A generalization is fallacious when it is based on insufficient or unfair evidence, or when it is not warranted by the facts available. For example, "All hippies are dirty," "All welfare recipients are lazy," and so on.

### ERRORS IN CAUSAL INDUCTION

Fallacy in causal induction occurs when there is no logical relationship between a cause and an effect. Two most common cause-and-effect fallacies are *post hoc* (after this, therefore, because of this) and *non sequitur* (it does not follow).

---

*This section is taken with permission from Arthur Koch and Stanley B. Felber, *What Did You Say?* 3rd ed. (Upper Saddle River, NJ: Prentice Hall, 1985).

POST HOC.   *Post hoc* is the fallacy of thinking that an event that follows another is necessarily caused by the other. Thus, you might conclude that the Democratic party promotes war, that television viewing increases juvenile delinquency, and that an easing of censorship causes an increase in immorality.

The error in *post hoc* reasoning occurs because the reasoner ignores other factors that may have contributed to the effect. A survey of former college debaters revealed, for example, that they were considerably more successful in their chosen field of work than their nondebating counterparts. To assume from this that their experience as debaters was the cause of their success would be fallacious. Other factors must be considered: Students who become debaters usually possess superior verbal ability, have keen analytical minds, and are highly motivated by competition. No doubt these factors, which led them into debate, also contributed to their success.

NON SEQUITUR.   In this fallacy, the conclusion reached does not necessarily follow from the facts argued. The argument that because a man is kind to animals he will make a good husband ignores the possibilities that the man may make a bad husband, drink excessively, cheat, or beat his wife.

## BEGGING THE QUESTION

An argument begs the question when it assumes something as true when it actually needs to be proven. For instance, the declaration that "these corrupt laws must be changed" asserts the corruption but does not prove it, and consequently the conclusion is not justified.

Begging the question also occurs when we make a charge and then insist that someone else disprove it. For example, to answer the question "How do you know that the administration is honest?" would put the respondent in the position of trying to disprove a conclusion that was never proven in the first place. Remember, whoever makes an assertion has the burden of proof.

## IGNORING THE QUESTION

Ignoring the question occurs when the argument shifts from the original subject to a different one, or when the argument appeals to some emotional attitude that has nothing to do with the logic of the case. An example of the first would be a man replying "Haven't you ever done anything dishonest?" when accused of cheating on his wife. He ignores the question of his infidelity by shifting to a different argument.

An argument that appeals to the emotional attitudes of the reader or listener would be the statement "No good American would approve of this communistic proposal."

## FALSE ANALOGY

To argue by analogy is to compare two things that are alike in germane known respects and to suggest that they will also be alike in unknown respects. This method is accurate if the things being compared are genuinely similar: "George will do well in graduate school; he had an excellent academic record as an undergraduate." It is

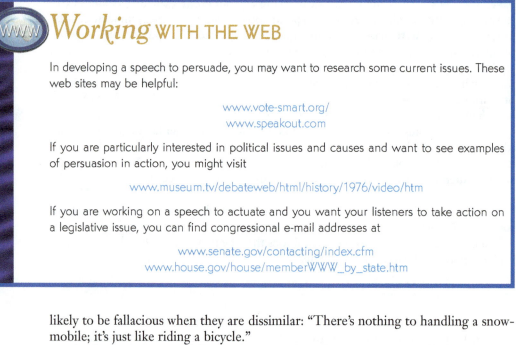

# Working WITH THE WEB

In developing a speech to persuade, you may want to research some current issues. These web sites may be helpful:

www.vote-smart.org/
www.speakout.com

If you are particularly interested in political issues and causes and want to see examples of persuasion in action, you might visit

www.museum.tv/debateweb/html/history/1976/video/htm

If you are working on a speech to actuate and you want your listeners to take action on a legislative issue, you can find congressional e-mail addresses at

www.senate.gov/contacting/index.cfm
www.house.gov/house/memberWWW_by_state.htm

likely to be fallacious when they are dissimilar: "There's nothing to handling a snow-mobile; it's just like riding a bicycle."

Analogies are more difficult to prove when the comparison is figurative rather than literal. In a political campaign, the incumbent might admonish the voter "not to change horses in the middle of the stream," while the opponent replies that "a new broom sweeps clean."

## EITHER/OR FALLACY

The either/or fallacy is reasoning that concludes there are only two choices to an argument when there are other possible alternatives. A tragic example would be the reasoning that escalated the Vietnam War. The argument was: Either we fight and win in Vietnam or Southeast Asia will fall to the Communists. Of course, we didn't win and Southeast Asia didn't fall to the Communists.

## AD HOMINEM

In this fallacy, the argument shifts from the proposition to the character of the opponent. Unfortunately, this abuse often occurs in politics, and the voters who fall for it wind up casting their votes against a candidate rather than for one. "I wouldn't trust him. He cheated on his wife," or "You're not going to believe a former convict?" are examples of this fallacy.

## RED HERRING

The red herring is similar to the ad hominem fallacy but does not attack the opponent's character. It gets its name from the superstition that if you drag a red herring across your path it will throw any wild animals following you off the track. Information is introduced that is not relevant to the question at hand in the hope that it will divert attention from the real issue. In politics, an opposing candidate is pictured as being overly religious, ultrarich, or divorced. If the trait has nothing to do with the way he will perform in office, the argument is a red herring.

## AD POPULUM

The *ad populum* argument appeals to the theory that whatever the masses believe is true. Make no mistake; popularity is not always an accurate determiner of truth. Consider the landslide victory of Richard Nixon in 1972. A typical ad populum fallacy is: "Unconditional amnesty is wrong, because most people are against it."

# TYPES OF PERSUASIVE SPEECHES

Persuasive speeches can be classified into three types: (1) speeches to convince, (2) speeches to reinforce, and (3) speeches to actuate. Careful audience analysis is essential in persuasive speaking. The type of persuasion a speaker chooses should be based on the attitudes of the audience prior to the speech and the specific changes sought.

## SPEECHES TO CONVINCE

At times a persuader must deal with an audience that is undecided, indifferent, or opposed to a proposition. President Bush defending his health plan, Jesse Jackson arguing against invading Haiti, a college debater attempting to prove that capital punishment is desirable, and a student senate leader trying to convince fellow students that the student senate is doing a good job are all cases of persuasion to convince.

Because speeches to convince appeal to the listener's intelligence rather than emotions, they employ logical rather than psychological or personal appeals. They must rely on clear reasoning and carefully selected evidence in order to get listeners to respond satisfactorily. Six forms of supporting evidence—examples, explanation, statistics, testimony, comparison and contrast, and visual aids—were presented in detail in Chapter 6 under supporting devices. A review of Chapter 6 should help you develop the speech to convince.

## SPEECHES TO REINFORCE

Rather than appealing to their intelligence, a speech to reinforce appeals essentially to the motives, attitudes, and sentiments of an audience. Rather than being undecided, indifferent, or opposed, the audience is in agreement with the speaker's point of view.

On Veterans Day, a speaker reminds the audience of the sacrifices made by those who fought and died so that each of them might enjoy this land of freedom. Those in the audience already believe that the sacrifices made by these veterans were important. However, the speaker wants to strengthen that belief, to reinforce that appreciation, or to deepen that concern.

The Independence Day orator, the speaker at a pep rally, the commencement speaker, the preacher, and the persons delivering eulogies, inaugural addresses, memorials, and testimonials are involved with persuasion to reinforce. Their purpose is to strengthen the existing attitudes, sentiments, emotions, and beliefs of their audience.

## SPEECHES TO ACTUATE

The speech to actuate calls for a specific action on the part of the audience. It asks them to buy, to join, to march, or to sign. A speech to convince may attempt to create an awareness in the audience as to the danger to our society caused by easy access to handguns; the speech to actuate seeks to get those in the audience to write to their representatives in Congress urging them to vote to get handguns off the streets. A speech to reinforce may seek to arouse greater concern for the plight of the hungry in our society; the speech to actuate would seek an overt response, asking the audience for a specific donation of food or money to respond directly to the problem.

A speech to actuate calls for the audience to take specific action, such as this speaker's message to "Join the Fight."

Although the speech to actuate may employ the logical and psychological appeals used in speeches to convince and reinforce, the purpose of this speech is to get specific action. For this reason, speeches to actuate are generally more successful when directed at audiences that basically agree with the speaker's point of view.

## SAMPLE SPEECH TO CONVINCE

Remember, a persuader must often deal with an audience that is undecided, indifferent, or even opposed to a proposition or an idea. Although few people would be opposed to the fact that Native Americans deserve respect, many are indifferent, or at least undecided. The following is a clear model of a speech to convince.

### American Indians Deserve Respect

What images come to mind when you hear the words redmen, chiefs, or warriors? For many people, these words are synonymous with sports. Maybe some of you went to a school whose sports team had an Indian name. Perhaps some of you have a favorite professional team that has an Indian name, like the Washington Redskins or the Atlanta Braves. Over the last few years, I've talked to many people who do not understand why American Indians object to "Indian" team names, mascots, and logos being used in school athletic programs and professional sports. "How can you complain? We're proud of our teams!" they say. "We love our Seminoles, our Chiefs, our Warriors. You should feel honored that we respect Native Americans enough to name our team after them and display their logos on our posters and t-shirts."

Well, we don't feel honored. As an American Indian and member of the Potawatomi Nation, I'm here to tell you why using "Indian" names and images for sports teams, logos, and mascots is highly insulting to American Indians. We don't feel honored, we are offended when we hear derogatory, offensive terms like Redskins and Red Men. We are offended when we see a logo caricature of an Indian running full speed wielding a spear or tomahawk or a fully armed Indian with painted face dancing a war dance. Besides the fact that these cartoonlike caricatures ridicule American Indian braves, they recall a very painful part of our history when these heroes fought to protect our people and lands from the United States government and greedy white men.

We also feel offended when you use objects sacred to us, such as the drum, eagle feathers, and face painting, in your publicity and games. These objects are important parts of our culture. We use many of them in sacred ceremonies and important social gatherings. All of them represent important values to American Indians. Some of them, like eagle feathers, are symbols of honor and valor. Others, like the drums and face painting, have significant meaning to us. To see ourselves depicted, along with these symbols, as mascots for some school or professional sports team is just one more demeaning, belittling insult to us.

When the white men came to North America, they came to a country inhabited by tribes of Indians who lived together in relative peace and harmony. These Native Americans had their own laws, culture, history, art, music, and poetry. In most cases, they welcomed the white man with friendship and goodwill.

In this land of opportunity, American Indians were given treaties, many of which were broken, had their land taken away from them by the government and greedy white men, were exterminated by being given disease-infected blankets, were taken on forced death marches, and were massacred in their own villages. If you want to get an honest account of what happened to American Indians in this country, read books like Howard Zinn's *A People's History of the United States* or Gary B. Nash's *Red, White, and Black*. These historians tell it the way it really was.

Names like Redskins and Warriors and mock-Indian behaviors, such as war-whooping and "scalping," promote a stereotype of American Indians that is totally false and racist. Many children in America grow up with this distorted image of the American Indian, as a buckskin-attired, poorly educated savage. We resent this stigmatization. My family and I are no different than any one of you. We wear the same kind of clothes, eat the same kind of food, do the same kind of work, and enjoy many of the same activities that you do. Depicting us as being different is hurtful and wrong and robs us of our dignity. Indian names, mascots, and logos should be eliminated from school and professional sports.

Note that there is no bibliography for this speech because it was developed from the speaker's own viewpoint and personal experience as a Native American.

## SAMPLE SPEECH TO REINFORCE

A eulogy is a formal speech praising a person who has recently died. In a eulogy at his brother Robert Kennedy's funeral service, Edward Kennedy gives his audience a mental picture of his brother. He tells what he and the other members of the Kennedy family thought of him, and he uses Robert's own words to give them an image of his brother as a person of intelligence, integrity, and goodwill.

### A Tribute to His Brother

Your Eminences, your excellencies, Mr. President:
On behalf of Mrs. Kennedy, her children, the parents and sisters of Robert Kennedy, I want to express what we feel to those who mourn with us today in this cathedral and around the world.

We loved him as a brother and as a father, and as a son. From his parents, and from his older brothers and sisters—Joe and Kathleen and Jack—he received an inspiration which he passed on to all of us. He gave us strength in time of trouble, wisdom in time of uncertainty, and sharing in time of happiness. He will always be by our side.

Love is not an easy feeling to put into words. Nor is loyalty, or trust, or joy. But he was all of these. He loved life completely and he lived it intensely.

A few years back, Robert Kennedy wrote some words about his own father which expresses the way we in his family felt about him. He said of what his father meant to him, and I quote: "What it really all adds up to is love—not love as it is described with such facility in popular magazines, but the kind of love that is affection and respect, order and encouragement, and support. Our awareness of this was an incalculable source of strength, and because real love is something unselfish and involves sacrifice and giving, we could not help but profit from it." And he continued, "Beneath it all he has tried to engender a social conscience. There were wrongs which needed attention. There were people who were poor and needed help. And we have a responsibility to them and this country. Through no virtues and accomplishments of our own, we have been fortunate enough to be born in the United States under the most comfortable conditions. We, therefore, have a responsibility to others who are less well off."

That is what Robert Kennedy was given. What he leaves to us is what he said, what he did, and what he stood for. A speech he made for the young people of South Africa on their Day of Affirmation in 1966 sums it up the best, and I would like to read it now:

"There is discrimination in this world and slavery and slaughter and starvation. Governments repress their people; millions are trapped in poverty while the nation grows rich and wealth is lavished on armaments everywhere. These are differing evils, but they are the common works of man. They reflect the imperfection of human justice, the inadequacy of human compassion, our lack of sensibility towards the suffering of our fellows. But we can perhaps remember—even if only for a time—that those who live with us are our brothers; that they share with us the same short moment of life; that they seek—as we do—nothing but the chance to live out their lives in purpose and happiness, winning what satisfaction and fulfillment they can.

Surely this bond of common faith, this bond of common goal, can begin to teach us something. Surely, we can learn, at least to look at those around us as fellow men. And surely we can begin to work a little harder to bind up the wounds among us and to become in our own hearts brothers and countrymen once again. The answer is to rely on youth—not a time of life but a state of mind, a temper of the will, a quality of imagination, a predominance of courage over timidity, of the appetite for adventure over the love of ease. The cruelties and obstacles of this swiftly changing planet will not yield to the obsolete dogmas and outworn slogans. They cannot be moved by those who cling to a present that is already dying, who prefer the illusion of security to the excitement and danger that come with even the most peaceful progress.

It is a revolutionary world which we live in, and this generation at home and around the world has had thrust upon it a greater burden of responsibility than any generation that has ever lived. Some believe there is nothing one man or one woman can do against the enormous array of the world's ills. Yet many of the world's great movements of thought and action have flowed from the work of a single man. A young monk began the Protestant reformation; a young general extended an empire from Macedonia to the borders of the earth; a young woman reclaimed the territory of France; and it was a young Italian explorer who discovered the New World, and the 32-year-old Thomas Jefferson who claimed that all men are created equal."

These men moved the world, and so can we all. Few will have the greatness to bend history itself, but each of us can work to change a small portion of events, and in the total of all those acts will be written the history of this generation. It is from numberless diverse acts of courage and belief that human history is shaped. Each time a man stands up for an ideal, or acts to improve the lot of others, or strikes out against injustice, he sends forth a tiny ripple of hope, and crossing each other from a million different centers of energy and daring, those ripples build a current that can sweep down the mightiest walls of oppression and resistance.

Few are willing to brave the disapproval of their fellows, the censure of their colleagues, the wrath of their society. Moral courage is a rarer commodity than bravery in battle or great intelligence. Yet it is the one essential, vital quality for those who seek to change a world that yields most painfully to change. And I believe that in this generation those with the courage to enter the moral conflict will find themselves with companions in every corner of the globe.

For the fortunate among us there is the temptation to follow the easy and familiar paths of personal ambition and financial success so grandly spread before those who enjoy the privilege of education. But that is not the road history has marked out for us. Like it or not, we live in times of danger and uncertainty. But they are also more open to the creative energy of men than any other time in history. All of us will ultimately be judged, and as the years pass we will surely judge ourselves on the effort we have contributed to building a new world society and the extent to which our ideals and goals have shaped that event.

The future does not belong to those who are content with today, apathetic toward common problems and their fellow man alike, timid and fearful in the face of new ideas and bold projects. Rather it will belong to those who can blend vision, reason and courage in a personal commitment to the ideals and great enterprises of American society.

Our future may lie beyond our vision, but it is not completely beyond our control. It is the shaping impulse of America that neither faith nor nature nor the irresistible tides of history, but the work of our own hands, matched to reason and principle, that will determine our destiny. There is pride in that, even arrogance, but there is also experience and truth. In any event, it is the only way we can live."

That is the way he lived. That is what he leaves us.

My brother need not be idealized, or enlarged in death beyond what he was in life, to be remembered simply as a good and decent man, who saw wrong and tried to right it, saw suffering and tried to heal it, saw war and tried to stop it.

Those of us who loved him and who take him to his rest today, pray that what he was to us and what he wished for others will some day come to pass for all the world.

As he said many times, in many parts of this nation, to those he touched and who sought to touch him:

"Some men see things as they are and say why.

I dream things that never were and say why not."

*Vital Speeches* XXXIV: 18 (July 1, 1968), pp. 546–47

# Chapter Review

After reading this chapter, you should be able to

- Define persuasion and identify different types of persuasive messages in your everyday life.
- Explain the importance of personal proof in persuasion.

- List and explain the five ways to project a positive image of yourself to your listeners.
- Define psychological proof, and describe specific motive appeals and how they are used in persuasion.
- Give an example of deductive reasoning.
- Give an example of inductive reasoning.
- Construct a three-step syllogism, and identify supporting materials to get your audience to agree with your major and minor premises and accept your conclusion.
- Describe specific types of fallacies and when they are likely to occur.

## Key Terms

Persuasion (p. 170)

Personal proof (p. 170)

Credibility (p. 173)

Psychological proof (p. 173)

Motive (p. 173)

Logical proof (p. 176)

Reasoning (p. 176)

Argumentation (p. 176)

Deductive reasoning (p. 177)

Syllogism (p. 177)

Inductive reasoning (p. 178)

Generalization (p. 179)

Causal reasoning (p. 180)

Fallacies (p. 180)

## Exercises

1. Make a list of all the attempts to persuade that you encounter in a given day, including TV or magazine ads, flyers, billboards, and communication with family, friends, and others in your community. Make a similar list of your own attempts to persuade others. Compare your lists. Are you more of a consumer of persuasive messages? Or the one trying to persuade others? How frequent are persuasive messages in your daily life?

2. Create a sample TV commercial or print advertisement for a product you know and like. What is the audience for this product? What type of appeals do you need to use to persuade your audience that this is a good product or a product that they need? What evidence do you need to gather to support your argument?

3. Survey your classmates about a controversial issue, as you did in earlier chapters. Taking into account the different viewpoints represented, what would be the most effective way to develop a speech about this topic? What organizational pattern would you use? Create a specific purpose and central idea statement for the speech. What will be your main points? What evidence do you need to support your purpose? How will you establish your credibility?

## Speech Assignments

1. *Persuasion to Reinforce*

Develop a three-to-four-minute speech to reinforce. Remember, persuasion to reinforce is directed at an audience that already agrees with you. You are seeking to make that agreement stronger. Rely chiefly on psychological proof. Appeal to your audience's motives, attitudes, and sentiments.

*Delivery.* The speech to reinforce seeks to strengthen the audience's beliefs. It is imperative that they believe that the speaker is sincere. The more relaxed and spontaneous you are, the more likely it will be that you will succeed.

### Sample Central Ideas

1. We are all unique.
2. You can make a difference.
3. We owe senior citizens a lot.
4. Be proud of our flag.

2. *Persuasion to Convince*

Develop a three-to-four-minute speech supporting a point of view you feel many in your audience are either undecided about or are against. Appeal to your audience's intelligence. Present your material objectively and fairly. An audience will react negatively to a speaker whom they perceive as being biased.

### Suggestions

1. Try to establish a common bond with your audience.
2. Try to show your listeners that your motives are sincere.
3. Don't attempt too much in this assignment. If you can get those in your audience to modify their views even slightly, you will have been effective.

### Sample Central Ideas

1. The United States should adopt a system of socialized medicine.
2. The U.S. government should prohibit the sale of handguns.
3. The death penalty should be re-established (abolished) in our state.
4. Our military budget should be reduced by one-third.

3. *Persuasion to Actuate*

Develop a two-to-three-minute speech to persuade your audience to act in a particular way. Make clear to your audience exactly what you want them to do. Remember, you are asking your audience to act: to sign, to vote, to buy, to march, to donate, or to participate. Be realistic. Don't ask them to do something they are unlikely to do.

### Sample Central Ideas

1. Begin an exercise program.
2. Do a fire check of your home.
3. Hug a loved one today.
4. Avoid using loaded words.

# Appendix: Sample Persuasive Speech Topics

The Internet leads to invasion of privacy

Illegal immigrants should be sent home

Support federal funding for stem cell research

Support our troops in Iraq

Withdraw our troops from Iraq

Global warming is affecting our weather

Global warming is hype

Oil companies are guilty of price gouging

FEMA needs to be overhauled

The new SATs are flawed

Fast food is the cause of obesity

Barry Bonds should be applauded

Barry Bonds' records should not stand

Girls outperform boys in college

Airline security still has problems

Education leads to a better job

# CHAPTER 11

## *Group* COMMUNICATION

IF YOU ARE like most people, you participate in some form of group discussion almost daily. There are all kinds of group discussions. They may be planned or spontaneous, structured or unstructured, formal or informal, or permanent or temporary. Some discussions take place with a group of friends over coffee or with fellow workers during the lunch hour. Others occur in the home where everything from the high cost of living to what to do about the neighbor's dog may be covered. More and more, however, discussions are occurring more formally in organized committees and action groups.

Since the 1990s, citizens have become increasingly involved in the affairs of their communities. Organizations like MADD (Mothers Against Drunk Driving) and CUB (Citizens' Utility Board) have sprung up as a result of people demanding to have a voice in determining policies that affect their lives.

Discussions are also a vital part of formal education. Many instructors employ a lecture–discussion format, and group discussion is often used in classes to promote learning. The advantages of becoming a more effective participant in discussion are obvious. A study of the principles of group discussion, together with guided practice, will help you achieve this goal.

## THE FUNCTIONS OF DISCUSSION

In general, discussion has four functions: social, educative, therapeutic, and problem solving.

### SOCIAL DISCUSSION

**Social discussion:**
Discussion that is temporary, unstructured, and informal.

**Social discussion** usually occurs spontaneously and is temporary, unstructured, and informal. A typical example of social discussion would be a group of students sitting around a table in the student union discussing federal budget cuts in aid-to-education programs. Another example might be a group of businessmen discussing federal budget cuts from an entirely different viewpoint over cocktails at the nineteenth hole of the local country club. Neither group will resolve the problem they are discussing. However, many of the participants will benefit from the interchange of ideas, the reinforcement of attitudes, and the enjoyment that social discussion groups provide.

### EDUCATIVE DISCUSSION

**Educative discussion:**
Discussion that seeks to gain knowledge and information.

The function of **educative discussion** (sometimes called *information-seeking discussion*) is to make you better informed about the topic discussed. Examples of educative discussion groups include garden clubs, Bible study groups, musical societies, and book clubs. One of the most familiar examples of educative discussion is classroom discussion, which is particularly well suited to the speech class. A brief discussion following each classroom speech can provide valuable feedback to both the speaker and the audience. An all-class discussion of the textbook and the exams will help students better understand speech principles and what is expected of them in the class.

### THERAPEUTIC DISCUSSION

**Therapeutic discussion:**
Discussion with the goal of personal improvement of each member.

A third function of discussion is the therapeutic group. The leader of a **therapeutic discussion** group is almost always a trained therapist whose goal is the personal improvement of each member. Examples of therapeutic groups include alcohol and drug rehabilitation groups, marriage counseling groups, religious encounter groups, and weight watching groups. These provide a supportive atmosphere where individuals can learn why they act the way they do and what they can do to change their behavior.

## PROBLEM-SOLVING DISCUSSION

Group problem solving is superior to individual problem solving for a number of reasons. First, an individual's background and experience can seldom match those of a group. The more people working on a problem, the more information available to solve it. Second, the more people you have looking at a problem, the more likely you are to solve it correctly. In a group, an error by one individual is likely to be spotted by someone else.

As our society grows increasingly complex, more and more problems that must be dealt with are surfacing. The majority of them will be addressed in **problem-solving group discussion**. In governmental committee meetings, business conferences, church councils, legislative sessions, classroom meetings, and the like, problems are being solved, policies are being determined, and decisions are being made that affect the lives of millions of people. As an educated person, you will be called on to participate in a variety of discussion situations. A study of the principles of group communication, together with guided practice, will help you develop the knowledge and skill necessary for effective participation.

> **Problem-solving group discussion:** Discussion that seeks to use group members' expertise to solve a problem.

# TYPES OF DISCUSSION

Because the discussion groups you participate in will most likely be either educative or problem solving, the rest of this chapter concentrates only on these. The six basic types of discussion are the roundtable, the panel, the symposium, the lecture forum, the dialogue, and the interview.

## THE ROUNDTABLE

In the roundtable discussion, the participants sit at a round table or in a circle. There are two reasons for this seating arrangement: (1) when seated in a circle, everyone is in a position to maintain eye contact with the others while speaking or listening to them, and (2) no one is seated in a superior "head of the table" position. Each participant is in a position equal to that of his or her neighbor. Everyone, including the moderator or leader if there is one, is involved in a roundtable discussion. There is no audience. This type of discussion is particularly suited to council and committee meetings, conferences, and classroom discussions. Although roundtable discussions usually involve from three to fifteen members, an effective classroom discussion can be held with as many as twenty-five.

## THE PANEL

A panel usually consists of from three to six panelists and a moderator. The members sit in front of an audience or judge in a circle or semicircle so they can see and react to each other. The language used by panel members is usually informal and conversational. Although panel participants are often made aware of the discussion problem beforehand, most panels are unrehearsed to ensure spontaneity and enthusiasm during the presentation.

A panel discussion group typically sits in front of an audience so that the group members can see and react to each other. The language used by the panelists is usually informal and conversational.

Panels that are followed by an audience participation period, or forum, are usually timed. For example, for a one-hour program, forty minutes might be set aside for the panel and twenty minutes for the forum period. It is the moderator's job to summarize the discussion and field the questions from the audience.

## THE SYMPOSIUM

Unlike roundtable and panel discussions, which are like magnified conversations, the symposium consists of a series of prepared speeches, each dealing with a specific aspect of the same topic. The number of speakers for a symposium usually ranges from three to five. A time limit is given to each speaker, who talks directly to the audience. The moderator opens the discussion, introduces each speaker and topic, and summarizes the discussion at the conclusion. If there is a forum period following the summary, the moderator fields the questions, rephrasing them when necessary.

## THE LECTURE FORUM

The lecture forum involves a moderator and a lecturer who delivers a prepared speech on a subject. The speech is followed by a forum period. The job of the moderator is to introduce the subject and speaker and preside during the forum period. The lecture forum technique has long been used by classroom teachers and political candidates, who then field questions from the audience.

Another variation of the lecture forum is the film forum. The success of this technique largely depends on the quality of the film shown and the ability of the moderator to deal effectively with any questions the audience may have regarding the film.

## THE DIALOGUE

A dialogue is an interchange and discussion of ideas between two people. It is highly successful when both participants know their subjects well. The dialogue can be a useful classroom exercise. It is an excellent means of communicating information. For best results, the dialogue should be carefully planned so both participants know where the discussion is heading.

## THE INTERVIEW

A carefully planned interview can be an excellent way to communicate information. In the discussion interview, the participants should plan the questions in advance so both will know where the discussion is going. A good interviewer can elicit a wealth of information from a well-informed interviewee.

## ROLE-PLAYING

An excellent way to introduce a discussion problem is through the technique of **role-playing**. In role-playing, the players take part in a brief drama built on a *real-life* problem. The actors in the drama each take the part of a specific character in the problem. They then act out the situation, expressing the views they believe that the character they are playing would have. The drama is unrehearsed, and the problem is usually given to the participants on the day the role-playing is to take place.

**Role-playing:** A technique to introduce a discussion problem by participating in a brief drama based on a real-life problem or situation.

Role-playing can be an effective way of pretesting a situation. Skill in handling oneself in an interview could make the difference between a student's getting a job or missing it. A series of mock interviews with students playing the roles of personnel director and interviewee provides excellent practice. Students will derive a greater feeling of confidence toward the interview situation and an increased understanding of management's position as well.

Role-playing is particularly useful in clarifying a situation. Often, after seeing the roles played, a group can more fully understand the problem. Role-playing, for example, can be used to facilitate the case problem approach to discussion. In discussing case problem 8 on page 205, a group may decide that to solve the problem Natalie should tell Joy that her husband-to-be had touched her indecently. At this point, the instructor might step in and say, "All right, class, let's see how well that solution will work. Joan, would you play the role of Natalie? And Sandy, how about you playing the role of Joy?"

SELECTING A ROLE-PLAYING PROBLEM.     The problems below have been prepared with today's college student in mind. Additional problems may be developed by members of a group in a discussion situation or by individual students as part of a class assignment.

One final note: After engaging in role-playing these problems, allow time for those in the audience to give their views and reactions to the drama.

1. A student who is of legal age is asked by his friends to buy the liquor for a weekend beach party. He knows he can get charged with contributing to the delinquency of minors if he is caught. He also wants to keep the status he has among his friends. What should the student do?

2. A new employee in a plant has a mother who must have open heart surgery. She lives in another state, and the employee would like to take a four-day leave of absence to be with her. The plant is behind in filling orders, and everyone is working a seven-day week. How should the employee handle the situation?

3. The students in an English class believe that the instructor assigns an excessive amount of homework each day. The instructor is teaching the course for the first time. How should the students handle the situation?

4. A student who will graduate in three weeks is offered a job that will start on the morning of his last exam. His instructor has indicated that he will give no early or makeup exams. What should the student do?

5. A secretary has recently begun a new job for an insurance company. The fringe benefits are excellent and the pay is good, but she runs into a problem. Her immediate supervisor is constantly making advances toward her that she resents. How should she handle the situation?

6. A first-year bank employee has been late for work on an average of two or three times a week for the last month. His wife, who is in the hospital, will remain there for at least another week. The reason he has been late is that he has to feed, dress, and drive his three school-age children to school each day. His supervisor has called him in to talk about his tardiness. How should the bank employee handle the situation?

#### ADDITIONAL SUGGESTIONS FOR ROLE-PLAYING

1. You have just graduated and are being interviewed for your first job.
2. A persistent salesman refuses to leave when you tell him to.
3. A policeman is about to ticket your car as you arrive on the scene.
4. A clerk who waited on you fifteen minutes ago now refuses to accept a return because you misplaced the receipt.
5. A teacher wrongfully accuses you of cheating.
6. A friend denies that he owes you $20.

## PARTICIPATING IN DISCUSSION

To a great extent, successful discussion depends on the participants. Sometimes discussions fail because the participants have little knowledge of the subject and, consequently, little to offer in solving the problem. At other times, a discussion ends in aimless argument because of the inflexibility or refusal to compromise. Breakdowns in communication, an unfriendly atmosphere, and a tendency to stray from the subject also contribute to the failure of discussion. Effective participation in discussion requires both ability and understanding. Following are the duties of a participant in a discussion.

### LISTEN CAREFULLY

**Critical listening:** An active process of listening that requires attention and concentration.

**Critical listening** is essential to effective discussion. It is an active process requiring both attention and concentration. All too often discussants respond to what they *thought* someone meant. If you are unclear as to the meaning of something that was said during a discussion, say so before the discussion continues.

## BE PREPARED

Every member of a discussion has a responsibility to be well informed on the topic being discussed. This means that if you have little knowledge of the subject, you spend time and effort researching it. If you are delivering a lecture or are a member of a symposium panel, prepare and practice your speech carefully so you can deliver it extemporaneously with good eye contact.

## BE SPONTANEOUS

Participate whenever you have something relevant to say. Although you must not interrupt another speaker, if you have something important to say, interject it when there is a pause in the conversation. A relevant comment in the right place can often save the group time.

## SHARE THE SPOTLIGHT

Although you should participate when you have a worthwhile contribution, don't monopolize the discussion. Group thinking can be thought of as thinking out loud. Unless all members contribute, the full value of their knowledge and experience will not be brought to bear on the problem.

## BE COURTEOUS

The old saying "You catch more flies with honey than with vinegar" is especially appropriate to the group discussion situation. Group discussion requires flexibility and compromise. It is unlikely that either will occur in a hostile atmosphere.

## BE COOPERATIVE

Participants in group discussion must put the best interests of the group above their own personal interests. The goal of discussion is to arrive at a solution acceptable to all members of the group. This means that group members must be willing to work cooperatively to avoid conflict.

## BE OBJECTIVE

For a discussion to be successful, each member must approach the question in an unbiased, objective way. If for some reason you have a strongly held attitude that would prevent you from discussing a topic objectively, excuse yourself from the discussion group.

## STICK TO THE POINT

Few things are more frustrating to a group than when a member introduces material that is completely off the subject. It is every member's responsibility to keep the discussion on track. Always be aware of where the discussion is heading and contribute only when your remarks are pertinent.

## (www) *Working* WITH THE WEB

If you want to learn more about communicating in groups, you can visit the web site of the nonprofit Center for the Study of Work Teams at the University of North Texas, which provides excellent links to a wide range of topics about small group communication, including working in teams and leadership. You can also access their newsletter. Go to

www.workteams.unt.edu

### USE TIME WISELY

A discussion participant should avoid belaboring a point. Once agreement is reached in regard to some aspect of the problem, move on. To explain to the group why you made the same decision as another member is counterproductive.

### SPEAK CONCISELY

Unless the listener understands the message, communication does not occur. If you want to be understood, articulate your words carefully and pronounce them correctly. Speak with adequate volume and emphasize important points so the other members of the group know exactly where you stand.

### BE NATURAL

No matter which form of discussion you are involved in, be yourself. Speak in a conversational manner with which you are comfortable. If you try to change your way of speaking, you are liable to sound stilted and unnatural.

## MODERATING THE DISCUSSION

Most discussion forms require a moderator. Seven specific duties of a moderator are listed here:

1. Start the discussion by introducing the topic and the lecturer or discussion participants to the audience.
2. Direct the discussion by seeing to it that the subject is adequately discussed and that the group moves steadily toward a solution or conclusion.
3. Encourage participation. Members who do not take part in the discussion contribute little or nothing to the outcome.
4. Resolve conflicts by using tact and diplomacy to minimize tension.
5. Control the time to make sure all aspects of the problem are discussed.
6. Provide transitions and summaries to help participants see what has been accomplished and what remains to be done.
7. Take charge of the forum period. Field all questions, rephrasing when necessary.

# A PATTERN FOR PROBLEM SOLVING

## IDENTIFYING THE PROBLEM

The first step in problem-solving discussion is to have the members pinpoint the problem. Many discussions fail because the problem is not clearly understood by all. Next, the problem must be carefully worded. When wording the problem for discussion, the group should adhere to the following guidelines:

1.  The problem should be worded in the form of a question. A properly worded question holds up a problem in such a way as to motivate discussants to seek solutions to it.
2.  It should be phrased to avoid a yes or no answer. Participants who answer yes or no to a question often feel committed to defend that answer. The result is that what started out as objective discussion turns into subjective debate.
3.  It should be stated in an impartial way. A discussion question should never indicate bias. The question "When will we stop the stupid sale of handguns?" is prejudiced. It would be far better to ask "How can the sale of handguns be effectively regulated?"

A problem-solving discussion group involves analyzing and exploring the nature and causes of the problem, as well as brainstorming solutions. People at other sites may be able to participate in the discussion via videoconferencing.

4. It should be worded specifically. The question "What should the government do to prevent terrorism?" is far too vague. Which government are we talking about? Where will the terrorism take place? A better question would be "What steps should the federal government take to prevent terrorists from illegally entering the United States?"

5. It should be sufficiently restricted. The question "What should be done to stop world hunger?" is so broad that it could not be adequately covered in a set period of time. A better question would be, "What should be done to stop hunger in Detroit?"

## ANALYZING THE PROBLEM

After identifying and wording the problem, the nature and causes of the problem should be explored. The group should consider such questions as these: What is the history of the problem? How serious is it? Who is affected by it? What are the causes?

The process of analysis usually requires research. Participants should research the discussion problem just as they would research the topic for a speech. A thorough investigation of the problem will give discussants a clear understanding of what conditions need correcting.

The final step in analysis is to decide on guidelines to evaluate proposed solutions. These guidelines should be agreed on before possible solutions are proposed. A typical list of guidelines might include it must be safe, it must be affordable, it must be obtainable, and it must not create new problems.

## FINDING THE BEST SOLUTION

At this point, members of the group should suggest possible solutions. It is a good idea to identify as many solutions as possible before evaluating any of them. An effective way to compile an adequate list of solutions is by using a technique called *brainstorming*.

In a discussion, the brainstorming technique can be handled in two ways. The first is to have members of the group write down whatever solutions come to mind as quickly as they can. They should jot them down in phrases or sentences without evaluating them. After five minutes, the exercise stops, and each list of solutions is read aloud. The second technique has one member of the group proposing a solution, another posing a different one, and so on. The brainstorming continues for a set period of time or until the group has no more solutions to offer. One member should be assigned to write down all the ideas.

Once a list of solutions has been established, the group can quickly eliminate any that are illogical or repetitive. The remaining solutions can then be evaluated according to the guidelines established earlier. It is wise for the group to evaluate each solution on the list before making their choice.

Finally, the group should make every effort to reach agreement as to the best solution or solutions. If they cannot reach a consensus, a majority vote should be taken.

## ACTUATING THE SOLUTION

Once the group has agreed on a solution, it is necessary to take action. This might mean drafting a letter and sending it to the appropriate representatives in Washington, framing a petition and collecting signatures, or planning and staffing a fund-raising event. Perhaps the proposed solution will take the form of an oral report to the mayor and city council or to your instructor and the rest of the class. Sometimes a solution will require a written report. Whatever action is taken, the last job the group has is to implement the solution it chooses.

## Chapter Review

After reading this chapter, you should be able to

- List and explain the four functions of group discussion.
- Describe the six basic types of discussion.
- Explain the duties of a participant in group discussion.
- Describe the duties of a group discussion moderator.
- Identify and explain the steps in problem-solving discussion.

## Key Terms

Social discussion (p. 194)          Problem-solving group discussion (p. 195)
Educative discussion (p. 194)       Role-playing (p. 197)
Therapeutic discussion (p. 194)     Critical listening (p. 198)

## Exercises

1. If possible, try to observe a group in action, either on campus, at your church, in your community, or even among friends discussing an issue or a decision to be made. Make note of what the various group members do. Does everyone participate? Are ideas exchanged in a friendly, cooperative way? Do you observe breakdowns in communication or behaviors that could lead to breakdowns? Does the group stay on track and make good use of its time? Is there a moderator? What does that person do to facilitate discussion? Fill out the Discussion Rating Form in Figure 11.1 and share your findings with the class.

2. **Case Problems:** The best way to develop ability in group discussion is through guided practice. The use of case problems as discussion questions is an effective way of practicing. The following problems are typical of those that occur in everyday life and are the kinds of situations you are likely to encounter at school, at work, or at home.

   There are no *right* or *wrong* solutions to these problems. However, each problem is constructed in such a way that choosing a solution poses a dilemma. For each problem there are two alternative solutions, both of which are undesirable. The job of the group is to choose the solution they see as being the least undesirable.

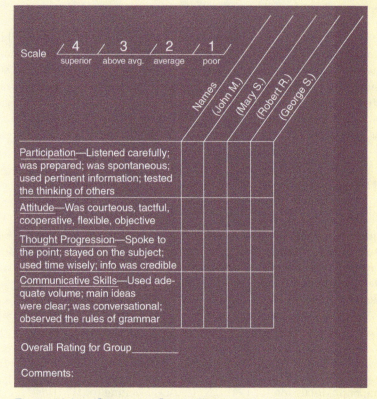

**Figure 11.1 ▪ Discussion Rating Form**
This form can be used by students and instructors to evaluate group members' participation.

Remember, the group should make an effort to reach agreement on a solution for each problem. If they cannot reach a consensus, the solution should be chosen by majority opinion.

1. Joan and Donna have been friends since childhood. Lately, Donna has been seeing a lot of an older, married man. Joan advises Donna to break this off, but Donna is convinced that the man plans to get a divorce and marry her. Donna has told her parents that she will be visiting Joan for the weekend so she and the man can go off together. What should Joan do?

2. John, a white student at a small out-of-state technical college, has fallen in love with Cindy, a black student at the same school. He plans to take her home for Christmas, but he doesn't plan to tell his parents before-hand that she is black. He argues that his parents have always insisted that they are unprejudiced, and

Problems 1–10 have been taken with permission from Arthur Koch and Stanley B. Felber, *What Did You Say?* 3rd ed. (Upper Saddle River, NJ: Prentice Hall, 1985).

now he will be able to judge by their reaction if they are honest. Cindy does not agree. How should the situation be handled?

3. While you are riding home with Ed, a good friend, he backs into a parked car, causing considerable damage. Although he has liability insurance, he declines to leave his name, explaining that he has already had two accidents this year and that another will result in his insurance policy's cancellation. Ed drives you to and from work every day. What should you do?

4. Fred and John, close personal friends, work together part-time stocking shelves at a local supermarket. Fred has been working to buy himself a new car while John has taken the second job to help support his widowed mother and nine brothers and sisters. One night after closing time, Fred notices John carrying a case of powdered milk out to his car. What should Fred do?

5. Carl's fifteen-year-old daughter, Ann, has recently begun a part-time job babysitting his employer's young children. After her second night on the job she confides to Carl that the children have told her they are often beaten by their father. She says she has seen the marks of this abuse. She feels that the authorities should be notified. Carl is concerned about losing his job. What should Carl do?

6. Paul found what he believed were LSD tablets in his sister's room. When he questioned her about it, she insisted they were antibiotics for a cold. He has noticed that she has become unusually withdrawn lately. He has revealed all this to his parents who have told him not to let his imagination run away with him. What should he do?

7. Don and Alice are required by law to take a blood test before marriage. During the examination it is discovered that Don has had a venereal disease. When Alice questions him about it, he refuses to answer her. What should Alice do?

8. Joy and Natalie have been friends since childhood. On the following Saturday, Natalie will be the maid of honor at Joy's wedding. After the rehearsal dinner Joy's husband-to-be drives Natalie home because her car didn't start. When he parks in front of her apartment, he touches her indecently. When she resists his advances, he begs her not to tell Joy. What should Natalie do?

9. A few days before the final examination you learn by chance that another student in one of your courses has a copy of the questions to be used on the test and that he is passing it among his friends in the course. You know that several students in the course have already seen it and you suspect that nearly a third of those in the course have seen it. What should you do?

10. Sandy and Kim have been best friends since childhood. A year ago Kim married and moved to another town. When Sandy visits her for two weeks during the summer, she discovers that Kim is being physically abused by her husband. One evening after Kim has been severely beaten, Sandy tells Kim that she is going to call the police. Kim begs her not to, explaining that her husband only beats her when he was drunk and he has promised to quit. Sandy is afraid Kim will be killed or seriously injured. What should she do?

# Glossary

**Actuate:** To put into action; in the case of a persuasive speech, gives audience instruction as to what action you want them to take: to buy, to sell, to join, to protest, and so on.

**Analogy:** A figurative comparison that describes similarities between things that are otherwise different, used to make a connection.

**Analysis:** The process of breaking a topic into parts and examining them; the process of breaking down a situation or concept in order to examine each part separately, to determine who, what, why, when, where, and how.

**Argumentation:** The reasoning process used to attempt to influence others' beliefs.

**Articulation:** The physical process of forming the consonant and vowel sounds of words.

**Attention factors:** Techniques, such as humor, suspense, and novelty, used to get and hold the attention of your audience.

**Audience analysis:** The collection and consideration of information about the characteristics, values, and attitudes of your listeners.

**Audience-centered speech:** A speech that is prepared with a specific audience, a specific collection of individuals, in mind.

**Blog:** An Internet feature that allows a person to create a public, online forum that expresses his or her personal opinion or agenda.

**Body:** The main points and supporting materials of a speech that develop the speaker's purpose and message.

**Brainstorming:** A technique used to generate ideas for speech topics by spontaneously coming up with as many ideas as possible without pausing to evaluate them.

**Causal reasoning:** A process that links cause and effect.

**Central idea:** A clear, one-sentence statement or thesis around which the entire speech is developed.

**Clustering:** The second step in the brainstorming process that involves writing down all related ideas about a topic to provide a framework for the important points of a speech.

**Combined supports:** Supporting materials that are used in combination with one another.

**Comfort zone:** Your self-concept and the belief systems and rules established by past experiences and personal knowledge.

**Common-ground approach:** A way of dealing with an audience opposed to your speech topic or viewpoint by finding a means of identifying with audience members.

**Communication breakdown:** A failure in the communication process traced to one of the five elements in the process.

**Conclusion:** A closing that signals to the audience that the speech is ending and reinforces your purpose.

**Content:** What is said in a speech, including the subject, main idea, supporting materials, organization, and the way the speech is worded.

**Contrast:** Compares differences between things that are physically different as a means of emphasizing the differences.

**Credibility:** The speaker's ability to be believable to the audience and worthy of its confidence and trust.

**Critical listening:** An active process of listening that requires attention and concentration.

**Deductive reasoning:** A three-step process of reasoning from a general rule to a specific conclusion.

**Delivery:** The way the speech is communicated, including through eye contact, facial expression, body movement, personal appearance, and voice.

**Delivery outline:** A speaking outline that contains key words and phrases from your complete sentence outline, used to deliver an extemporaneous speech.

**Demographic audience analysis:** The collection and consideration of the audience's vital statistics, including age, gender, educational level, and ethnic, cultural, or racial background.

**Demonstration speech:** A speech to show an audience how to do something.

**Description speech:** A speech that makes use of sensory appeals to give the listener a clear picture of what is being described.

**Descriptive gestures:** Hand gestures, including signs that communicate information about what you are discussing, such as the size or shape of objects.

**Educative discussion:** Discussion that seeks to gain knowledge and information.

**Emphatic gestures:** Gestures that emphasize or reinforce what you are saying.

**Ethics:** The moral standards and values that influence our decisions and behaviors.

**Evaluation:** Another form of analysis that reviews and assesses material or performance.

**Example:** A specific, representative instance used to clarify and reinforce a point.

**Explanation:** The process of explaining something to make it clear and understandable.

**Explication:** A form of analysis that clarifies what is not clear or only implied.

**Exposition:** A precise statement that provides information or an explanation to the listener to increase understanding.

**Expository speech:** A speech that explains a concept, process, idea, or belief, the primary purpose of which is to inform.

**Extemporaneous speech:** A speech that is carefully planned in advance and includes a complete sentence outline, but the not the exact wording of the speech.

**Fallacies:** Arguments based on incorrect or flawed reasoning.

**General purpose:** A clear goal established for your speech, with a desired response from the audience: informing, persuading, or entertaining.

**Generalization:** A general conclusion based on examining specific examples or details.

**Hypothetical example:** An imaginary or fabricated situation or story used to illustrate a point.

**Impromptu speech:** A speech that is developed on the spur of the moment, with little or no preparation.

**Inductive reasoning:** The process of reasoning from a specific observation or experience to a general conclusion.

**Informative communication:** Communication that adds to a listener's knowledge and understanding of a subject.

**Internet:** A system that provides an unlimited number of resources by connecting computers worldwide.

**Introduction:** An opening that gets the audience interested in listening to the speech, presents the central idea, and previews the main points.

**Isometric exercise:** A procedure during which you contract a muscle for about 8 to 10 seconds, against resistance, in order to release nervous energy.

**Kinesics:** The study of how the body, face, and eyes communicate; also known as "body language."

**Literal comparison:** Compares similarities between things that are physically alike.

**Logical proof:** The use of evidence to appeal to the audience's ability to reason, used to support the speaker's argument.

**Manuscript speech:** A speech that is completely written out in advance and read.

**Memorized speech:** A speech that is written out first, committed to memory, and then delivered.

**Motivated sequence:** An organizational pattern involving a five-step plan of action, developed specifically for persuasive speaking.

**Motive:** The inner drive or impulse that stimulates behavior.

**Nonverbal communication:** Behaviors, including body movement, facial expression, voice, and personal appearance, that are part of our communication.

**Overconcern:** The anxiety about what others will think of us.

**Paralanguage:** The vocal elements that are apparent in how you say something and influence your message.

**Personal proof:** The image the speaker presents to the audience, including competence, goodwill, integrity, and credibility.

**Persuasion:** A deliberate attempt to influence the thought and behavior of others through the use of personal, psychological, and logical appeals.

**Plagiarism:** Presenting someone's words or ideas as your own without giving proper or adequate credit.

**Planning outline:** A tentative plan of what the speaker wants to say, allowing for review and changes.

**Preview statement:** A clear explanation of the main ideas to be covered in the speech.

**Problem–solution speech:** A speech that encourages the audience to take specific action to solve the problem identified in the speech.

**Problem-solving group discussion:** Discussion that seeks to use group members' expertise to solve a problem.

**Pronunciation:** Articulating the accepted consonant and vowel sounds with the proper accent.

**Psychological proof:** An appeal to the attitudes and motives of the listeners.

**Ready reference:** A phone service provided by many libraries that allows a caller to gain information from a reference librarian over the phone.

**Reasoning:** The process of drawing conclusions from evidence.

**Rhetorical question:** A question used to gain listeners' attention, where the audience is not expected to give an answer out loud.

**Role-playing:** A technique to introduce a discussion problem by participating in a brief drama based on a real-life problem or situation.

**Search engine:** A way of navigating the millions of web sites on the World Wide Web by quickly locating sources of information on a specific topic.

**Social discussion:** Discussion that is temporary, unstructured, and informal.

**Specific purpose:** A more detailed statement of what you want to accomplish with your speech.

**Speech communication process:** The act or process of sending and receiving a message, involving five elements: a speaker, a message, a channel (through which the message is sent), an audience, and a response.

**Statistics:** Numerical data that provide a representative sampling.

**Supporting materials:** Materials used to support the points in a speech that make the ideas clear or persuasive to the audience.

**Syllogism:** A three-step pattern of deductive reasoning, which moves from a major premise to a minor premise to a conclusion.

**Testimony:** The words of an expert or authority on a particular subject, used to support a point.

**Therapeutic discussion:** Discussion with the goal of personal improvement of each member.

**Transitions:** Words or phrases that act as guideposts for listeners to connect ideas in the speech and move from one point to the next.

**Visual aid:** An instructional devise that appeals mainly to vision.

**Visual imagery:** A technique for behavior change; when used to mentally rehearse a speech, helps develop confidence in public speaking.

**World Wide Web:** A global tool to help users access information on the Internet.

# Index

# Photo Credits

p. 2, © Dick Blume/Syracuse Newspapers/The Image Works; p. 7, © Davis Barber/PhotoEdit; p. 10, © Gary Conner/PhotoEdit; p. 20, © David Young-Wolff/PhotoEdit; p. 26, © Mike Theiler/epa/CORBIS; p. 29, © BananaStock/Jupiter Images; p. 35, © Roger L. Wollenberg/UPI/Landov; p. 42, © Simon Hollington/Photoshot/Landov; p. 48, © Mel Yates/Photodisc Red/Getty Images; p. 51, © Tom Grill/age fotostock; p. 56, © Jessica Rinaldi/Reuters/Landov; p. 60, © Viviane Moos/CORBIS; p. 64, 67, © AP Images; p. 72, © John Neubauer/PhotoEdit; p. 77, © Ellen B. Senisi; p. 81, © Elizabeth Crews/The Image Works; p. 86, © Image Source/Getty Images; p. 91, © Jon Feingersh/Masterfile; p. 94, © AP Images; p. 104, © Michael Newman/PhotoEdit; p. 110, © JP Laffont/Sygma/CORBIS; p. 112, © John Terence Turner/Getty Images; p. 118, 122, © AP Images; p. 125, © Charles Gupton/CORBIS; p. 130, © Robert Sorbo/Reuters/Landov; p. 137, © Joe McBride/Getty Images; p. 148, © Larry Downing/Reuters/Landov; p. 151, © Michael Newman/PhotoEdit; p. 155, © Bob Mahoney/The Image Works; p. 161, © AP Images; p. 168, © Jamie Rector/Bloomberg News/Landov; p. 172, © AP Images; p. 176, © Stockbyte/Getty Images; p. 184, © AP Images; p. 192, © Steve Chenn/CORBIS; p. 196, © Bob Daemmrich/PhotoEdit; p. 201, © Photodisc/Getty Images.

# Text Credits

Pages 32–34:  Used with permission of E. Fuller Torrey, M.D. and the Treatment Advocacy Center, Arlington, VA.

Pages 33–35: From Koch, Arthur and Felber, Stanley B., *What Did You Say? A Guide to Communication Skills*, Third Edition, © 1985, pp. 89–92, 297. Reprinted by permission of Pearson Education, Inc., Upper Saddle River, NJ.

Page 41: © 1964 Tom Lehrer. Used by permission.

Page 46: From William J. Seiler and Melissa Beall, *Communication: Making Connections*, Sixth Edition. Published by Allyn and Bacon, Boston MA., Copyright © by Pearson Education, Reprinted by permission of the publisher.

Page 55: *Congressional Record*. Speech given by Hon. John Conyers, Jr., of Michigan in the House of Representatives, November 25, 1969.

Page 65: Reprinted by arrangement with the Estate of Martin Luther King, Jr., c/o Writers House as agent for the proprietor New York, NY. Copyright 1968 Martin Luther King, Jr., copyright renewed 1996 Coretta Scott King.

Page 112: From Douglas Ehninger, Bruce Gronbeck, Ray McKerrow, and Alan Monroe, *Principles and Types of Speech Communication*, Tenth Edition (Glenview, IL: Scott Foresman, 1986), page 153.

Page 127: Adapted from William J. Seiler and Melissa Beall, *Communication: Making Connections*, Sixth Edition. Published by Allyn and Bacon, Boston MA., Copyright © by Pearson Education, Reprinted by permission of the publisher.

Pages 133–134: From Robert C. Jeffrey and Owen Peterson, *Speech: A Text with Adapted Readings* (New York: Harper & Row, Publishers, 1971), pages 385–386.

Page 155: Excerpt used with permission from  Arthur Koch and Stanley B. Felber, *What Did You Say?*, Third Edition (Upper Saddle River, NJ: Prentice Hall, 1985).

Page 156: Excerpt from speech: Quoted in George Breitman, ed., *Malcolm X Speaks*, p. 50; copyright © 1965 by Merit Publishers and Betty Shabazz.

Page 156: Excerpt from Paul Kuenning, *A Worldly Christianity* (Lima, Ohio: Fairway Press, 1995), pages 48–49.

Page 157: Duane Rodriguez, *The MATC Times*, Milwaukee Area Technical College.

Page 158: From Roger Garrison, *How a Writer Works* (New York: Harper & Row, 1981), page 4.

Page 180: Excerpt used with permission from  Arthur Koch and Stanley B. Felber, *What Did You Say?*, Third Edition (Upper Saddle River, NJ: Prentice Hall, 1985).

Pages 186–188: From Vital Speeches XXXIV: 18 (July 1, 1968), pages 546–547.

Pages 204–205: Used with permission from  Arthur Koch and Stanley B. Felber, *What Did You Say?*, Third Edition (Upper Saddle River, NJ: Prentice Hall, 1985).

# NOTES

# NOTES

# NOTES

# NOTES

# NOTES

# NOTES

# NOTES

# NOTES

# NOTES

# NOTES

# NOTES

# NOTES

# NOTES

# NOTES

# NOTES

# NOTES